THE PAPER CANOE

Eugenio Barba, director, theorist and founder of Odin Teatret, is today one of the major points of reference for contemporary theatre. *The Paper Canoe* is the first major study of theatre anthropology; it distils all the research of ISTA, the International School of Theatre Anthropology, and focuses upon the pre-expressive level of the performer's art. Barba defines this as the basic technique which creates 'presence' on stage; a dilated and effective body which can hold and guide a spectator's attention.

The Paper Canoe alternates between detached analysis and the observations of an ardent traveller who reveals the value of theatre as a discipline and a revolt. It comprises a fascinating dialogue with the masters of Asian performance and the makers of twentieth-century theatre, such as Stanislavski, Meyerhold, Craig, Copeau, Brecht, Artaud and Decroux, making their thoughts and techniques accessible and relevant to contemporary practice.

The Paper Canoe establishes beyond doubt the importance of Barba's practical and theoretical work for today's students and practitioners of performance.

Eugenio Barba is the Founder and Director of Odin Teatret, and Director of the International School of Theatre Anthropology. He is also Examining Professor at Aarhus University in Denmark and the author of *Beyond the Floating Islands* and *The Dictionary of Theatre Anthropology*.

Richard Fowler, Artistic Director of Primus Theatre in Canada, has also translated *A Dictionary of Theatre Anthropology: The Secret Art of the Performer* by Eugenio Barba and Nicola Savarese (1991) and *The Actor's Way* (1993).

THE PAPER CANOE

A Guide to Theatre Anthropology

Eugenio Barba
Translated by Richard Fowler

Routledge
Taylor & Francis Group

LONDON AND NEW YORK

First published in English 1995
by Routledge
11 New Fetter Lane, London EC4P 4EE

Simultaneously published in the USA and Canada
by Routledge
29 West 35th Street, New York, NY 10001

Reprinted 2002, 2003 (twice)

Routledge is an imprint of the Taylor and Francis Group

Originally published as *La Canoa di carta* by
Società editrice il Mulino, Bologna,
and © 1993 Eugenio Barba.
© 1993 Società editrice il Mulino, Bologna.

English edition – © 1995 Eugenio Barba

Typeset in Garamond by
Ponting-Green Publishing Services, Chesham, Bucks
Printed and bound in Great Britain by
TJ International Ltd, Padstow, Cornwall

British Library Cataloguing in Publication Data
A catalogue record for this book is available from
the British Library

Library of Congress Cataloging in Publication Data
Barba, Eugenio.
[Canoa di carta. English]
The paper canoe: a guide to theatre anthropology / Eugenio
Barba; translated by Richard Fowler.
p.   cm.
Includes bibliographical references and index.
1. Theater. 2. Anthropology. 3. Experimental theater.
I. Title..
PN2041.A57B3713   1994
792-dc20   94-7809

ISBN 0-415-10083-6 (hbk)
ISBN 0-415-11674-0 (pbk)

To Judy and Nando

and to the builders of canoes
Else Marie
Torgeir
Iben
Tage
Roberta
Julia

with gratitude

CONTENTS

CONTENTS

PREFACE

I wrote this book in Holstebro, but I conceived it during long, silent rehearsals and on journeys, while seeing performances and meeting theatre people from various continents. It grew during involved discussions or 'brainstorms' dealing with questions which at first seemed childish or foolish: What is the performer's presence? Why, when two performers execute the same actions, is one believable and the other not? Is talent also a technique? Can a performer who does not move hold the spectator's attention? Of what does energy in the theatre consist? Is there such a thing as pre-expressive work?

A friend, gentle and insistently curious, made me sit down and put everything on paper. From then on, my room was invaded by books, by memories of and dialogues with my 'ancestors'.

There is a land-less country, a country in transition, a country which consists of time not territory, and which is confluent with the theatrical profession. In this country, the artists who work in India or Bali, my Scandinavian companions, or those from Peru, Mexico or Canada, in spite of the distance between them, work elbow to elbow. I am able to understand them even if our languages separate us. We have something to exchange and so we travel in order to meet. I owe a great deal to their generosity. Their names, dear to me, are remembered in the following pages.

When one is working, to be generous means to be exigent. From *exigent* comes *exact*. Precision, in fact, has something to do with generosity. And so in the following pages, precision, exactness, will also be discussed. Something which appears to be cold anatomy on paper, in practice demands maximum motivation, the heat of vocation. 'Hot' and 'cold' are adjectives which are in comfortable opposition when one is talking about the work of the performer. I have also tried to alternate 'hot' pages with 'cold' pages in this book. But the reader should not trust appearances.

The 'ancestors' are the most exacting. Without their books, their tangled words, I could not have become an auto-didact. Without a dialogue with them, I would not have been able to hollow out this canoe. Their names have a double existence here: within the current of questions, they are live presences; in the bibliographical notes, they are books.

It was Fabrizio Cruciani who, with his exacting gentleness, obliged me to sit down and put this book together. He imposed a commitment upon me, he bound me to a contract. When he read the manuscript his first reaction was one of satisfaction, because the notes to the text had the required precision: 'He wrote them just as we would have done', he said of me to a mutual friend. By saying 'we', he meant 'historians'. The pain I felt when he died is slowly becoming pride.

I asked my companions from Odin Teatret and ISTA to read the manuscript. Some of them found errors or inaccuracies, proposed changes, made their demands and their tastes heard with insistence. I am a fortunate author.

The abbreviation ISTA, which stands for the International School of Theatre Anthropology, and which is, like all abbreviations, rather forbidding, represents the attempt to give form and continuity to something which evolved almost on its own. It was a strange environment, in which performers, directors and theatre historians gathered together, most often in Italy. Odin Teatret was at the centre of this environment. Once it was given a name and a mobile structure, scientists and artists from other continents joined it. ISTA became increasingly international: a Babel of languages in a shared village where it is not always easy to distinguish between artists, technicians and 'intellectuals', and where Orient and Occident are no longer separable. With time, the familiar yet remote figure of Sanjukta Panigrahi became an integral part of this village.

The Paper Canoe comes from this village and is for those who, even though they may not have known it, even when it no longer exists, will miss it.

E.B.
Holstebro, 25 February 1993

1

THE GENESIS OF
THEATRE ANTHROPOLOGY

It is often said that life is a journey, an individual voyage which does not necessarily involve change of place. One is changed by events and by the passage of time.

In all cultures, there are certain fixed events which mark the transition from one stage of this journey to another. In all cultures, there are ceremonies which accompany birth, establish the entry of the adolescent into adulthood, mark the union of man and woman. Only one stage is not sanctioned by a ceremony, the onset of old age. There is a ceremony for death, but none to celebrate the passage from maturity to old age.

This journey and these transitions are lived with lacerations, rejections, indifference, fervour. They take place, however, within the framework of the same cultural values.

This much *is known*. But what is it that *I know*? What would I say if I had to talk about *my* journey, about the stages and transitions in the contrasting landscapes of collective order and disorder, of experiences, of relationships: from childhood to adolescence, from adulthood to maturity, to this annual countdown where every birthday, fifty, fifty-one, fifty-five, is celebrated by recalling my past achievements?

If memory is knowledge, then I know that my journey has crossed through various cultures.

The first of these is the culture of faith. There is a boy in a warm place full of people singing, fragrant odours, vivid colours. In front of him, high up, is a statue wrapped in a purple cloth. Suddenly, while bells ring, the smell of incense becomes more pungent and the singing swells, the purple cloth is pulled down revealing a risen Christ.

This is how Easter was celebrated in Gallipoli, the village in southern Italy where I spent my childhood. I was deeply religious. It was a pleasure to the senses to go to church, to find myself in an atmosphere of darkness and candlelight, shadows and gilt stucco, perfumes, flowers and people engrossed in prayer.

I waited for moments of intensity: the elevation of the Host, Holy Communion, processions. Being with other people, feeling a bond with them, sharing something, filled me with a sensation which even now resonates in my senses and in their subconscious.

So I can still feel the pain I felt in my knees when I saw a friend's mother one Good Friday in Gallipoli. The procession of Christ with the cross on His shoulders, accompanied only by men, wound through the narrow streets of the old town. The procession of the Virgin, calling after Her Son, followed, half a kilometre behind. This distance between Mother and Son was poignant, announcing the final separation and emphasizing it through a vocal contact: the 'lament' of the Mother of Christ, accompanied only by women. Those whose prayers had been answered followed Her on their knees. Among them was my friend's mother. I was not expecting to see her, and at first reacted with the embarrassment typical of children who see their parents, or those of their friends, behaving in an unusual way. But immediately afterwards I was struck by the stabbing pain one feels when one walks hundreds of metres on one's knees.

I lived with an elderly woman for a number of years. She must have been about seventy. In the eyes of a ten-or eleven-year old boy, she was very old. I slept in her room. She was my grandmother. Every morning, at five o'clock, she got up and made very strong coffee. She would wake me and give me a little. I enjoyed the sweet warmth of the bed, in the cold room in that southern village with no heating in the winter. I was warm, and my grandmother, wearing a long, white, embroidered nightdress, would go over to the mirror, let loose her hair, and comb it. She had very long hair. I watched her from behind; she looked like a slender adolescent. I could just make out the withered body of an old woman, wrapped in a nightdress, and at the same time I saw a young girl dressed as a bride. Then there was her hair, very long and beautiful, yet white, dead.

These images, and others as well, which I recall from the culture of faith, all contain a 'moment of truth', when opposites embrace each other. The most transparent is the image of the old woman who, to my eyes, is both woman and child, her hair flowing sensuously, but white. A portrait of coquettishness, vanity, grace. And yet, I had only to look from another angle and the mirror reflected back a face worn and etched by the years.

All these images are brought together by physical memory: the pain I felt in my knees on seeing my friend's mother, the sensation of warmth while I watched my grandmother combing her hair. Revisiting this culture of faith, the senses are the first to remember.

My journey through this culture was happy, yet it was punctuated by profound sorrows. I lived through a harrowing experience which, at that time, did not take place in the anonymity of a hospital but in the intimacy of the family. I stood by my father's deathbed, witnessing his long agony. As it dragged on into the night, I felt bewilderment, which became certainty and dismay. Nothing was said explicitly, and yet I realized from the faces and behaviour of those present, from their silences and their glances, that something irreparable was happening. As the hours passed, dismay gave way to impatience, unease, tiredness. I began to pray that my father's agony would end soon, so that I wouldn't have to remain standing any longer.

Again a 'moment of truth', opposites embracing each other. I observed simultaneously the elusiveness of life and the materiality of the corpse. I was about to lose forever one of the people I loved most and yet was discovering in myself impulses, reactions and thoughts which impatiently invoked the end.

At fourteen I went to a military school. Here, obedience demanded physical submission, and obliged us mechanically to carry out martial ceremonies which engaged only the body. A part of myself was cut off. We were not permitted to show emotion, doubt, hesitation, any outburst of tenderness or need for protection. My presence was shaped by stereotyped conduct. The highest value was placed on appearances: the officer who demanded respect and believed that he received it; the cadet who cursed or silently mouthed obscenities, concealing anger or scorn behind the impassive façade of standing to attention. Our behaviour was tamed through codified poses which conveyed acquiescence and acceptance.

I have an image of myself in the culture of faith: singing, or not singing, but involved with my whole being, on my own but nevertheless in unison with a group, amid singing women, lights, incense, colours. In the new culture, the image is of an impassive and immobile me, lined up geometrically with dozens of my peers, supervised by officers who do not permit us the slightest reaction. This time the group has swallowed me up; it is Leviathan, in whose belly my thinking and my sense of being whole within myself crumble. I was in the culture of corrosion.

Before, feeling and doing were the two simultaneous phases of a single intention; now, there was a split between thought and action; cunning, insolence, and cynical indifference were presumed to be determined self-assurance.

There is the immobility of the believer at prayer. There is the immobility of the soldier at attention. Prayer is the projection of the whole of oneself, a tension towards something that is at one and the same time within and outside oneself, an outpouring of inner energy, the intention-action taking flight. Attention on parade is the display of a stage set, the façade which exhibits its mechanical surface while the substance, the spirit, the mind, may be elsewhere. There is the immobility which transports you and gives you wings. There is the immobility which imprisons you and makes your feet sink into the earth.

Thus, my senses recall my passage through these two cultures, where immobility acquired such diverse charges of energy and meaning.

Like an acid, the culture of corrosion ate into faith, ingenuousness and vulnerability. It made me lose my virginity, in all ways, physically and mentally. It generated in me a need to feel free and, as happens when one is

3

seventeen, to dissent from and deny all geographical, cultural and social constraints. So I set off into the culture of revolt.

I rejected all the values, aspirations, demands and ambitions of the culture of corrosion. I longed not to integrate, not to put down roots, not to drop anchor in any port, but to escape, to discover the world outside and to remain a stranger. This longing became my destiny when, not yet eighteen, I left Italy and emigrated to Norway.

If one of our senses is mutilated, the others become sharpened: the hearing of a blind man is particularly acute, and for the deaf, the slightest visual details are vivid and indelible. Abroad, I had lost my mother tongue and grappled with incomprehensibility. I tried to get by as an apprentice welder among Norwegian workers who, because of my Mediterranean 'exoticism', treated me sometimes like a teddy bear and sometimes like a simpleton. I was plunged into the constant effort of scrutinizing behaviour which was not immediately decipherable.

I concentrated my attention on intercepting movements, frowns, smiles (benevolent? condescending? sympathetic? sad? scornful? conniving? ironic? affectionate? hostile? wise? resigned? But above all, was the smile for me or against me?).

I tried to orient myself in this labyrinth of recognizable yet unknown physicality and sounds, in order to explain to myself the attitudes of others with respect to me, what their behaviour towards me meant, what intentions lurked behind compliments, conventions, banal or serious discussions.

For years, as an immigrant, I experienced every single day the wearing see-saw of being accepted or rejected on the basis of 'pre-expressive' communication. When I boarded a tram, I certainly did not 'express' anything, yet some people withdrew to make room for me, while others withdrew to keep me at a distance. People simply reacted to my presence, which communicated neither aggression nor sympathy, neither desire for fraternization nor challenge.

The need to decipher other people's attitudes towards me was a daily necessity which kept all my senses alert and made me quick to perceive the slightest impulse, any unwitting reaction, the 'life' which flowed through the smallest tensions, and which took on for me, attentive observer that I was, special meanings and purposes.

During my journey as an immigrant, I forged the tools for my future profession as a theatre director, someone who alertly scrutinizes the performer's every action. With these tools I *learned to see*, I learned to locate where an impulse starts in the body, how it moves, according to what dynamic and along which trajectory. For many years I worked with the actors of Odin Teatret as a *maître du regard* searching out the 'life' which was revealed, sometimes unconsciously, by chance, by mistake, and identifying the many meanings that it could take on.

But still another scar marks my physical memory: the period from 1961 to

1964 that I spent in Opole, Poland, following the work of Jerzy Grotowski and his actors. I shared the experience that few in our profession are privileged to have, an authentic moment of transition.

Those few we call rebels, heretics or reformers of the theatre (Stanislavski and Meyerhold, Craig, Copeau, Artaud, Brecht and Grotowski) are the creators of a theatre of transition. Their productions have shattered the ways of seeing and doing theatre and have obliged us to reflect on the past and present with an entirely different awareness. The simple fact that they existed removes all legitimacy from the usual justification, often made in our profession, which maintains that nothing can be changed. For this reason, their successors can only emulate them if they themselves live in transition.

Transition is itself a culture. Every culture must have three aspects: material production by means of particular techniques, biological reproduction making possible the transmission of experience from generation to generation, and the production of meanings. It is essential for a culture to produce meanings. If it does not, it is not a culture.

When we look at photographs of productions by the 'rebels', it may be difficult to understand what, on a technical level, is novel about them. But the novelty of the meaning that they gave to their theatre in the context of their times is undeniable. Artaud is a good example. His productions left no traces. Yet he is still with us because he distilled new meanings for that social relationship which is theatre.

The importance of the reformers resides in their having breathed new values into the empty shell of the theatre. These values have their roots in transition, they are the rejection of the spirit of the time and cannot be possessed by future generations. The reformers can only teach us to be men and women of transition who invent the personal value of *our own* theatre.

At first, Grotowski and his actors were part of the traditional system and the professional categories of their time. Then, slowly, the gestation of new meaning began, through technical procedures. Day after day, for three years, my senses absorbed, detail by detail, the tangible fulfilment of this historic adventure.

I believed that I was *in search of a lost theatre*,[1] but instead I was learning to be in transition. Today I know that this is not a search for knowledge, but for the unknown.

After the founding of Odin Teatret in 1964, my work frequently took me to Asia: to Bali, Taiwan, Sri Lanka, Japan. I witnessed much theatre and dance. For a spectator from the West, there is nothing more suggestive than a traditional Asian performance *seen in its context*, often in the open tropical air, with a large and reactive audience, with a constant musical accompaniment which captivates the nervous system, with sumptuous costumes which delight the eye, and with performers who embody the unity of actor-dancer-singer-storyteller.

At the same time, there is nothing more monotonous, lacking action and development, than the seemingly interminable recitations of text, which the performers speak or sing in their (to us) unknown languages, melodiously yet implacably repetitive.

In these monotonous moments, my attention developed a tactic to avoid giving up on the performance. I attempted to concentrate tenaciously on and follow just one detail of a performer: the fingers of one hand, a foot, a shoulder, an eye. This tactic against monotony made me aware of a strange coincidence: Asian performers performed with their knees bent, *exactly like the Odin Teatret actors*.

In fact, at Odin Teatret, after some years of training, the actors tend to assume a position in which the knees, very slightly bent, contain the *sats*, the impulse towards an action which is as yet unknown and which can go in any direction: to jump or crouch, step back or to one side, to lift a weight. The *sats* is the basic posture found in sports – in tennis, badminton, boxing, fencing – when you need to be ready to react.

My familiarity with my actors' *sats*, a characteristic common to their individual techniques, helped me see beyond the opulence of the costumes and the seductive stylization of the Asian performers, and *to see bent knees*. This was how one of the first principles of Theatre Anthropology, the change of balance, was revealed to me.

Just as the Odin Teatret actors' *sats* made me see the bent knees of the Asian performers, their stubborness provided the opportunity for new conjecture and speculation, this time far from Asia.

In 1978, the actors all left Holstebro in search of stimuli which might help them shatter the crystallization of behaviour which tends to form in every individual or group. For three months, they dispersed in all directions: to Bali, India, Brazil, Haiti and Struer, a small town about fifteen kilometres from Holstebro. The pair who had gone to Struer to a school of ballroom dancing learned the tango, Viennese waltz, foxtrot and quickstep. Those who had gone to Bali studied *baris* and *legong*; the one who had been in India, *kathakali*; the two who had visited Brazil, *capoera* and *candomble* dances. They had all stubbornly insisted on doing what, in my view, ought absolutely to be avoided: they had learned styles – that is, the results of other people's techniques.

Bewildered and sceptical, I watched these flashes of exotic skills, hurriedly acquired. I began to notice that when my actors did a Balinese dance, they put on another skeleton/skin which conditioned the way of standing, moving and becoming 'expressive'. Then they would step out of it and reassume the skeleton/skin of the Odin actor. And yet, in the passage from one skeleton/skin to another, in spite of the difference in 'expressivity', they applied similar principles. The application of these principles led the actors in very divergent directions. I saw results which had nothing in common except the 'life' which permeated them.

What was later to develop into Theatre Anthropology was gradually defining itself before my eyes and in my mind as I observed my actors' ability to assume a particular skeleton/skin – that is, a particular scenic behaviour, a particular use of the body, a specific technique – and then to remove it. This 'putting on' and 'taking off', this change from a daily body technique to an extra-daily body technique and from a personal technique to a formalized Asian, Latin American or European technique, forced me to ask myself a series of questions which led me into new territory.

In order to know more, to deepen and verify the practicability of these common principles, I had to study stage traditions far removed from my own. The two Western scenic forms that I could have analysed (classical ballet and mime) were too close to me and would not have helped me establish the transcultural aspect of recurring principles.

In 1979, I founded ISTA, the International School of Theatre Anthropology. Its first session was held in Bonn and lasted a month.[2] The teachers were artists from Bali, China, Japan and India. The work and the research confirmed the existence of principles that, on the pre-expressive level, determine scenic presence, the body-in-life able to make perceptible that which is invisible: the intention. I realized that the artificiality of the forms of theatre and dance in which one passes from everyday behaviour to 'stylization' is the prerequisite for making a new energy potential spring forth, resulting from the collision of an effort with a resistance. In the Bonn session of ISTA, I found the same principles among Asian performers that I had seen at work in Odin Teatret actors.

It is sometimes said that I am an 'expert' on Asian theatre, that I am influenced by it, that I have adapted its techniques and procedures to my practice. Behind the verisimilitude of these commonplaces lies their opposite. It has been through knowledge of the work of Western performers – Odin Teatret actors – that I have been able to see beyond the technical surface and the stylistic results of specific traditions.

However, it is true that some forms of Asian theatre and some of their artists move me deeply, just as do the actors of Odin Teatret. Through them I find again the culture of faith, as an agnostic and as a man who has reached the last stage of his journey: the count-down in reverse. I rediscover a unity of the senses, of the intellect and of the spirit, a tension towards something which is both inside and outside myself. I find again the 'moment of truth', where opposites merge. I meet again, without regrets, nostalgia or bitterness, my origins and the entire journey which seemed to distance me from them and which has in fact brought me back to them. I find again the old man that I am and the child that I was, in the midst of the colours, the smell of the incense, and the singing women.

In every one of Odin Teatret's productions, there is an actor who, in a surprising way, divests her/himself of her/his costume and appears, not nude, but in the splendour of another costume. For many years I thought this was a *coup de théâtre* inspired by *kabuki*, the *hikinuki*, in which the protagonist, with the help of one or more assistants, suddenly divests himself of his costume and appears totally changed. I once believed I was adapting a Japanese convention. Only now do I understand this *détour* and return: it is the moment of Life when, in Gallipoli, the purple cloth fell and I saw, in a statue, the risen Christ.

It can sometimes make sense to confront a theory with a biography. My journey through cultures has heightened my sensorial awareness and honed an alertness, both of which have guided my professional work. Theatre allows me to belong to no place, to be anchored not to one perspective only, to remain in transition.

With the passing of the years, I feel pain in my knees and a sensual warmth, as an artisan in a craft which, at the moment of its fulfilment, vanishes.

2

DEFINITION

Theatre Anthropology is the study of the pre-expressive scenic behaviour upon which different genres, styles, roles and personal or collective traditions are all based. In the context of Theatre Anthropology, the word 'performer' should be taken to mean 'actor and dancer', both male and female. 'Theatre' should be taken to mean 'theatre and dance'.

In an organized performance the performer's physical and vocal presence is modelled according to principles which are different from those of daily life. This extra-daily use of the body-mind is called 'technique'.

The performer's various techniques can be conscious and codified or unconscious but implicit in the use and repetition of a theatre practice. Transcultural analysis shows that it is possible to single out recurring principles from among these techniques. These principles, when applied to certain physiological factors – weight, balance, the use of the spinal column and the eyes – produce physical, pre-expressive tensions. These new tensions generate an extra-daily energy quality which renders the body theatrically 'decided', 'alive', 'believable', thereby enabling the performer's 'presence' or scenic *bios* to attract the spectator's attention *before* any message is transmitted. This is a logical, and not a chronological 'before'.

The pre-expressive base constitutes the elementary level of organization of the theatre. The various levels of organization in the performance are, for the spectator, inseparable and indistinguishable. They can only be separated, by means of abstraction, in a situation of analytical research or during the technical work of composition done by the performer. The ability to focus on the pre-expressive level makes possible an expansion of knowledge with consequences both in the practical as well as in the historical and critical fields of work.

In general, the performer's professional experience begins with the assimilation of technical knowledge, which is then personalized. Knowledge of the principles which govern the scenic *bios* make something else possible: *learning to learn*. This is of tremendous importance for those who choose or who are obliged to go beyond the limits of specialized technique. In fact, *learning to learn* is essential for everyone. It is the condition that enables us to dominate technical knowledge and not to be dominated by it.

Performance study nearly always tends to prioritize theories and utopian ideas, neglecting an empirical approach. Theatre Anthropology directs its attention to empirical territory in order to trace a path among various specialized disciplines, techniques and aesthetics that deal with performing. It does not attempt to blend, accumulate or catalogue the performer's techniques. It seeks the elementary: *the technique of techniques*. On one hand this is a utopia. On the other, it is another way of saying, with different words, *learning to learn*.

Let us avoid equivocation. Theatre Anthropology is not concerned with applying the paradigms of cultural anthropology to theatre and dance. It is not the study of the performative phenomena in those cultures which are traditionally studied by anthropologists. Nor should Theatre Anthropology be confused with the anthropology of performance.

Every researcher knows that partial homonyms should not be confused with homologies. In addition to cultural anthropology, which today is often referred to simply as 'anthropology', there are many other 'anthropologies'. For example: philosophical anthropology, physical anthropology, paleo-anthropic anthropology and criminal anthropology. In Theatre Anthropology the term 'anthropology' is not being used in the sense of cultural anthropology, but refers to a new field of investigation, the study of the pre-expressive behaviour of the human being in an organized performance situation.

The performer's work fuses, into a single profile, three different aspects corresponding to three distinct levels of organization. The first aspect is individual, the second is common to all those who belong to the same performance genre. The third concerns all performers from every era and culture. These three aspects are:

(i)   the performer's personality, *her/his* sensitivity, artistic intelligence, social persona: those characteristics which render the individual performer unique and uncopiable;

(ii) the particularities of the theatrical traditions and the historical-cultural context through which the performer's unique personality manifests itself;

(iii) the use of the body-mind according to extra-daily techniques based on transcultural, recurring principles. These recurring-principles are defined by Theatre Anthropology as the field of pre-expressivity.

The first two aspects determine the transition from pre-expressivity to performing. The third is the *idem*, that which does not vary; it underlies the various personal, stylistic and cultural differences. It is the level of the scenic *bios*, the 'biological' level of performance, upon which the various techniques and the particular uses of the performer's scenic presence and dynamism are founded.

The only affinity connecting Theatre Anthropology to the methods and fields of study of cultural anthropology is the awareness that what belongs to our tradition and appears obvious to us can instead reveal itself to be a knot of unexplored problems. This implies a displacement, a journey, a *détour* strategy which makes it possible for us to single out that which is 'ours' through confrontation with what we experience as 'other'. Displacement educates our way of seeing and renders it both participatory and detached. Thus a new light is thrown on our own professional 'country'.

Among the different forms of ethnocentrism that often blinker our point of view, there is one which does not depend on geography and culture but rather on the scenic relationship. It is an ethnocentrism that observes the performance only from the point of view of the spectator, that is, of the finished result. It therefore omits the complementary point of view: that of the creative process of the individual performers and the ensemble of which they are part, the whole web of relationships, skills, ways of thinking and adapting oneself of which the performance is the fruit.

Historical understanding of theatre and dance is often blocked or rendered superficial because of neglect of the logic of the creative process, because of misunderstandings of the performer's empirical way of thinking, and because of an inability to overcome the confines established for the spectator.

The study of the performance practices of the past is essential. Theatre history is not just the reservoir of the past, it is also the reservoir of the new, a pool of knowledge that from time to time makes it possible for us to transcend the present. The entire history of the theatre reforms of the twentieth century, both in the East and in the West, shows the strong link of inter-dependence between the reconstruction of the past and new artistic creation.

Often, however, theatre historians come face to face with *testimonies* without themselves having sufficient experience of the craft and process of theatre making. They run the risk, therefore, of not writing history but of accumulating the deformations of memory. They do not possess a personal knowledge of the theatre with which to compare the testimonies of the past and therefore they cannot interpret them and restore the living and auto-nomous image of the theatre life of other times and cultures.

The historian without awareness of the practical craft corresponds to the 'artist' shut within the confines of her/his own practice, ignorant of the whole course of the river in which her/his little boat is navigating, and yet convinced of being in touch with the only true reality of the theatre.

This results in a yielding to the ephemeral. The non-expert in history and the non-expert in practice involuntarily unite their strengths to defile the theatre.

Those who have fought against a defiled theatre and who have sought to transform it into an environment with cultural, aesthetic and human dignity have drawn strength from books. Often they have themselves written books, especially when trying to liberate scenic practice from its enslavement to literature.

11

The relationship that links *theatre* and *books* is a fertile one. But it is often unbalanced in favour of the written word, which remains. Stable things have one weakness: their stability. Thus the memory of experience lived as theatre, once translated into sentences that last, risks becoming petrified into pages that cannot be penetrated.

3

RECURRING PRINCIPLES

Theatre Anthropology is a study *of* the performer and *for* the performer. It is a pragmatic science which becomes useful when it makes the creative process accessible to the scholar and when it increases the performer's freedom during the creative process.

Let us consider, to begin with, two different categories of performer which, according to the common way of thinking, are often identified as 'Oriental Theatre' and 'Western Theatre'. This is an erroneous distinction. In order to avoid false associations with specific cultural and geographic areas, we will turn the compass around and use it in an imaginary way, speaking of a North Pole and a South Pole.

The North Pole performer is apparently less free. S/he models her/his scenic behaviour according to a well-proven system of rules which define a style or a codified genre. This code of the physical or vocal action, fixed in its own particular and detailed artificiality (whether it be that of ballet or one of the classical Asian theatres, modern dance, opera or mime), is susceptible to evolution and innovation.

At the beginning, however, every performer who has chosen this type of theatre must conform to it and begins her/his apprenticeship by de-personalizing her/himself. S/he accepts a model of a scenic *persona* which has been established by a tradition. The personalization of this model will be the first sign of her/his artistic maturity.

The South Pole performer does not belong to a performance genre characterized by a detailed stylistic code. No repertoire of specific rules to be respected has been provided. The performer must construct the rules of support by her/himself. The apprenticeship begins with the inherent gifts of her/his personality. S/he will use as points of departure the suggestions contained in the texts to be performed, the observation of daily behaviour, the emulation of other performers, the study of books and pictures, the director's instructions. The South Pole performer is apparently freer but finds greater difficulty in developing, in an articulate and continuous way, the quality of her/his own scenic craft.

Contrary to what at first may appear to be the case, it is the North Pole

13

performer who has greater artistic freedom, while the South Pole performer easily becomes the prisoner of arbitrariness and of a lack of points of support. But the freedom of the North Pole performer remains completely within the genre to which s/he belongs and is paid for with a specialization which makes it difficult for her/him to go beyond known territory.

Theoretically, one knows that absolute scenic rules do not exist. They are *conventions* and an 'absolute convention' would be a contradiction in terms. But this is only true in theory. In practice, in order for a well-proven complex of rules actually to be useful to the performer, it must be accepted *as if* it was a complex of absolute rules. In order to realize this explicit fiction, it is often useful to keep one's distance from other styles.

Numerous anecdotes relate how many great Asian and European masters (such as Etienne Decroux) prohibit their students from approaching, even if only as simple spectators, other performance forms. They maintain that only in this way is the purity and quality of their own art preserved and only in this way does the student demonstrate her/his dedication to the path s/he has chosen.

The merit of this defence mechanism is that the pathological tendency which often derives from the awareness of the relativity of rules is avoided: moving from one path to another in the illusion that one can thereby accumulate experience and widen the horizon of one's own technique. It is true that one path is as good as another, but only if one follows it to the end. A long-term commitment which, for a long time, does not allow one to think of any other possibility, is necessary. 'Impose simple rules on yourself and never betray them', declared Louis Jouvet.[1] He was aware that the principles first used by a performer must be defended as her/his most valuable possession, which would be irremediably polluted by a too hasty process of syncretism.

Today, the theatrical environment is restricted but has no frontiers. Performers often travel outside their own cultures or host foreigners, theorize and diffuse the specificity of their art in foreign contexts, see other theatres, remain fascinated by and therefore tempted to incorporate into their own work some of the results which have interested or moved them. To be inspired by such results often leads to misunderstandings. These misunderstandings can be fertile; it suffices to think of what Bali meant to Artaud, China to Brecht and English theatre to Kawagami. But the knowledge which lies behind those results, the hidden technique and the vision of the craft which bring them alive, continue to be ignored.

This fascination with the surface, which today because of the intensity of contacts risks subjecting the evolution of traditions to rapid accelerations, can lead to homogenizing promiscuity.

How does one manage to 'eat' the results obtained by others, while also having the time and chemistry to digest those results? The *opposite* of a colonized or seduced culture is not a culture which isolates itself but a culture which knows how to cook in its own way and to eat what it takes from or what arrives from the outside.

But performers have used, and continue to use, not only the many principles which belong to each tradition but also certain similar principles. It is possible to use these principles without practising any form of promiscuity.

To trace these *recurring principles* is the first task of Theatre Anthropology. 'The arts', Decroux has written, 'resemble each other because of their principles, not because of their works.'[2] We could add: neither do performers resemble each other because of their techniques, but because of their principles.

Studying these principles, Theatre Anthropology renders a service both to the performer who has a codified tradition and to the performer who suffers from the lack of same; both to the performer who is caught by the degeneration of routine as well as to the performer who is menaced by the decay of a tradition; both to North Pole performers and to South Pole performers.

Daily and extra-daily

North Pole performers (dancers, mimes of the Decroux school, actors modelled by the tradition of a small group who have elaborated their own personal codifications, actors of the classical Asian theatres, modelled by rigorous traditions) possess a quality of energy which stimulates the spectator's attention even when they are giving a cold, technical demonstration. In such a situation, these performers are not attempting to express anything and yet they have a core of energy, an unpremeditated, knowing and suggestive irradiation, which captures our senses.

One might think that this is due to the performers' 'power' acquired through years and years of experience and work, to a technical quality. But a 'technique' is a particular use of the body. The body is used in a substantially different way in daily life than in performance situations. In the daily context, body technique is conditioned by culture, social status, profession. But in performance, there exists a different body technique. It is therefore possible to distinguish between a daily technique and an extra-daily technique.

The more daily techniques are unconscious, the more functional they are. For this reason, we move, we sit, we carry things, we kiss, we agree and disagree with gestures which we believe to be natural but which are in fact culturally determined. Different cultures determine different body techniques according to whether people walk with or without shoes, whether they carry things on their heads or with their hands, whether they kiss with the lips or with the nose. The first step in discovering what the principles governing a performer's scenic *bios*, or life, might be, lies in understanding that the body's daily techniques can be replaced by extra-daily techniques which do not respect the habitual conditionings of the use of the body.

Daily body techniques generally follow the principle of minimum effort,

15

that is, obtaining a maximum result with a minimum expenditure of energy. Extra-daily techniques are based, on the contrary, on the wasting of energy. At times they even seem to suggest a principle opposite to that which characterizes daily techniques: the principle of maximum commitment of energy for a minimal result.

When I was in Japan with Odin Teatret, I wondered about the meaning of the expression which spectators used to thank performers at the end of a performance: *otsukaresama*. The meaning of this expression – one of many in Japanese etiquette used particularly for performers – is: 'You have tired yourself out for me'.

But the waste of energy is not alone sufficient to explain the power which characterizes the performer's life.

The difference between this *life* and the *vitality* of an acrobat or even of certain moments of great virtuosity in Peking Opera and other forms of performance is obvious. In such cases, the acrobat shows us 'another body' which uses techniques so different from daily techniques that they seem to have no connection with them. It is no longer a question of extra-daily techniques but simply 'other techniques'. In this case, there is not the dilation of energy which characterizes extra-daily techniques when they replace daily techniques. In other words, there is no longer a dialectic relationship but only distance, or rather, the inaccessibility of a virtuoso's body.

Daily body techniques are used to communicate; techniques of virtuosity are used to amaze. Extra-daily techniques, on the other hand, lead to information. They literally *put* the body *into form*, rendering it artificial/artistic but *believable*. Herein lies the essential difference which separates extra-daily techniques from those which merely transform the body into the 'incredible' body of the acrobat and the virtuoso.

Balance in action

The observation of a particular quality of scenic presence leads us to a differentiation between daily, virtuosic techniques and extra-daily body techniques. It is these latter which determine pre-expressivity, the life of the performer, *characterizing it even before this life attempts to express something*.

The preceding affirmation is not easy to accept. Is there perhaps a level of the performer's art in which s/he is alive, present, without either representing anything or having any meaning? The performer, because of the very fact of facing spectators, seems perforce to be obliged to represent something or someone. And yet there are performers who use their presence to represent their own absence. This might seem no more than a mental game; it is, however, a fundamental aspect of Japanese theatre.

In *nō*, *kyōgen* and *kabuki*, one can distinguish an intermediate profile between the two possibilities (the real identity and fictional identity) which usually define the performer. For example, the *waki*, the secondary actor in *nō*, often expresses his own non-being, his absence from the action. He engages a complex extra-daily body technique which is not used to impersonate but to 'draw attention to his ability not to impersonate'. This artistically elaborated negation is also found when the main actor, the *shite*, exits. Now stripped of his character, he is nevertheless not reduced to his daily identity. He withdraws from the spectators with the same quality of energy which brought his performance to life.

The *kokken*, the men dressed in black who assist the main performer, are also asked to 'perform absence'. A *kokken*'s presence neither expresses nor represents anything but draws so directly from the sources of the performer's energy and life that connoisseurs claim that it is more difficult to be a *kokken* than a performer.

These extreme examples show that there exists a level at which extra-daily body techniques engage the performer's energy in a pure state, that is, on the pre-expressive level. In classical Japanese theatre, this level is sometimes openly displayed, sometimes concealed. It is, however, always present in every performer, in every tradition or genre. It is the substance of scenic presence.

To speak of the performer's 'energy' means using a term which lends itself to a thousand misunderstandings. The word energy must be immediately given operative value. Etymologically it means 'to be at work'. How does it happen, then, that the performer's body is at work on a pre-expressive level? What other words could replace the word 'energy'?

Translating the principles of Asian performers into a European language, one uses words like 'energy', 'life', 'power' and 'spirit' for the Japanese terms *ki-ai, kokoro, io-in,* and *koshi,* the Balinese *taksu, virasa, chikara,* and *bayu,* the Chinese *kung-fu, shun toeng,* and the Sanskrit *prana, shakti.* The practical meanings of the principles of the performer's life are obscured by complex terms imprecisely translated.

Let us try to get ahead by going backwards: how should our term 'energy' be translated?

'We say that a performer has, or does not have, *koshi,* to indicate that he has, or doesn't have, the right energy while working', *kabuki* performer Sawamura Sojurō translates for me. In Japanese, *koshi* is not an abstract concept but a very precise part of the body, the hips. To say 'you have *koshi,* you do not have *koshi*' means 'you have hips, you do not have hips'. But, for a performer, what does 'not having hips' mean?

When we walk using daily body techniques, the hips follow the movement of walking. In the *kabuki, nō,* and *kyōgen* performers' extra-daily techniques, the hips, on the contrary, must remain fixed. To block the hips while walking, it is necessary to bend the knees slightly and, using the trunk as a single unit, to engage the vertebral column, which presses downwards. In this way, two different tensions are created in the upper and lower parts of the body, respectively, and dictate a new point of balance. It is a way of engendering the performer's life and only secondarily does it become a particular stylistic characteristic.

In fact, the performer's life is based on an alteration of balance.

Suriashi, 'feet which lick': this is the name given to the way of walking in Japanese *nō* theatre. The performer never lifts his feet from the ground. He moves forward, or turns around, lifting only the toes. One foot slides forward, the front leg is slightly bent, the back leg is stretched, the weight of the body – contrary to what is natural – is on the back leg. The stomach and buttocks are contracted, the pelvis tilts forward and down as if one thread was pulling its front part downwards and another thread was pulling its back part upwards. The spinal column is stretched 'as if one had swallowed a sword'. The shoulder blades are held as closely together as possible, thus lowering the shoulders. The neck and the head are aligned with the trunk. The body – according to an image employed by Meyerhold for one of his bio-mechanical exercises – is like the keel of a boat whose structure is inspired by the skeleton of a fish, but unlike a fish, it is not flexible and instead is held by a firm axis.

This elaborate net of tensions, the details of which are concealed beneath heavy and sumptuous costumes, is the source of the suggestive presence of *nō* performers. They say: '*Nō* is a walking dance.'

Kabuki is also a 'walking dance'. Here, the performer follows two distinct criteria: *aragoto* and *wagoto*. In *aragoto*, the 'rough' style, the 'law of diagonals' is applied. The head is one end of an acute diagonal line while one of the feet, stretched out to the side, is the other end. The entire body, supported by one leg, maintains an altered and dynamic balance.

The *wagoto* is the so-called 'soft' or 'realistic' style. The performer uses a sinuous way of moving which reminds one of the *tribhangi* of classical Indian dance. *Tribhangi* means 'three arches'. In Indian Odissi dance, the performer's body must be curved like an '*S*' which passes through the head, shoulders and hips. The principle of *tribhangi* sinuosity is clearly visible in all classical Indian statues, just as it is in Greek statuary after Praxiteles. In *kabuki*'s *wagoto*, the performer moves his body with a lateral, undulating movement which produces a constant amplification of the imbalance in the relationship between the body weight and its base, the feet.

In Balinese theatre, the performer supports her/himself on the soles of the feet while at the same time lifting the toes and the front of the feet as much as possible, thus reducing contact with the ground by almost a half. To avoid falling, s/he must spread the legs and bend the knees.

The Indian *kathakali* performer supports himself on the sides of the feet. But the consequences are the same: this new base produces a radical change of balance resulting in a posture with legs spread and knees bent.

In another codified form, classical ballet, the intention to oblige the performer to assume a precarious balance is found in the basic positions themselves. If, on a typical day, we join the beginners' class at the Ballet School of the Royal Theatre of Copenhagen, founded by Bournonville in 1830, we hear the teacher repeat to the seven-or eight-year old children: 'Squeeze your buttocks. Imagine that your legs have been zipped together. Weight in front, not on the heels. The heels must be just barely lifted from the floor. Not too much! Just enough to slide a sheet of paper underneath them. The audience must not realize that they are lifted. The trunk is immobile, like a box which is carried by the legs. Stand straight! As if you are hungry and your stomach is stretched. You must stretch up with the trunk, as if I was pulling you by the hair.' It is this exhausting balance of the basic posture which leads to the marvel and lightness of the *arabesques* and *attitudes*.

All codified performance forms contain this constant principle: a deformation of the daily technique of walking, of moving in space, and of keeping the body immobile. This extra-daily technique is based on an alteration of balance. The aim is a permanently unstable balance. Rejecting 'natural' balance, the performer intervenes in space with a 'luxury' balance: complex, seemingly superfluous and costing excessive energy. 'One can be born with grace or rhythm but not with the balance I am thinking of.'[3]

It could be claimed that this 'luxury' balance is a formalization, a stylization, a codification . . . However, these terms are usually used without questioning the motives which have led to the choice of physical positions that hamper our 'natural' way of being, our way of using the body in daily life.

What exactly is happening?

Balance – the human ability to keep the body erect and to move through space in that position – is the result of a series of relationships and muscular tensions. When we amplify our movements – by taking longer steps or by holding our heads more forwards or backwards than usual – our balance is threatened. A whole series of tensions is then set in action just to keep us from falling. The tradition of modern mime is based on this *déséquilibre*, as a means to dilate scenic presence, just like being 'off-balance' in modern dance.

Anyone who has seen a Marcel Marceau performance will certainly have stopped for a moment to consider the strange fate of the mime who appears alone on the stage for a few seconds, in between Marceau's numbers, holding up a card on which is written the title of the next piece.

Pierre Verry, the mime whose task it was to present Marceau's title cards, has described how he sought to achieve the maximum degree of scenic existence during the brief instant in which he appeared on the stage, without having – and without being able – to do anything. In order to reach this result, in his few seconds on stage, he concentrated on finding a 'precarious balance'. Thus his static posture became a dynamic immobility. Verry had to reduce himself to the essential, and he discovered the essential in the alteration of balance.[4]

When we are standing erect, we can never be immobile. Even when we think we are motionless, minute movements are displacing our weight. With a continuous series of adjustments, our weight presses now on the front, now on the back, now on the left, now on the right sides of the feet. Even in the most absolute immobility, these micro-movements are present, sometimes condensed, sometimes enlarged, more or less controlled, according to our physiological condition, our age, our profession.

There are scientific laboratories specialized in the analysis of balance by means of the measurement of the various types of pressure applied by the feet on the ground. From these analyses result diagrams in which anyone can see how many complicated and laborious movements are made to maintain a standing position. Experiments have been conducted with professional performers. If they are asked to imagine themselves carrying a weight, running, walking, falling or jumping, this imagining in itself immediately produces a modification in their balance. No modifications occur in the balance of non-performers, for whom imagination remains a mental activity without perceptible physical consequences.[5]

All this can tell us a great deal about balance and about the relationship between mental processes and muscular tensions. It does not, however, tell us anything new about the performer. In fact, to say that performers are accustomed to controlling their own presence and translating their mental images into physical impulses simply means that performers are performers. But the series of micro-movements revealed in scientific laboratories in which balance is measured puts us on another track: they are the life-source which gives birth to the performer's presence.

Let us return to the *nō* theatre. The spirituality which is characteristic of its performances varies according to the styles of the principal actors' families. These stylistic differences are related to the various procedures used to compose a 'luxury' balance. A specialist in Japanese theatre writes:

> My general impression from seeing a number of different actors has been that the body is tilted slightly forward. However, Shiro said that in the Kanze and Kongō schools of *nō* there are enough individual differences that one cannot generalize; in the Hōshō school the body tends to lean back slightly; and in the Kita and Konparu schools flexing of the knees is emphasized so that the body looks as if it is sunk rather than tilted either forward or back. As a general rule, Shiro said, too much forward tilting makes the body appear unstable and reduces the actor's stage presence, while too much leaning backward prevents the energy from being projected forward. I interpret this to mean that each individual must find the critical degree of tilt that is right for his own basic posture.
>
> Normally, when a person stands erect, the body's weight is distributed equally over the soles of the feet – but this is not the case in *nō*. Kita Nagayo, a *nō* actor of the Kita school, explained to his class during the 1981 UCLA Summer Institute program that the weight should be placed on the balls of the feet, a description I have heard from other *nō* and *kyōgen* actors as well. Nomura Shiro, however, said that when he stands, weight is on the heels of his feet ... The

20

particular placement of weight in the feet may also be the result of the overall body carriage that a given *nō* actor considers to be most effective for himself.[6]

The basic positions of the classical forms of Asian theatre and dance are further examples of a conscious and controlled distortion of balance. The same can be said of the basic ballet positions and of Decroux' mime system, where daily balance technique is abandoned, and a luxury balance which dilates the tensions in the body is adopted instead.

I have given these examples because this luxury balance is evident to the spectator and is codified for the performer by very precise rules. The same principles, not as evident but just as conscious, can however be observed in every skilled performer, even one from a non-codified tradition and even when her/his style is realistic.

'Do you ask whether the way you walk on the stage is different from the gait you use on the street? Yes it is.' In this way, Torzov-Stanislavski began his course in plasticity, distinguishing the gait of the dramatic actor from the choreography of the dancer. He explains the differences between the two, the dangers of the exaggeration of both, and the conditions necessary for the plasticity which is 'an energy rising from the deepest wells of their beings. . . . As it flows down the network of your muscular system, arousing your inner motor centres, it stirs you to external activity.' He dwells upon the correct scenic gait, on systems for developing and adjusting it. 'In other words, let us learn how to walk all over again from the beginning, both on the stage and off it.'

Torzov-Stanislavski proposes one exercise after another, explaining the consequences which result from various types of footwear: the type used by Chinese women, 'tight shoes to transform the human feet into hooves such as cows have', the walk of women of his day which is 'sacrificed on the altar of fashion and silly heels'. He explains the structure of the leg and of the foot, the various ways the foot is in contact with the ground, the phase of movement when the body weight passes from one foot to the other, how to 'rise into the air . . . not upwards but forwards in a horizontal line'. He analyses the function of the hips and pelvis: 'They have a double function. In the first place, like the spinal column, they moderate side shocks and the swaying of the torso from side to side when we walk. Secondly, they thrust the whole leg forward each time we take a step.' As part of this analysis, he describes a scene which had made a strong impression upon him: a parade of soldiers. The soldiers were behind a stockade; only their chests, shoulders and heads were visible. 'They did not appear to be walking at all but rolling along on skates or skis over an absolutely smooth surface. One had the sense of their gliding . . . the upper parts of their bodies positively floated by behind the fence in a horizontal line.'[7]

Meyerhold maintained that he recognized an actor's talent by the way the

21

actor used his feet, by the dynamism with which they were in contact with the ground and with which they moved. He conjures up for the actor the image of the vigorous, functional, inelegant gait of a sailor on the deck of a pitching ship. For one of his exercises, he even spoke about the 'ecstasy of the legs' which reveal the actor's reaction at the end of an action.[8] He claimed to have discovered the fundamental law of movement by reflecting on his reactions when, one day, he slipped on an icy street. He was falling to the left and automatically moved his head and arms to the right as a counterweight.[9]

In bio-mechanics, said Meyerhold, each movement must be consciously reconstructed so that it keeps the dynamism implicit in the automatic reactions which maintain one's balance, not in a static way, but by losing it and then regaining it with a series of successive adjustments.[10] This principle is identical with that of *fall/recovering* upon which Doris Humphrey constructed her dance method: one begins to walk by falling; in the next phase, one controls the falling weight.

Charles Dullin often said that it is typical of a beginning actor not to know how to walk on stage. He developed numerous exercises and themes for improvisation on ways of moving and analysed their effect on muscular tonus, posture, rhythm, and the use of the eyes.[11]

'The feet are the centre of expressivity and communicate their reactions to the rest of the body.'[12] This conviction of Grotowski's had notable consequences on the composition training he developed with his actors, involving dozens of exercises and tasks for developing new postures and dynamics.

At Odin Teatret, *gangene*, the ways of moving, walking and stopping, is something to which the actors constantly return in their individual training, irrespective of how many years they have been working.

'All the technique of the dance', says Sanjukta Panigrahi, describing Indian Odissi dance but referring to a general principle governing the performer's life, 'is based on a division of the body into two equal halves according to a vertical line which passes through it, and on the unequal distribution of weight, sometimes more on one half of the body, sometimes more on the other half.'

The dance amplifies, as if under a microscope, those continuous and minute shifts of weight which we use to remain still while standing and which laboratories specializing in balance measurement reveal by means of complicated diagrams.

It is this *dance of balance* that performers reveal in fundamental principles common to all scenic forms.

Fei-cha, 'flying feet': this is the name given to a basic step in Peking Opera.

The dance of oppositions

In the search for the principles from which the performer's life springs no account whatsoever is taken of the distinctions between theatre, dance and mime.

Such distinctions are, in any case, fluid. Gordon Craig, scorning the contorted images used by critics to describe the English actor Henry Irving's way of walking, simply explained that Irving did not walk on the stage, but danced on it.

The same affirmation, but this time in a negative sense, was used to deprecate Meyerhold's research. After his production of *Don Juan*, some critics wrote that it was not real theatre but ballet. They were not yet able to see what was already evident to Meyerhold himself: the essence of scenic movement, based on contrasts – which later he defined as bio-mechanics – is common to both genres, danced performance as well as spoken performance. But we will discuss this 'ballet' – bio-mechanics – in a subsequent chapter.

> Is raising the eyes dancing? When the eyes cannot go any higher, is raising the head dancing? No, the gaze follows its course. But if, in order to continue seeing something which continues to move away, it is necessary to tilt the neck backwards, then the chest, waist, pelvis in turn ... where does the dance begin? At the neck or at the thigh.[13]

The rigid distinction between dance and theatre reveals a profound wound, a void with no tradition, which continuously threatens to draw the actor towards a muting of the body and the dancer towards virtuosity. To a classical Asian performer, such a distinction would seem absurd, just as it would have seemed absurd to European performers in other historical periods, to a jester or a commedia dell'arte or Elizabethan actor. We can ask a *nō* or *kabuki* performer how he would translate the word 'energy' into the language of his work, but he would shake his head if we asked him to explain the rigid distinction between dance and theatre.

'Energy', said *kabuki* actor Sawamura Sojurō, 'could be translated as *koshi*.' And according to *nō* actor Hideo Kanze: 'My father never said, "use more *koshi*". He taught me what it was about by making me walk while he held me by the hips.' To overcome the resistance of his father's grasp, he was forced to incline his torso slightly forwards, bend his knees, press his feet upon the floor and slide them forward rather than taking a normal step: an efficient means of obtaining the basic *nō* walk. Energy, like *koshi*, is not the result of a simple and mechanical alteration of balance, but of a tension between opposing forces.

At the *nō* school of the Kita family, a different means is used. The performer must imagine that above him is suspended a ring of iron which pulls him upwards and he must resist this pull in order to keep his feet on the ground. The Japanese term which describes these opposing tensions is *hippari hai*, which means 'to pull someone towards oneself while being pulled in turn'. *Hippari hai* takes place between the upper and lower parts of the performer's body, as well as between the front and back. There is also *hippari hai* between the performers and the musicians. They interact in discordant harmony, trying to diverge, alternately surprising each other, interrupting each other's tempo, yet not moving so far apart as to lose either the contact between them or their particular bond of opposition.

Expanding this concept, we could say that extra-daily body techniques have a *hippari hai* relationship with the techniques of daily usage. We have in fact seen that extra-daily techniques are different from daily techniques, but nevertheless maintain a tension with them without becoming separated from them.

The performer's body reveals its life to the spectator by means of a miriad of tensions between opposing forces. This is the *principle of opposition*. Certain traditions constructed elaborate composition systems on the basis of this recurring principle, which all performers use, consciously or unconsciously.

The codified movement system of the Peking Opera performer is built on this principle: every action must begin from the direction opposite to that in which it will be carried out. All forms of traditional Balinese theatre are based on the construction of a series of oppositions between *keras* and *manis*. *Keras* means strong, hard, vigorous; *manis*, delicate, soft, tender. The terms *manis* and *keras* can be applied to different movements, to the positions of the various parts of the body in a dance, to the various sequences of the same dance. If one analyses an *agem*, one of the basic positions of Balinese dance, one observes that it contains a conscious alternation of parts of the body in *keras* position with parts of the body in *manis* position.

The dance of oppositions characterizes the performer's life on different levels. But, in general, in the search for this dance, the performer has a compass with which to orientate her/himself: unease. *Le mime est à l'aise dans le mal-aise* ('it is in discomfort that the mime feels comfortable'), says Decroux,[14] and his maxim is echoed by masters from all traditions. Tokuho Azuma, master of Japanese *buyo* dance, repeatedly told her students to use pain as a means to verify whether or not a position had been correctly assumed. If the position did not hurt, then it was incorrect. And, smiling, she would add: 'But if it hurts, this does not necessarily mean that it is correct.' The same advice is given by Sanjukta Panigrahi, by the masters of Peking Opera, of classical ballet or Balinese dance. Discomfort is used, then, as a control system, a kind of internal radar with which the performer observes her/himself while performing. This observation is not done with the eyes, but through physical perceptions which confirm that non-habitual, extra-daily tensions are at work in the body. 'Actor, my friend, my brother, you live only by contrariness, contradiction and constriction. You live only in the "contra".'[15]

When I ask Balinese master I Made Pasek Tempo what the performer's principal gift is, he answers that it is *tahan*, 'the ability to resist'. The same awareness is found in the working language of the Chinese performer, who has mastery when he has *kung-fu*, literally, the 'ability to hold fast, to resist'. This terminology brings to mind something which in another language could

24

be translated by the word 'energy', the ability to persist in work. We will discuss this further in chapter 5.

Katsuko Azuma explains, for example, which forces are at work in the movement found in both *buyo* and *nō*, when the body leans slightly forwards and the arms are stretched out in front of the body in a gentle curve. She speaks of forces which are acting in the direction opposite to that which is apparent: the arms are not stretching outwards, but it is as if they are clasping a large box to the chest. Hence, while moving outwards they are in fact pressing inwards, in the same way that the torso, as if being pushed backwards, opposes a resistance and leans forwards.

In the various daily techniques of the body, the forces which bring alive the actions of extending or withdrawing an arm, the legs, or the fingers of one hand, act one at a time. In extra-daily techniques, the two opposing forces (extending and withdrawing) are in action simultaneously. Or better, the arms, the legs, the fingers, the spine, the neck, extend as if resisting a force which obliges them to bend.

Anyone with a rudimentary knowledge of anatomy could object that this procedure is not essentially different from what happens in the natural mechanics of movement in daily life. It is different, however, from what we normally *perceive* in our bodies and in the bodies of others. The extra-daily techniques dilate, bring into view for the spectator, and therefore render meaningful, one aspect which is hidden in daily behaviour: *showing* something engenders interpretation.

This is one of the objectives of every artistic technique. A line by Goethe says: 'Love and art amplify the small things.'

Consistent inconsistency and the virtue of omission

The term 'stylization' often distracts one from observing how North Pole performers deform natural postures without apparent motivation. They apply norms which are completely inconsistent with the economy of action and even demand great effort simply to stand still doing nothing.

If we limit ourselves to repeating that this is nothing more than a question of 'stylization', we risk making two errors in the understanding of the facts. On the one hand, by limiting ourselves to the idea that every culture has its particular conventions, we ignore the evidence of their immediate kinaesthetic effectiveness, an effectiveness apparent even to those who know little or nothing of the conventions themselves. On the other hand, if we take 'stylization' as a sign with which to recognize and define each individual tradition and therefore as a fact sanctioned by historical differences, we dull our ability to marvel and be curious. The diverse ways of constructing a scenic behaviour which is artificial but believable then seem no more strange to us than the obvious differences between the various spoken languages. We thus disregard the way of thinking implicit in the practice of extra-daily techniques: consistent inconsistency.

It is interesting to observe how some performers abandon the techniques of daily behaviour even when they have to carry out simple actions (standing up, sitting down, walking, looking, speaking, touching, taking). But even more interesting is the fact that this inconsistency, or initial lack of adherence to the economy of daily practice, is then organized into a new, systematic consistency.

The puzzling artificiality which is characteristic of the extra-daily techniques elaborated by North Pole performers leads to another quality of energy. The performer, through long practice and continuous training, fixes this 'inconsistency' by a process of innervation, develops new neuro-muscular reflexes which result in a renewed body culture, a 'second nature', a new consistency, artificial but marked with *bios*.

Let us take an example. Our hands and fingers are continuously changing tensions and positions, both when we speak (and gesticulate) and when we are acting or reacting in order to take something, to support ourselves, to caress. In the case of an action or reaction, the position of each finger changes as soon as the eyes have transmitted the relevant information, depending on whether we are about to pick up a piece of broken glass or a bread crumb, a heavy dictionary or an inflated balloon. Our fingers, before reaching the object, already assume the muscular tonus suitable to the weight and tactile quality of the object. The manipulatory muscles are already at work. The asymmetry of the fingers is a sign of life, of credibility, manifest by means of the tensions of the manipulatory muscles, which are ready to act according to the weight, the temperature, the volume, the fragility of the object towards which the hand is extended, but also according to the affective reaction which the object elicits in us.

The hand acts, and in so doing, speaks.

In daily life, these actions and reactions occur according to a non-reflex organicity, the result of automatisms which are genetically transmitted and culturally learned. If no blocks – embarrassment, fear, illness – interrupt the process, we say that the hand moves 'naturally'.

South Pole performers, when they are at the peak of their craftsmanship, know how to overcome the blocks resulting from the artificial situation of the stage and succeed in making their actions and reactions flow, even down to those minute processes governed by the refined automatisms of daily life.

North Pole performers, however, do not have recourse to the verisimilitude of daily behaviour. When their craftsmanship is of high quality, they transform a codified system into a 'second nature', whose logic is equivalent to the logic of organic life.

In India, the *hasta mudra* are the basis for the elaboration of a 'second nature' of the hands. In Sanskrit, *hasta* (hand) *mudra* (seal) refers to a cipher-language articulated by means of the positions of the hands and the fingers.

It originated in sacred statues and in prayer practices. When used by performers to emphasize or translate the words of a text or to add descriptive detail to them, the *mudra* assume, above and beyond their ideogrammatic value, a dynamism, a play of tensions and oppositions whose visual impact is decisive in determining their believability in the eyes of the spectator. In spite of the 'stylized' artificiality of the gestures, the spectator perceives a consistency which is equivalent to, although different from, that which is manifest in daily life.

Balinese performers, although belonging to Hindu culture, have lost the meanings of the *mudra*, but have kept the richness of their micro-variations and the vibrant asymmetry of the life they contain. A symphony of alternations between vigour and softness (*keras* and *manis*), between immobility and movement, in every individual finger and in the entire hand, changes the artificiality into a consistent and vital quality.

Let us listen now to a spectator describing a performance:

> I once saw Kongō Iwao play the Chinese beauty Yang Kuei-fei in the *nō* play *Kōtei*, and I shall never forget the beauty of his hands showing ever so slightly from beneath his sleeves. As I watched his hands, I would occasionally glance down at my own hands resting on my knees. Again, and yet again, I looked back at the actor's hands, comparing them with my own; and there was no difference between them. Yet strangely the hands of the man on the stage were indescribably beautiful, while those on my knees were but ordinary hands.[16]

Another significant example is found in the use of the eyes and the way of directing the gaze.

We normally look straight ahead and at an angle of about thirty degrees below the horizon. If we keep the head in the same position and raise the eyes thirty degrees, a muscular tension will be created in the neck and in the upper part of the trunk, which will in turn have repercussions on our balance.

The *kathakali* actor follows his hands with his eyes, composing the *mudra* slightly above his normal field of vision. Balinese performers look upwards. In all of the Peking Opera *liang-xiang* ('sudden freezing of positions'), the eyes look upwards. *Nō* actors describe how they lose all sense of space, and how they have difficulty keeping their balance, because of the tiny slits in their masks, which limit their vision. This is another explanation for their way of walking, in which their feet never leave the floor – rather like blind men who slide along, feeling their way, always ready to stop in case of unforeseen obstacles.

All of these performers use a different angle of vision when performing than they do in daily life. Their physical posture is changed, as is the muscular tonus of the torso, the pressure of the feet on the ground, the balance. The consistent inconsistency of the extra-daily way of using the eyes brings about a qualitative change of energy.

When these elements of scenic behaviour are woven together they seem to be much more complex than daily movements. In fact, they are the result of simplification: they are composed of moments in which the oppositions governing the body's life are manifest at the simplest level. This occurs because a well-defined number of forces – oppositions – are isolated, amplified, and assembled, simultaneously or in succession. Once again, this is an uneconomical use of the body, because in daily techniques, the forces tend to combine, with a subsequent saving of time and energy.

Decroux says that mime is a 'portrait of work',[17] accomplished by the body. He makes a point which can also be applied to other traditions. Sometimes this bodily 'portrait of work' is made visible in a direct way, at other times it is concealed, as is the case with ballet dancers, for example, who hide their weight and effort behind an image of lightness and grace.

The principle of oppositions, which are the essence of energy, is connected to the principle of simplification. Simplification in this case means the omission of certain elements in order to put other elements into relief, thus making these other elements seem essential.

Dario Fo explains that the power of a performer's movement is the result of 'synthesis', of the concentration, into a small space, of an action which uses a large amount of energy and reproduces only those elements essential to the action, any accessory elements being eliminated.

Decroux considers the body as being limited essentially to the trunk and treats the movements of the arms and legs as anecdotes. These movements, if they originate only in the joints – shoulder, elbow, wrist, knee, ankle, etc. – do not involve the trunk and therefore do not change the body's balance. They remain pure gesticulation. They become scenically alive only if they are a prolongation of an impulse or a micro-action which occurs in the spinal column.[18] The same concept is found in the teachings of all masters of 'physical actions', from Stanislavski to Grotowski (even if the 'method of physical actions' is not limited to this aspect only and can imply a detailed composition of internal images).

From the foregoing can be drawn a valuable orientation for our craft: we can go down the same street in the opposite direction. Macro-actions, if they are really such and not gesticulations, can be absorbed by the trunk, while their original is preserved. The actions become transformed into impulses, into micro-actions of a nearly immobile body which is acting. This process, according to which the space the action occupies is restricted, can be defined as the absorption of the action.

The consequence of the process of the absorption of an action is an intensification of the tensions which enliven the performer and is perceived by the spectator irrespective of the size of the action.

The opposition between one force pushing towards action and another force holding back is translated into a series of rules according to which an opposition is established between energy employed in space and energy employed in time. Some performers say that it is as if an action continues rather than actually finishing where the gesture has stopped in space.

Both *nō* and *kabuki* use the expression *tameru*, which can be represented by a Chinese ideogram meaning 'to accumulate' or by a Japanese ideogram meaning 'to bend something which is both flexible and resistant', like a cane of bamboo. *Tameru* defines the action of holding back, of retaining. From *tameru* comes *tame*, the ability to keep energy in, to concentrate into an action limited in space the energy necessary for a much larger action. A performer's skill is measured by the degree to which he possesses this ability. In order to say that a student has or doesn't have sufficient scenic presence, the master tells him that he has, or doesn't have, *tame*.

All this may seem like an overly complicated and excessive codification of the performer's art. In fact, it derives from an experience which is common to performers from many different traditions: the compression, into restricted movements, of the same physical energies necessary to accomplish a much larger and heavier action. Engaging the whole body to light a cigarette, for example, as if the match was as heavy as a large stone, or as if it was incandescent; leaving the mouth slightly open with the same force needed to bite something hard. This process, which composes a small action as if it was much larger, conceals the energy and makes the performer's entire body come alive, even when immobile.

It is probably for this reason that many famous performers have been able to turn so-called 'stage business' into great scenes. When they have to stop acting and stay on the sidelines while other performers develop the principal action, they are able to conceal, in almost imperceptible movements, the force of actions which they are denied.

'Stage business' does not belong only to the Western tradition. In the seventeenth and eighteenth centuries, the *kabuki* performer Kaneko Kichizaemon, in a treatise on the performer's art entitled *Dust in the Ears*, refers to a statement made by Matsumoto Nazaemon: in certain performances, when only one performer is dancing, the other performers turn their backs to the audience, sit in front of the musicians and relax. 'I myself do not relax', says Matsumoto Nazaemon. 'Even though I am there in front of the musicians, I am performing the dance in my mind. If I did not do so, the view of my back would be so displeasing that the performance would be brought to a halt.'[19]

The theatrical virtue of omission does not consist in 'letting oneself go' into something undefined, into non-action. On the stage, for the performer, omission means, rather, 'retaining' that which characterizes scenic presence without squandering it in an excess of expressivity and vitality. The beauty of omission, in fact, is the suggestiveness of indirect action, of the life which is revealed with a maximum of intensity in a minimum of activity.

This way of thinking and proceeding reaches its extreme manifestation in *i-guse*, a particular sequence in *nō*. The main performer, the *shite*, is seated in the centre of the stage, as immobile as a rock, his head very slightly inclined, while the chorus sings and speaks. To the uninitiated spectator, it seems as if the *shite*'s position is inert and that it does not require any ability whatsoever. The performer, however, is dancing. Inside himself. Technique is negating itself, it is possessed and surpassed. It is theatre which transcends itself. The *i-guse* is called 'the action of silence' or 'to dance with the heart'.

The great *nō* performer Hisao Kanze, who died in 1977, once said, when referring to the *i-guse*, in which the performer seems to be doing nothing for such a long time:

> I want to exist on the stage as a flower might, one which by chance has just happened to blossom there. Each member of the audience too sits brooding over various images of his own. Like a single flower. The flower is alive. The flower must breathe. The stage tells the story of the flower.[20]

Equivalence

If we put some flowers in a vase, we do so in order to show how beautiful they are, to please our senses of sight and smell. We can also make them take on ulterior meanings: filial or religious piety, love, recognition, respect. But beautiful as they might be, flowers have a shortcoming: taken out of their own context, they continue to represent only themselves. They are like the performer described by Decroux: the man condemned to resemble a man, the body imitating a body. This may well be pleasing but it is not sufficient to be considered art. 'For art to be', adds Decroux, 'the idea of one thing must be given by another thing.'[21] Flowers in a vase are, however, irremediably flowers in a vase, sometimes subjects of works of art, but never works of art themselves.

But suppose we imagine using cut flowers to represent the struggle of the plant to grow, to rise up from the earth into which its roots sink ever deeper as it reaches up to the sky. Let us imagine wanting to represent the passage of time, as the plant blossoms, grows, droops, fades and dies. If we succeed, the flowers will represent something other than flowers and will be a work of art. We will have made an *ikebana*.

The ideogram for *ikebana* means 'to make flowers live'.

The life of the flowers, precisely because it has been interrupted, can be represented. The procedure is clear: something has been wrenched from the normal conditions of its life (this is the fate of our daily flowers arranged in a vase), and those conditions have been replaced and rebuilt using other, equivalent rules.

We cannot represent the flowers' blossoming and withering in temporal terms. But the passage of time can be suggested with an analogy in space. One can bring together – compare – one flower in bud with another already in full bloom. With two branches, one thrusting upwards and the other pointing downwards, one can draw attention to the directions in which the plant is developing, to the force which binds it to the earth and to the force which pushes away. A third branch, extending along an oblique line, can show the combined force which results from the other opposing tensions. This composition seems to derive from refined stylization but is, however, the consequence of the analysis and dissection of a phenomenon, that is, the transposition of energy acting in time into a composition of lines which, with a principle of equivalence, extend in space.

This equivalent transposition opens the composition to new meanings, different from the original ones. The branch which is reaching upwards becomes associated with Heaven, the branch extending downwards, with the Earth, and the branch in the centre with the intermediary between these two opposing entities: Man. The result of a schematic analysis of reality and the transposition of this reality following principles which represent it without reproducing it, becomes an object for philosophical contemplation.

'The mind has difficulty maintaining the concept of the bud because the thing thus designated is prey to an impetuous development and shows – in spite of our thought – a strong impulse not to be a bud but a flower.' These are words which Bertolt Brecht attributes to Hu-jeh, who adds: 'Thus, for the thinker, the concept of the flower bud is already the concept of something which aspires to be other than what it is.'[22] This 'difficult' thought is exactly what *ikebana* proposes to be: an indication of the past and a suggestion of the future, a representation through immobility of the continuous motion which turns the positive into the negative and vice versa.

Abstract meanings derive from *ikebana* through the precise work of analysis and transposition of a physical phenomenon. If one began with these abstract meanings, one would never reach the concreteness and precision of *ikebana*, whereas by starting from precision and concreteness, one does attain these abstract meanings. Performers often try to proceed from the abstract to the concrete. They believe that the point of departure can be what one wants to express, which then implies the use of a technique suitable for this expression.

Ikebana shows how certain forces which develop in time can have an equivalence in spatial terms. Decroux insists on this use of equivalence, which is a recurring principle. His mime is based on the rigorous substitution of extra-daily tensions equivalent to those necessary for the body's daily techniques. Decroux explains how an action from daily life can be believably represented by acting in *exactly* the opposite way. The action of pushing something is shown not by projecting the chest forward and pressing down with the back foot – as one does in the daily action – but by arching the spine concavely, as if instead of pushing it was being pushed, and bending the arms towards the chest and pressing downwards with the front leg and foot. This consistent and radical inversion of the forces characteristic of the daily action produces the work involved in the daily action. It is a fundamental principle of the theatre: on stage, the action must be real, but it is not important that it be realistic.

Everything takes place as if the performer's body was taken apart and then recomposed according to successive and antagonistic movements. The performer does not relive the action; s/he recreates the life of the action. At the end of this work of decomposition and recomposition, the body no longer resembles itself. Like the flowers in our vase or like Japanese *ikebana*, the performer is cut from the 'natural' context in which daily techniques dominate. Like the flowers and branches in *ikebana*, performers, in order to be scenically alive, cannot present *what they are*. They must represent what they want to show by means of forces and procedures which have the same value and the same effectiveness. In other words, they must give up their own 'spontaneity', that is, their own automatisms.

The various codifications of the performer's art are, above all, methods to break the automatic responses of daily life and to create equivalents to them.

Naturally, this rupture of automatisms is not expression. But without this rupture, there is no expression.

An actor, speaking to his director, explains his own criteria for acting:

> I speak in the third person and name someone, but I wait for a moment before indicating him or turning towards him. Or, I describe a fact. When I want to underline the text with physical actions, I delay them. First I speak and then I 'describe' physically.[23]

'Kill the breathing. Kill the rhythm', Katsuko Azuma's master repeated to her. To 'kill' breathing and to 'kill' rhythm means to be aware of the tendency automatically to link gesture to the rhythm of breathing, speaking and music, and to break this link. The opposite of linking automatically is consciously to create a new connection.

The precepts which demand the killing of rhythm and breathing, as expressed by Katsuko Azuma's master, show how the search for oppositions can result in the rupture of the automatisms of the body's daily techniques. Killing the rhythm in fact implies creating a resistance, a series of tensions to prevent the flow of words from coinciding with the actions which accompany them and to prevent the movements of the dance from synchronizing automatically with the cadences of the music. Killing the breathing means slowing down or withholding the exhalation – which is a moment of relaxation – by means of a contrary force.

All these principles are not aesthetic ways of suggesting how to add beauty to the performer's body nor how to 'stylize' it. They are means *to remove* what is obviously the body's daily aspect, in order to avoid it being only a human body condemned to resemble itself, to present and represent only itself.

A decided body

'True expression', said Grotowski at an ISTA conference in Bonn in 1980, 'is that of a tree.' And he explained: 'If an actor *wants* to express, then he is divided. One part of him is doing the willing, another the expressing; one part is commanding and another is carrying out the commands.'

Many European languages have an expression which might be chosen to epitomize what is essential for the performer's life. It is a grammatically paradoxical expression, in which a passive form assumes an active meaning, and in which an indication of energized availability for action is presented as a form of passivity. This expression is not ambiguous, it is hermaphroditic, combining within it both action and passion, and in spite of its strangeness, it is commonly used. One says, in fact, *essere deciso, être décidé, to be decided*. And this does not mean that someone or something decides for us or that we submit to a decision. Neither does it mean that we are deciding, nor that we are carrying out the action of deciding.

Between these two opposite conditions flows a current of life which language does not seem able to represent and around which it flutters with images. Only direct experience, not explanation, shows what it means 'to be decided'. To explain it with words, we must refer to innumerable associations of ideas, to examples, to the construction of ingenious situations. Yet everyone thinks s/he knows what the expression 'to be decided' means. All the complex images and abstruse rules which are applied to performers, the elaboration of artistic precepts and their sophisticated aesthetics, are vaultings and acrobatics to explain experiences. To explain the performer's experience one must use a complicated strategy to create artificially the conditions in which that experience can be reproduced.

Let us imagine that we are once again entering the intimate world of the work which takes place in Tokyo between Katsuko Azuma and her master, Tokuho Azuma. When Tokuho judges that she has succeeded in passing her experience on to her student, she will also pass on her name. Azuma, then, says to the future Azuma: 'Find your *ma*.' To an architect, *ma* means space; to a musician, tempo. And also, interval, pause, rest, rhythm. And this is what it means to a performer: 'To find your *ma* you must kill the rhythm, that is, you must find your *jo-ha-kyu*.'

The expression *jo-ha-kyu* describes the three phases into which all of a Japanese performer's actions are divided. The first phase is determined by the opposition between a force which tends to increase and another force which holds back (*jo* means 'to retain'); the second phase (*ha*, 'to break') occurs at the moment when one is freed from the retaining force, until one arrives at the third phase (*kyu*, 'speed'), where the action culminates, using up all of its force in order to stop suddenly, as if faced with a resistance, a new *jo* ready to start again.

To teach Azuma to move according to *jo-ha-kyu*, her master holds her by the waist and then suddenly lets her go. Azuma strives to make the first steps (while being held), bending her knees, pressing the soles of her feet to the ground, inclining her trunk slightly. Then, released by her teacher, she advances quickly to a specified point, where she suddenly stops, as if a deep ravine had opened up a few centimetres in front of her. When a performer has learned, as second nature, this artificial way of moving, s/he appears to have been cut off from everyday space-time and seems to be 'alive': s/he is 'decided'.

The three phases of *jo-ha-kyu* impregnate the atoms, the cells, the entire organism of a Japanese performance. They apply to every one of a performer's actions, to each gesture, to breathing, to the music, to each scene, to each play, to the composition of an entire day of *nō* performances. It is a kind of code which runs through all the levels of organization of theatres and classical music in Japan.

All the teachings which Azuma the master imparts to Azuma the student are aimed at the discovery of the centre of the individual's own energy. The methods of the search are meticulously codified, the fruit of generations of experience. The result is uncertain, impossible to define with precision, and differs from person to person.

Today, Katsuko Azuma says that the principle of her life, of her scenic presence, can be defined as a centre of gravity found at the midpoint of an imaginary line between the navel and the coccyx. Every time she performs, she tries to find her balance around this centre. In spite of all her experience, in spite of the fact that she has been the student of one of the greatest masters and that she herself is now a master, she doesn't always find it. She imagines (or perhaps these are the images with which her master tried to transmit the experience to her) that the centre of her energy is a ball of steel, covered with many layers of cotton, at the centre of a triangle formed by lines connecting the hips and the coccyx. The Balinese master I Made Pasek Tempo nods approvingly and observes: 'Everything that Azuma does is really like this – *keras*, vigour, covered by *manis*, softness.'

* * *

Having followed the traces of the performer's *bios*, we can now glimpse its essence:

1 in the amplification and activation of the forces which are at work in balance;
2 in the oppositions which guide the dynamics of movements;
3 in the application of a consistent inconsistency;
4 in the breaking of automatisms by means of extra-daily equivalents.

Extra-daily body techniques consist of physical procedures which appear to be based on a recognizable reality but which follow a logic which is not immediately recognizable.

These techniques operate by means of a process of reduction and substitution which brings out what is essential in the actions, separates the performer's body from daily techniques, and creates a tension and a difference of potential through which energy passes.

In the Western tradition, the performer's work has been orientated towards a network of fictions, of 'magic ifs' which deal with the psychology, the behaviour and the history of her/his person and that of the character which s/he is playing. The pre-expressive principles of the performer's life are not cold concepts concerned only with the body's physiology and mechanics. They also are based on a network of fictions and 'magic ifs' which deal with the physical forces that move the body. What the performer is looking for, in this case, is a *fictive body*, not a fictive person.

In order to break the automatisms of daily behaviour, each of a North Pole performer's actions is dramatized, carried out by imagining that one is pushing, lifting, touching objects of a particular form, dimension, weight and consistency. This is a veritable psycho-technique which does not, however, attempt to influence the performer's psychic state, but rather her/his physical dynamism. It belongs, therefore, to the terminology performers use when speaking to themselves, or to the master's comments to the student, but does not pretend to mean anything to the spectator who is watching.

To find the body's extra-daily techniques, the performer does not study psychology but creates a network of external stimuli to which s/he can react with physical actions.

The great Danish physicist Niels Bohr, an avid Western film fan, wondered why, in all the final shoot-outs, the hero shoots faster even if his adversary is the first to reach for his gun. Bohr asked himself if some physical truth might not explain this convention. He came to the conclusion that such a truth did indeed exist: the first to draw is the slowest because he *decides* to shoot, and dies. The second to draw lives because he is faster, and he is faster because he doesn't have to decide, *he is decided*. This brilliant discovery was the result of a whimsical empirical research: Bohr and his assistants went off to a toy shop, bought water pistols, and back in their laboratory, duelled for hours and hours.[24]

4

NOTES FOR THE PERPLEXED
(AND FOR MYSELF)

Eftermaele means, literally, 'that which will be said afterwards'. An appropriate translation of this Norwegian word would require two English words, *renown* and *honour*, or, better still, *meaning* and *value*.

Time will decide the meaning and value of our actions. But, in fact, time is *the others*, those who will come after us. This is a paradox: theatre is the art of the present.

Do those who act through the theatre also have a responsibility towards those 'spectators' who will never see them? Is their professional identity, created and lived in the present, part of a legacy?

* * *

In the age of electronic memory, of film and reproducibility, theatre performance appeals to living memory, which is not a museum but metamorphosis. This relationship defines it.

We can leave as a legacy to others only that which we ourselves have not wholly consumed. A testament does not pass on everything, nor to everyone. It is useless to ask oneself: who will be my heirs? Yet it is essential to remember that there will be heirs.

* * *

To make theatre means practising an activity in search of meaning. Considered on its own, the theatre is an archeological relic. And yet this archeological relic, which has lost its immediate utility, is loaded with ever-changing values. We can adopt the values of the spirit of the times and of the culture in which we live. Or we can search for *our own* values.

* * *

The word *honour* seems to belong to past ages and to archaic social constraints. But it also suggests the existence of a superior value. It implies an obligation not towards ourselves and our surroundings, but towards that which transcends us.

Constraints, including that of acting in an ephemeral reality, can become springboards. You can only talk to unknown heirs through the people who surround you today.

Some think of the *message* to be transmitted to others as a truth that our own history, our tradition, our experience and personal knowledge have made us discover and that we wish to communicate.

I imagine it as a picture painted by a blind artist whose expert hand makes movements he cannot see dance on the canvas. Through the techniques which we master, the stories which attract us, our intimate wounds and revelations, we must reach something which is no longer ours, which no longer carries our name and which cannot be possessed either by those who do it or by those who see it.

The true message is the unforeseen and unprogrammed result of a voyage towards a conscious obscurity: anonymity.

Eftermaele, honour, renown. Can a good name and anonymity go hand in hand?

* * *

Generalizations prevail in the books which relate the history of theatre: one reads of confluences and confrontations of styles, of genres, of tendencies, of poetics, of cultures and nations. The real protagonists of these histories are formulas which become personifications like 'French Theatre', 'Spanish Theatre', 'Chinese Theatre', 'Commedia dell'Arte', 'Kathakali', 'Naturalistic Theatre', 'Romantic Theatre', 'Stanislavski Method', 'Brechtian Theatre', 'Grotowskian Theatre', etc. And then there are even more abstract generalizations: 'Medieval Theatre', 'Western Theatre', 'Oriental Theatre'.

Everyone knows that these are ways of speaking, conventions and abbreviations which stand for clusters of events, intricate or parallel histories. But ways of speaking turn into ways of thinking, into illusory characters.

Beneath these formulas, beneath these collective subjects, living memory is suffocated. A meaning is lost, the meaning of the irreducible, contradictory presence of those men and women who, by socializing their needs and their own personal visions, their autobiographical wounds, their loves and hates and even their own egoism and solitude, have invented the *meaning* of the theatre, have constructed, piece by piece, the mental geography and the history through which our theatrical craft navigates. These men and women, not the great historical generalizations, are *our* real past.

* * *

There is an anonymity which is the result of acquiescence to the spirit of the times. It is the anonymity of repletion. Our voice is suffocated by everything that has been poured into us by others, by culture, by society and by the tradition which surround us. We are anonymous because the ideas received have baptized us and given us a name.

But there is also another anonymity, an anonymity of emptiness arrived at through personal effort and consisting not of *what is known*, but of *what I know*.

This other anonymity is the result of a personal revolt, of nostalgia, of refusal, of the need to find oneself and to lose oneself. It is the necessity to dig so deep as to discover underground caverns covered by rocks and hundreds of metres of compacted earth.

There is a technique one can use to fulfill these intentions: launching and wrecking.

You have to plan your own performance, know how to construct it and steer it towards the whirlpool where it will either break up or assume a new nature: meanings at first not thought of and which its 'authors' will look upon as enigmas.

It is not possible to use this technique without working on the living tissue which is the pre-expressive level. In order to do so, one needs to be able to neutralize one of the brain's antennae, in order not to perceive all the messages, the meanings, the contents, the connections, the associations which emanate from the performance material on which one is working. One part of the brain, of the guidance system, must discover silence. The other works on microscopic sequences, as if it was confronted with a symphony of details of life, impulses, physical and nervous dynamisms, but in a process which, as yet, does not attempt to represent or narrate anything. Then, from that vibrating silence, emerges an unexpected meaning, so profoundly personal that it is anonymous.

All these metaphors are but meaningless words if there is no technique, no attention to details and to the most minute tensions, if there is no science of physical and vocal actions. But without metaphors and obsessions of this kind, the technique, the science, the perfectionism and the precision of the details become theatre deprived of sense.

* * *

Zeami, Stanislavski, Appia, Meyerhold, Craig, Copeau, Artaud, Brecht, Eisenstein, Decroux . . . Can we consider their writings as experience passed on as a legacy?

It is similar to what happens when you live in a foreign country for a long time without knowing the language. Thousands of unknown sounds penetrate your ears and are stored there. In a short time you can master the *grammelot* of the language, you can imitate it. You recognize it, but do not understand it. It is a confused mass of sounds punctuated here and there by the odd intelligible word. Then you are given a grammar book and a dictionary. The written signs help you to recognize the familiar and confusing sounds which gradually find an order, a classification, a reason. Now you are capable of learning by yourself. You know how to help yourself and to what you must pay particular attention, if you want to learn.

The books of the rebels, the reformers, the visionaries of the theatre, can only be understood if we come to them full of experience to which we have not yet been able to give a name. Their words shake up our opaque *grammelot* and give it the clarity of articulate consciousness.

They are excellent books, capable of interesting their readers. But their secret effectiveness lies beneath the literary and technical surface, in the hidden net which can capture those of our experiences which still elude us.

The legacy, like an occult science, catches its own heirs.

* * *

The theatre's raw material is not the actor, nor the space, nor the text, but the attention, the seeing, the hearing, the mind of the spectator. Theatre is the art of the spectator.

Like the poet with the particularly acute senses spoken of by Baudelaire, every spectator, even when not aware of doing so, uses a pair of imaginary binoculars, sometimes perceiving the performance through the large lenses, sometimes through the small lenses. S/he observes the whole from a distance, then becomes engrossed by a detail.

Theatre Anthropology singles out the principles which the performer must put to work in order to make this dance of the senses and mind of the spectator possible. It is the performer's duty to know these principles and to explore their practical possibilities incessantly. In this consists her/his craft. It will then be up to her/him to decide how and to what ends to use this dance. This is her/his ethic.

Theatre Anthropology does not give advice on ethics; it is the premise of ethics.

* * *

Does Theatre Anthropology have a scientific nature?

It does not take measurements, it does not use a statistical method, it does not try to draw consequences for the performer's behaviour from the knowledge of medicine, biology, psychology, sociology or the communication sciences.

It is based on empirical research, from which it extracts general principles. It takes place in an operative dimension with a view to the effectiveness of scenic action. It defines a field of investigation and forges the theoretical instruments to explore it. It singles out pragmatic laws.

Is it, then, a science?

* * *

The language which one chooses to transmit certain precise, technical, and comprehensible experiences gives birth to numerous misunderstandings.

Artaud appears to be a visionary. Craig, a seductive and spoiled dandy. Decroux, a rather pedantic poet. Stanislavski, a wanderer in the subtle land of the soul.

Many people become perplexed when confronted with an apparent contradiction: why, precisely at the moment in which we are attempting to go beyond the obvious knowledge about the theatre, do words refuse to become scientific, clear, free from ambiguous nuances? Why do they become lyrical, suggestive, emotive, intuitive, flying from one metaphor to another, without indicating directly and unequivocally the things to which they refer?

This perplexity often leads to a sterile answer; if the words seem imprecise, it must mean that what they describe is also imprecise; if they are personal, it must mean that they stand for something which is exclusively personal.

The serpent bites its tail; writers – it is said – can reveal only their interior and imaginary world, their dreams, the obsessive metaphors which are inherent in their spiritual biographies and art.

And so, books which are intended to open the way towards objective knowledge, to orientate the action and construct the mechanics of the performer's scenic *bios*, become opaque tomes, closed unto themselves.

Artaud – it is said – spoke only of Artaud. We read Artaud to learn about Artaud. And that is enough.

But *for whom* is it enough?

* * *

One knows/I know

Niels Bohr was once asked how – at such a young age – he made the discovery of the periodicity of elements which brought him the Nobel prize. He replied that he did not begin from what 'one knew' but from what 'he knew'.

I reflect on what *I know*, on what circumstances have put within my grasp, and I realize that throughout my life as a theatrical craftsman, which began in 1964, all I have needed is two Norwegian words: *kraft* and *sats*.

I have used these two words to explain to my actors what did not work in their actions.

Kraft means force, power.

I said to the actor: 'You have no *kraft*.' Or: 'You are showing too much of your *kraft*.' Or: 'The *kraft* in this action is too similar to that in the previous one.'

Sats can be translated with the words 'impulse' or 'preparation', 'to be ready to . . .' In the language of our work it indicates, among other things, the moment in which one is ready to act, the instant which precedes the action, when all the energy is already there, ready to intervene, but as if suspended, still held in the fist, a tiger-butterfly about to take flight.

I said to the actor: 'You have no *sats*.' Or: 'Your *sats* is not precise.' Or again: 'You are marking the *sats* too much.'

These two words have guided our work and are sufficient to explain the results my companions and I have obtained. The Odin Teatret 'method' could be concentrated into these two words.

All of Theatre Anthropology is basically a way of developing, in objective terms, that knowledge for which, in the practice of our group, we only need two rather vague words.

I find the same technical content, with the same operative precision, in the terminology of other masters, in apparently very different words: 'second nature', 'bio-mechanics', 'cruelty', 'Über-Marionette' . . .

* * *

The history of culture shows that each time one advances into little-explored territory, one invents images, metaphorical and evocative terms, linguistic contrapositions, daring clusters of words like 'electric current', 'electro-magnetic waves', 'force of inertia', 'Oedipus complex'. Then these extravagant linguistic approximations crystallize into conventions shared by an ever-increasing number of people, and in the end they seem to stand for precise things in a direct way, literally. Personal languages become languages of work, and these in turn become common languages.

In the theatre, the groups of people who share the same terminologies are few. There is not much discussion about the performer's practice. The languages of work, which characterize the communication within a group, and which, for its members, are useful professional indications, to outsiders seem prosaic, insignificant, abstruse or purely metaphorical.

One cannot write, speak to the outside world with the conventions of one's own working language.

But, at the same time, if one wants to relate a concrete experience which is not known to everyone, one must shun prefabricated definitions, the verbal networks which are only a parasitic imitation of the languages of other sciences and other learning.

The exact languages of the sciences, when transposed in order to give the effect of concreteness or the appearance of seriousness to one's own arguments, become a screen which is even more opaque than lyrical, suggestive, or emotive images.

The principal danger does not reside in the unavoidable risk of equivocation, but in the continuous reference to an ostensible scientific clarity which exploits what is already known and spares the researcher one of the most fertile of efforts: that of also searching for one's own words.

* * *

Wer sich selbst und andre kennt,
Wird auch hier erkennen:
Orient und Okzident
Sind nicht mehr zu trennen.

Sinnig zwischen beiden Welten
Sich zu wiegen, lass' ich gelten;

> Also zwischen Ost und Westen
> Sich bewegen sei zum Besten!

These two quatrains from one of Goethe's posthumously published poems are part of the *Occidental-Oriental Divan*. 'He who knows himself and others is also certain of this: Orient and Occident can no longer be separated. I make a rule of staying in a conscious balance between the two worlds, thus always choosing to move between East and West.'

The theatre of the twentieth century lives in this *movement*, in the search for a new meaning for that archeological relic which is its present condition.

Stanislavski, Meyerhold, Copeau, Craig, Artaud, Brecht, Decroux, Beck, Grotowski, are not, if we are to be precise, the so-called 'Occidental tradition'. Nor do they belong, obviously, to the Oriental tradition. They are Eurasian theatre:

> Orient and Occident
> Can no longer be separated.

My entire theatrical apprenticeship has taken place in that *movement* between East and West which I now call Eurasian theatre. *Kathakali* and *nō*, *onnagata* and *barong*, Rukmini Devi and Mei Lanfang, Zeami and the Natya Shastra were alongside the books of the Russian, French and German masters, and alongside Grotowski, my Polish teacher.

It was not only the memory of their theatrical creations which fascinated me, but above all the detailed artificiality of their performer-in-life.

The long nights of *kathakali* in 1963 helped me catch a glimpse of the limits which the performer can reach. But it was the dawn which revealed to me these performers' secrets, at the Kalamandalam school in Cheruthuruthy, in Kerala. There, young boys, barely adolescents, diligently repeating exercises, steps, songs, prayers, gymnastics, eye movements and votive offerings, crystallized their own *ethos* as artistic behaviour and ethical attitude.

I compared our theatre with theirs.

Today the very word 'comparison' seems inadequate to me; it has to do with the epidermises of different theatres, their diverse conventions and customs.

But beneath the luminous and seductive epidermises, I discern the organs which keep them alive, and the poles of the comparison blend into a single profile, without limits or fissures. Yet again, Eurasian theatre.

* * *

It is possible to consider the theatre in terms of ethnic, national, group or even individual traditions. But if in doing so one seeks to understand one's own *identity*, it is also essential to take the opposite and complementary point of view: to think of one's own theatre in a transcultural dimension, in the flow of a 'tradition of traditions'.

Why, as opposed to what happens in other countries, does our actor-singer become specialized separately from the actor-dancer and, in turn, the actor-dancer separately from the actor ... What should we call her/him? The talking actor? The actor-interpreter-of-texts?

Why, in our part of the world, does the performer tend to confine her/himself within the skin of only one character in each production?

Why does s/he only very rarely explore the possibility of becoming the context of an entire story, with many characters, with leaps between levels of action, with sudden changes from the first to the third person, from the past to the present, from the whole to a part, from person to thing?

Why, with us, does this possibility remain relegated to masters of story-telling or to exceptions like Dario Fo, while elsewhere it is characteristic of every theatre, every type of performer, both when s/he acts-sings-dances alone and when s/he is part of a performance with other performers and many characters?

Why, in our part of the world, do nearly all forms of classical theatre accept that which here seems admissible only in opera: the use of words whose meaning the majority of the spectators cannot understand?

These questions have specific answers on the historical plane. But they become professionally useful when they stimulate one to imagine how one's own identity can develop without going against one's own nature and history but rather extending beyond the boundaries which imprison it more than define it.

It suffices to look from the outside, from distant countries and times, to discover the latent possibilities here and now.

*   *   *

Who would presume to investigate the history and theory of music without knowing the ABC of the piano?

In our culture, the understanding of the performer's work has often been blocked by the presumption of understanding.

Critics, scholars, theoreticians, and even philosophers such as Hegel and Sartre have tried to interpret the performer's creative process by starting from the assumption that they knew what they were talking about. In reality, they yielded to their spectator ethnocentrism. They often imagined a process which was only the deceptive, a posteriori projection of the effects achieved by the performers on the minds of their spectators.

They based their writings on conjectures, on episodic testimony, on their own impressions as spectators. They tried to make 'science' out of something of which they observed the result without being aware of its complementary aspect: the logic of the process. They spoke and wrote about an imaginary process as if making a scientific description based on empirical data.

This is an attitude which persists today. We could define it as the faith in the scientific 'power of attorney'.

This form of deceitful and imposing ignorance consists of the pretence of analysing theatrical behaviour by superimposing upon it paradigms which have proved their utility in other fields of research.

For Sainte-Albine and Diderot, it was the mechanics of passion; in Archer's time, psychology; then psychoanalysis; during the Brechtian period, it was the contraposition between idealism and materialism in the historical and social sciences; then semiology and cultural anthropology.

This scientific 'authority' is based on a superstitious mental attitude. It maintains that a theoretical paradigm is valid *unto itself* and therefore is a precise instrument even when it moves from one context to another.

Interpretative schemas which are valid in one specific context *can* be applied elsewhere. However, the pertinence of such applications must be proved each time.

In the case of the performer, it is usual to proceed like those professors who preferred to look at the sky through classical and prestigious books instead of through the crude instrument made by Galileo.

* * *

In spring of 1934, in Rome, a great many exponents of world theatre (but no performers and no-one from the classical theatres of Asia) met at a congress. A new theatrical architecture – some declared – could generate a new way of writing for the theatre. Others replied that a building had never given life to a play. It was then that Gordon Craig intervened: 'There is a theatre which comes before plays, but it is not a building of bricks and stones. It is the building consisting of the body and voice of the actor.' This was a sensible reflection, but was understood by everyone as a paradoxical metaphor.

Theatre Anthropology concerns itself with the reality of this metaphor.

* * *

Some people are perplexed and say: 'How is it possible to study the performer's creative processes without examining her/his historical and social context? How is it possible to compare various forms of scenic behaviour, isolate recurring principles, without taking into consideration that each of the examples belongs to culturally diverse and at times incomparable circumstances?' And they conclude: 'Theatre Anthropology ignores history; it ignores the fact that particular technical procedures have a specific symbolic or ideal meaning in the culture to which they belong; it reduces everything to the materiality of scenic *bios*.'

No, Theatre Anthropology does not reduce to . . . but concentrates on.

One cannot investigate anything if one does not proceed as if a portion of reality or a particular level of organization was separable from the rest. In reality, everything is part of everything else. But in the reality of the action of research one must know how to proceed as if a single detail or a single level of organization was a world unto itself.

Someone who studies the joints of the hand does not ignore the importance of the heart, even if s/he never mentions the heart.

If one's attention is not concentrated on a few specific questions and on the contexts pertinent to them, one cannot investigate in depth.

The continuous requests to consider also all the rest 'which must not be ignored' unwillingly collaborate in shifting only the surfaces, leaving things just as they are.

٭ ٭ ٭

The importance of studying the social and cultural contexts of various theatres is obvious.

But it is also obvious that it is not true that one understands nothing of a theatre if one does not consider it in the light of its socio-cultural context.

We often use the expression 'this phenomenon cannot be understood if it is not examined in the light of . . . '. It is a way of speaking, not an indication of method. No object of research automatically carries with it its own necessary context. It is not the correct relationship between the object considered on its own and its context which guarantees the validity of a research method. Every object, in fact, can belong to innumerable, diverse contexts, all equally pertinent. A good method is that in which the context is pertinent to the *questions* which have been put to the object under examination.

It would be foolish, for example, to question the 'meaning' of Indian theatre without considering it in the context of the culture in which it is practised and in which its past is rooted, without having a well-versed knowledge of the literature, social conflicts, religion and history of which it is a part, and above all without a profound knowledge of the Indian languages. But if one questions the influence of certain Indian theatres on European theatres in the nineteenth and twentieth centuries, the tools and the context which must be activated are very different. Reference contexts and tools change yet again if one investigates which elements in the practices of Indian performers can also be useful for other performers, or that which is common to both and which can therefore be adopted as a pragmatic principle or orientation for any performer.

To consider the problem in this way does not mean that one claims that the performers of any time or country are *substantially* equal. It means that one recognizes the obvious: performers who work in an organized performance situation individualize themselves through profound differences as well as profound similarities.

It is therefore possible to conduct research of a scientific kind which proposes to single out transcultural principles which, *on the operative level*, are the basis of scenic behaviour.

Theatre Anthropology proceeds from this hypothesis. That is why it is based on a Eurasian vision of the theatre and is not interested in specific study

45

of Asian theatres or those of European origin in their historical contexts, nor in their myth in Europe and the Americas, in Asia or Africa. It is not interested in these matters because it is concerned with something else, not because it denies the value of these other interests.

* * *

. . . And *Songlines*? and Australia? Polynesia? Africa? And all the autochthonous cultures of the Americas? So much theatre and so much dance is excluded by the expression 'Eurasian theatre'!

Eurasian theatre does not refer to the theatres contained within one geographic area, on the continent of which Europe is a peninsula. It suggests a mental and technical dimension, an active *idea* in modern theatrical culture. It includes that collection of theatres which, for those who have concentrated on the performer's problems, have become the 'classical' points of reference of research: from Peking Opera to Brecht, from modern mime to *nō*, from *kabuki* to Meyerhold's bio-mechanics, from Delsarte to *kathakali*, from ballet to *butō*, from Artaud to Bali . . . This 'encyclopedia' has been put together by drawing on the repertoire of the European and Asian scenic traditions. Whether we like it or not, whether it is just or unjust, this is what has happened.

When we speak of 'Eurasian theatre', we are recognizing the existence of a unity sanctioned by our cultural history. We can cross its borders but we cannot ignore them. For all those who in the twentieth century have reflected in a competent way on the performer, the borders between 'European theatre' and 'Asian theatre' do not exist.

* * *

In the context of the activity of ISTA and of discussions concerning Theatre Anthropology, Asian theatres in particular attract one's attention because they are little known. In some cases, however, they monopolize one's attention; hence the misunderstanding that the object of Theatre Anthropology is the study of the classical theatres of Asia. This misunderstanding is reinforced by the plurality of the meanings of the word 'anthropology' which many people automatically presume to be 'cultural anthropology', the study of those who are culturally different from oneself.

Theatre Anthropology does not propose an 'Orientalization' of Western theatre. Its field of study is not the 'Orient', but performer technique. Every craftsman belongs to her/his own culture, but also to the culture of the craft itself. S/he has a cultural identity and a professional identity. S/he can meet 'compatriots' who practise the same profession in other countries. This is why the *Wanderlehre*, the 'learning journey' beyond the borders of one's native country, was once part of the apprenticeship of even the most humble artisan.

The theatrical profession is also a country to which we belong, a chosen homeland, without goegraphical borders. Today we accept it as normal that a Mexican philologist has discussions with an Indian philologist, that a

Japanese architect shares experiences on an equal basis with a Swedish architect, just as it appears to us to be a form of cultural insufficiency that Chinese medicine and European medicine have not become two complementary aspects of a single body of knowledge. It is not strange that performers meet within the common borders of their profession. It is strange that it seems strange.

Those whose attention is monopolized by the frequent presence of Asian traditions in Theatre Anthropology tend to make two further mistakes. They object that in the investigation of these 'different' and 'foreign' theatres we do not take sufficiently into consideration the subjectivity of the observer, of our cultural categories. They maintain that Theatre Anthropology presumes an impossible scientific objectivity.

No, the point of view is strongly and explicitly objective, but partial. The questions and concerns which we raise in our field of investigation belong to the practice of the theatrical craft. We make use of that objectivity which is functional for theatre artisans.

Others believe that Theatre Anthropology turns to the 'Orient' in search of an Original Tradition of the Theatre, the traces of which have supposedly been lost in the West. It would be splendid if this were the case (perhaps). But we, in our *Wanderlehre*, are seeking only to render the knowledge of the potentialities of our profession wider and deeper.

*　*　*

Does Theatre Anthropology seek to analyse the scenic behaviour which has existed and exists in different cultures? Or does it seek to furnish rules for effective scenic behaviour? Is it for scholars or performers?

These two perspectives are not mutually exclusive. To single out models, recurring-principles, also means furnishing a range of orientations useful to scenic practice.

*　*　*

Anyone concerned with history is aware of the dialectic between the not always decipherable order of events (or rather, the context) and the linear and simple order of historiography (which transforms the context into text). This ought to be particularly relevant to all of us who work in a craft which leaves so few visible traces and whose results vanish quickly into time. So quickly that our professional *ethos* cannot acquire its own identity unless we have a strong awareness of our predecessors.

The cult of the past is unimportant. But memory guides our actions. It is memory which makes it possible for us to penetrate beneath the skin of the times and to find the numerous paths which lead to our origins, to our first day in our craft.

Louis Jouvet once said something both enlightening and enigmatic: 'There exists a legacy from us to ourselves.'

47

The choice of one thread rather than another in the telling of the tangle of events is first an ethical responsibility and then a scientific problem.

Ethics and science: the ancients used one word only – *discipline*.

*   *   *

An actress flips through the pages of this book and asks me: 'Of what use to me are all these analyses, all these examples, the same names over and over again?' And she adds: 'Your book is arid. I work alone, in an empty room, in what you call the Third World or the Third Theatre. I am already fighting everyday against my own aridity. This is not what I expect from a book about the actor.'

I answer: 'Here there are pipes, channels, a few reservoirs, all of them dry and empty. No-one can give you *your* water.'

She asks me: 'Do you mean that without all this, my water, if there is any, becomes a swamp?'

*   *   *

It is easy to banalize the words 'profession' or 'technique' by repeating: 'These are not the most important things.'

Yet, apart from one small element, finding *one's own meaning* in the theatre implies a personal invention of one's craft.

But what I call the 'small element' is the essential thing. It has to do with a part of ourselves which is subject to continuous disorientation, to periods of silence, tiredness, aridity, discouragement. It is a teeming and sombre sea which at times seems flooded with light and at times daunts us and is as bitterly infertile as the salt it contains.

One cannot remain with one's eyes fixed on the stars or one's heart abandoned to the sea for long. One needs the well constructed deck of a ship, the grease of the engines, the artificial fire of welders.

To invent one's own meaning means knowing how to search for the way to find it.

*   *   *

Sometimes, the shortest route between two points is an arabesque, the journey of a canoe gripped by the currents. This book is a paper canoe. The currents are the flowing multiplicity of theatres and their performers, experiences and memories. The canoe's route twists and turns, but according to a method.

*   *   *

If you can't bite, don't show your teeth.

I must concentrate on technical precision. I can only collaborate with those who know the art of self-discipline.

I believe only in the stubborn.

I write this 'treatise' for them.

Do not believe that it will be of use to you. Do not believe that you will be able to do without it.

5

ENERGY, OR RATHER,
THE THOUGHT

dual conciousness.

For the performer, energy is a *how*. Not a *what*.

How to move. *How* to remain immobile. *How* to make her/his own physical presence visible and *how* to transform it into scenic presence, and thus expression. *How* to make the invisible visible: the rhythm of thought.

And yet, it is very useful for the performer to think of this *how* in the same way as s/he would think of a *what*, of an impalpable substance which can be manoevred, modelled, facetted, projected into space, absorbed and made to dance inside the body. These are not mere fancies. They are efficient figments of imagination.

> Our thought pushes our gestures in the same way that the thumb of the sculptor pushes forms, and our body, sculpted from the inside stretches. Our thought, between its thumb and index fingers, pinches us along the reverse flap of our envelope and our body, sculpted from the inside, folds.[1]

Metaphors. Practical advice.

At the end of workshops, participants exchange impressions. Sometimes, after having focused on the way of modelling energy, I hear someone venture to comment: 'In reality, we have been working on the soul.' We can use whatever words we choose. But words can be dangerous. Sometimes they asphyxiate what we would like them to give birth to.

'Never again this word'

Certain words are treacherous because they stick in one's mouth. The word 'energy' can deceive us because, when we apply it to our actions, it can inflate and stiffen them.

A friend of mine, a director in Germany, wrote to me reminding me ironically of a tinker's promise I had once made: 'I will never again use the word energy with respect to the performer.' In the ten years which followed I never stopped talking and writing about it. It cannot be avoided. But I

50

remember that promise and how justified it was. It was made in a moment of impatience and was a reflection on the malignity of certain professional terms.

We were in Bonn, at the daily directors' meeting, early one morning in the autumn of 1980, during the first session of ISTA. The previous evening we had seen a performance. The actors had flooded the space with their vitality, using large movements, great speed and muscular strength, exhibiting vocal deformations, mechanical oppositions between the different phases of each action, exaggerated tensions, unreasonable emphases of physical impulses and *sats*. A rhythm that was overexcited, convulsive, boring. They were like raging elephants, caught up in the impetus of their own charge. Every once in a while, with the obvious intention of varying the flow of their squandered energy, they stopped, plunging into the extreme opposite: numbing pauses. Then they charged again.

Thinking of scenic presence in terms of energy can suggest to performers that the more they are able to force the theatre space and the senses of the observer, the more effective they can be. Thus, instead of dancing with the spectator's attention, the performers bombard it and alienate it. They *have decided* to expand their own power, to work with all their energies, to mobilize them. It is precisely for this reason that they *are not decided*.

In order to take the spectator's defences by storm (and the spectator has come to the theatre to have her/his senses taken by storm and thus be stimulated), one must use subtlety, feints and counterfeints. Only in rare, carefully planned cases is a powerful action effective.

Who is not familiar with the word *kung-fu*? A fighting style, a martial art. But wait, the name Confucius, Kung-fu-tsu, comes from *kung-fu*.

In Chinese, *kung-fu* means 'to hold firmly in one's hand', 'to grasp', 'to learn'. To know how to seize one's adversary. To perceive with certainty the slender thread in the labyrinth, the knowledge.

In the Chinese performer's profession, this word is very common, and paradoxical. To have *kung-fu* can mean to be in form, to be trained, to have talent, to have a personal quality which surpasses technique.

Above all, *kung-fu* means an exercise, a design of movements, a pattern of behaviour, a score of actions, but also that imperceptible something which is worked on and guided by means of the exercise, by means of a design of movements, by means of a pattern of behaviour or well-fixed scores of actions.

> When performing, the actor perceives *directions*, feels changes. He feels that he is continuously *oriented*. In this sense, the role is a succession of impulses, of movements of feeling. The actor is put to the test when he stops these movements because of his partner's cue.[2]

For the performer, to have energy means knowing *how* to model it. To be able to conceive of it and to live it as experience, s/he must artificially modify its routes, inventing dams, dikes, canals. These are the resistances against which s/he *presses* her/his intention – conscious or intuitive – and which make

51

her/his expression possible. The whole body thinks/acts, with another quality of energy. A free body-mind defies necessity and meticulously planned obstacles, submitting itself to a discipline which becomes discovery.

The actor's intelligence is his vitality, his dynamism, his action, his predispositions, his energy, a living feeling which provokes within him, to a certain degree, almost by habit, a deep examination, a *condensation* of his sensibility, a consciousness of himself. It is the *thought-action*.[3]

Jouvet claims that there exists an actor's philosophy, a way of perceiving and acting which is the result of an attitude, a practice, a method, a discipline. 'The actor is an empiricist who ends up thinking [. . .] The actor thinks by means of a tension of energy.'[4]

Seven-tenths – the energy of the absorbed action

A fact fundamental to our profession must be reaffirmed here: teaching is impossible; one can only learn. If words are evanescent, the reality which they represent is not necessarily so. Words can refer to experiences which are tangible, simple, and clear for those who have lived through them. Evanescent words are 'answers' in search of 'questions'. The questions, in this case, must be already present in the listener. Otherwise one has the impression of being presented with a theory in gibberish.

Let us see what happens when an intelligent but still inexpert student listens to a lesson by Meyerhold:

The master moves his fingers. His clear eyes are shining. He is holding a Javanese marionette. The golden hands of the master move the little golden hands of the puppet [. . .] Suddenly, the magician breaks the spell. He has in his hands two golden sticks and a piece of coloured cloth. [. . .] His lessons were mirages and dreams. We were struggling fever-ishly to write everything down. When I awoke, in the notebook was written: 'The devil only knows what this is about!'

That student, whose notebooks were of no help to him, was more than intelligent. He was Sergei Eisenstein, and he recalls:

Meyerhold's lessons were like the songs of the sirens [. . .] It is impossible to remember what he was saying.

Aromas, colours, sounds. And over everything, a kind of golden mist.

Elusive. Impalpable. Mystery upon mystery.

Veil upon veil.

The romantic 'I' listens, enchanted.

The rational 'I' mutters dully.

When will the veil be lifted from the 'mysteries'? When will we get to the system?

Another winter of intoxication, but nothing to show for it.[5]

'The devil only knows what this is about!', I said to myself at the theatre school in Warsaw during the winter of 1960, when Bogdan Korzeniewski, my directing teacher, talked to us about how to miniaturize a character's actions. Then, with an example, he revealed to us Stanislavski's subtle approach. He said:

> Two merchants who are in ruthless competition and who detest each other are seated at the same table at a reception, enjoying tea and exchanging pleasantries. In order to bring out the double flavour of their behaviour, Stanislavski asks the two actors to improvise a fight between two scorpions. He reminds them that these animals attack and kill with their tails. The impulse against the adversary must begin from the bottom of the spinal column. The actors improvise a merciless fight, walking, sitting down, standing on the chairs. The scene loses any realistic connotation. There are no longer two merchants, but two actor-scorpions. Ever alert, they pretend to ignore each other. Suddenly their tails attack. This broad and varied improvisation is then fixed and so begins the patient work of miniaturizing each individual phase: looks, rotations of the trunk, cautious or indifferent steps, feints, strikes, parries . . . of the tail.
>
> The result is a credible scene; two merchants who are in ruthless competition and who detest each other are seated at the same table at a reception, enjoying tea and exchanging pleasantries. Their rhythm – pouring tea, adding sugar, offering each other pastries, lifting cup to lip, smiling, nodding in agreement, chatting – is articulated exactly according to the individual phases and the intensity – now restrained – of the mortal fight of the two monstrous scorpions who have invaded the stage.

In his production of Gogol's *The Government Inspector*, Meyerhold applied the principle of the absorption of action, transposing it from the level of the individual actor to that which regulates the relationships between the characters. He set the thirty or more characters on a platform of reduced size (3.55 m. by 4.55 m.), with so steep an incline that it was difficult for the actors to keep their balance. Even the furniture, a divan and a table, was sloped. In this restricted space he created an atmosphere of swarming social interplay, by means of an uninterrupted flow of gesture, attitude, 'braking of rhythm', immobility.

> Stage acting is not a question of static groupings but of action: the action of time upon space. [. . .] When you look at a bridge you notice that it is a leap fixed in metal. In other words, not immobility but movement.

It is the tension expressed in the bridge which is essential to it, not the ornamentation of its railings. It is the same with the actor on stage.[6]

And Decroux: 'immobility is an act and, under the circumstances, a passionate one'[7].

> This cumulative, collecting, progressing kind of acting is best observed at rehearsals immediately before a performance, when the actors are only running through their parts, only sketching in gestures and vocal emphases. [. . .] Imagine, then, added to this, the direct turning to the public, but not intensified or 'suggestive' in any way. Observe the distinction between 'suggestive' acting and compelling, plastic acting.[8]

This cumulative technique of thinking on a large scale and then miniaturizing the resulting action can be observed among the most diverse performers. Craig noted it in Irving. Brecht valued it in Helene Weigel. Eduardo De Filippo refined it during the course of his long career and from it created the 'flower' of his old age.

Pina Bausch has often said how important it is for the dancer to be able to dance seated on a chair, apparently immobile, dancing in the body before dancing with the body. In her performances she has often 'immobilized' her performers' dances.

When the visible, the external (the body), does not move, then the invisible, the internal (the mind), must be in movement. Like a swan on water: it glides impassively, but its feet, hidden from view, are always working. Motionless while moving, in stillness not still.

'The static [. . .] is a movement set at a level which does not carry along the bodies of the spectators, but simply their minds.' This is how Matisse described the kinaesthetic effect of colours on flat canvases.[9]

It is often said that within good music can be heard the background of silence from which the music emerges or even that good music gives to the listener the gift of an extraordinary experience of silence. In the twenties, Alexei Granovski, the founder of the Goset Hebrew Theatre of Moscow, applied this way of thinking to the behaviour of actors. He is speaking paradoxically, on an abstract level, but what he says is loaded with good sense on the practical level:

> Immobility is the norm, movement is an occurrence. The word and the occurrence are abnormal states. Every movement must emerge and emanate from the immobility which is the background upon which the movement is designed.[10]

Movement emanating from immobility recalls the *sats*, which we will discuss in the next section. The term 'design', as we will see later, recalls one of the performer's principal problems: to compose a score or precise pattern of actions which form the banks and the variations in level through which energy flows, transforming the natural *bios* into scenic *bios* and bringing it into view. This topic is dealt with in chapter 7, 'A theatre not made of stones and bricks'.

Immobile and living presence is the ultimate limit of one of the performer's fundamental difficulties: keeping thought and action connected to each other. This connection keeps its tension by means of a difference of potential, which prevents it from weakening and being lost.

> The expression 'when you feel ten in your heart, express seven in your movements' refers to the following. When a beginner studying the *nō* learns to gesture with his hands and to move his feet, he will first do as his teacher tells him and so will use all his energies to perform in the way in which he is instructed. Later, however, he will learn to move his arms to a lesser extent than his own emotions suggest, and he will be able to moderate his own intentions. This phenomenon is by no means limited to dance and gesture. In terms of general stage deportment, no matter how slight a bodily action, if the motion is more restrained than the emotion behind it, the emotion will become the Substance and the movements of the body its Function, thus moving the audience.[11]

But Zeami warns against the mechanical application of the process of absorption. Immediately following the above, he recommends that the performer 'make use of the mind with the minutest attention to detail and the body with ample movements'.

Sats – *the energy can be suspended*

Energy can be suspended in immobility in motion.

Above and beyond the metaphorical uses to which it can be put, the word energy implies a difference of potential. Geographers, for example, refer to the *energy* of a region to indicate the arithmetic difference between maximum and minimum heights.

At school, we were taught that when a physical system contains a difference of potential, it is able to carry out work, that is, to 'produce energy' (water flowing down a slope makes the mill turn, the turbine creates electrical power).

The Greek word *enérgheia* means just that: to be ready for action, on the verge of producing work.

In physical behaviour, the transition from intention to action is a typical example of difference in potential.

In the instant which precedes the action, when all the necessary force is ready to be released into space but as though suspended and still under control, the performer perceives her/his energy in the form of *sats*, of dynamic preparation. The *sats* is the moment in which the action is thought/acted by the entire organism, which reacts with tensions, even in immobility. It is the point at which one decides to act. There is a muscular, nervous and mental commitment, already directed towards an objective. It is the tightening or the gathering together of oneself from which the action departs. It is the spring before it is sprung. It is the attitude of the feline ready for anything: to bound forward, to withdraw, to return to a position of rest. An athlete, a tennis player or boxer, immobile or moving, ready to react. It is John Wayne facing an adversary. It is Buster Keaton about to take a step. It is Maria Callas on the verge of an aria.

The performer knows how to distinguish the *sats* from the gesticulatory inertia in which movements roll over each other without internal power. The *sats* engages the entire body. The energy which is accumulated in the trunk and presses on the legs can be canalized into a caress of the hand or into the hurried steps of a run, into a slow movement of the eyes, into the leap of the tiger or the flight of the butterfly.

Sats is impulse and counterimpulse.

In the language of Meyerhold's work, we find the word *predigra*, 'pre-acting':

> Pre-acting is a trampoline, a moment of tension resulting in acting. Acting is a *coda* [musical term in Italian in original text], while pre-acting is the element which accumulates, develops and waits to be resolved.[12]

Another of Meyerhold's terms is *otkaz*, 'refusal', or – in musical terminology – the alteration of a note by one or two semitones which interrupts the development of the melody:

> The principle of *otkaz* implies the precise definition of the points at which one movement ends and another begins, a *stop* and a *go* at the same time. *Otkaz* is a clean stop which suspends the preceding movement and prepares the following one. It thus makes it possible to reunite dynamically two segments of an exercise; it puts the subsequent segment into relief, and gives it a push, an impulse, like a trampoline. The *otkaz* can also signal to a partner that one is ready to pass on to the next phase of the exercise. It is a very brief act, going against, opposite to, the overall direction of the movement: the recoil before going forward, the impulse of the hand being raised before it strikes, the flexion before standing.[13]

For Grotowski this 'pre-movement':

> can be done at different levels, like a kind of silence before the movement, a silence which is filled with potential or can occur as a stop of the action at a precise moment.[14]

Etienne Decroux, obviously, does not use the Norwegian word *sats*, but formulates the experience in this way:

This is immobile immobility; the pressure of water on the dike, the hovering of a fly stopped by the windowpane, the delayed fall of the leaning tower which remains standing. Then, similar to the way we stretch a bow before taking aim, man implodes yet again.[15]

Implosion should not necessarily make one think of a successive explosion, an impetuous, bursting, rapid action.

This does not mean that the *sats* must be so emphasized that the performer's action becomes 'staccato' or proceeds by *saccades*, by fits and starts. If the *sats* are too marked, they become inorganic, that is, they suppress the performer's life and dull the spectator's senses.

In his work, Ingemar Lindh describes Decroux' 'immobile immobility' as follows: to execute the intention in immobility. It is what ethologists call MI, *Movements of Intention*: the cat is not doing anything yet, but we understand that it wants to snatch a fly.

Sats is not something which belongs only to the 'sculptor who sculpts the body from the inside'. It is not connected only to dynamic immobility. In a sequence of actions, it is a small charge of energy which causes the action to change its course and intensity or suddenly suspends it. It is a moment of transition which leads to a new, precise posture, and thus to a change in the tonus of the entire body. In the action of sitting, for example, we can single out the moment when, as we bend, we are no longer able to control our weight and the body descends. If we stop just before that moment we are in a *sats*: we can return to a standing position or decide to sit. To find the life of the *sats*, the performer must play with the spectators' kinaesthetic sense and prevent them from foreseeing what is about to happen. The action must surprise the spectators.

The word 'surprise' should not be misunderstood. We are not referring to a level of organization which has to do with the macroscopic and more evident aspects of the scenic action. We are not referring, in short, to a performer who wants to provoke astonishment.

Rather, it is a question of subliminal surprises, which the spectator does not become aware of with the conscious 'eye' but with the 'eye' of the senses, with the kinaesthetic sense. To give life to the *sats*, to those continuous changes of muscular tonus which make the leaps of thought visible, the performer and her/his 'first spectator' – the director – must know how to control the action as if it was under a microscope.

Meyerhold:

The actor's work consists in a clever alternation of acting and pre-acting. [. . .] It is not acting as such which interests us, but *predigra*, pre-acting, because expectation arouses in the spectator a greater tension than that which is provoked in him by something already received or pre-digested. This is not theatre. The spectator wants to dive into the expectation of the action.[16]

Referring to an actress:

> I asked you to sit there, but you do it in much too obvious a way, you reveal my design to the spectator. First you should barely sit down, and then sit completely. You must conceal the outline of the plan that I, the director, have made.[17]

The performer knows what s/he is about to do, but must not anticipate it. The *sats* is the technical explanation of that commonplace according to which the performer's skill consists in knowing how to repeat the performance as if every action was being made for the first time.

The work on *sats* is the means by which one penetrates into the cellular world of scenic behaviour. It serves to eliminate the separation between thought and physical action which is often, for reasons of economy, characteristic of behaviour in daily life. It is essential, for example, to know how to walk without thinking about how to do it. The *sats* is a minute charge with which the thought innervates the action and is experienced as thought-action, energy, rhythm in space.

In Bali, the *sats* has a precise equivalent, *tangkis*, and is one of the four components of performative technique:

1 *agem*, attitude, base position;
2 *tandang*, to walk, to move in space;
3 *tangkis*, transition, the change from one posture, direction, level, to another;
4 *tangkep*, expression.

Tangkis literally means 'to escape', 'to avoid', but also, 'a way of doing'. It is the means by which the performer can 'escape' from the rhythm s/he is following and create a variation in the design of movements.

Tangkis can be a quick, vigorous micro-movement (unforgettable after having seen a Balinese performance). It is then defined as *angsel*, the essence of which is *keras*, strong. But it can also be *manis*, *alus*, gentle, in which case it is called *seleyog*, soft, and is supple, flowing, 'legato'.

I Made Bandem compares the *tangkis* moments with punctuation. They are the full stops which separate one sentence from another and 'avoid' the sense of being lost in an indistinct flow of words. He concludes: 'without *tangkis*, there is no *bayu* ("wind", energy) and therefore no dance. But a dance with only *tangkis* is *bayu* gone crazy.'

In Peking Opera, certain *sats* (impulse-counterimpulse) emerge in a particularly clear way. The performer rapidly executes an intricate design of movements and at the height of tension, stops in a position of precarious balance – *liang xiang* – ready to start off again in a direction which will surprise the spectator's expectations. During one of the sessions of ISTA, a Peking Opera master formulated the technical base of these dilated *sats* in this way: *Movement stop, inside no stop*. Perhaps because he spoke little English, or perhaps because a working language always tends towards extreme concision, he defined the nature and value of *sats* and its secret richness for the performer in the shortest possible way: one can hold the movement back without immobilizing it. Almost the exact same words turned up during the work with Ingemar Lindh.

'Many have observed, quite aptly, that the basis of *nō* dance lies in stopping each movement just at the moment when the muscles are tensed', writes Kunio Komparu, thus revealing the same principle of *movement stop, inside no stop*. This mastery of *sats* is the performer's objective. He adds: 'The times of action in *nō* exist for the sake of the times of stillness, and [. . .] the stance and carriage are the bases not of movement but of the acquisition of the technique of non-movement.'[18]

In Japan, this ability of the performer to continue an action even when it has been finished is called *io-in*. The term suggests the resonating sound of a bell after it has been struck by a clapper. This sound, which persists without any dynamic cause, creates a world of echoes and impressions for those who hear it.

Vakhtangov called the ability to assume a position and to justify its internal tension 'to live in the pauses'. He suggested to the actor: pose for a photograph; you are dancing, the music suddenly stops and you are ready to continue; in a restaurant, you are trying to listen to what is being said about you at a nearby table; you are in bed and are trying to identify a noise in the next room: a thief or a mouse?[19]

The *sats* is the tiny keystone of every physical action. It makes it possible for the performer to be technically precise even when working according to the 'magic if' and 'emotional memory' procedures.

Here is Stanislavski, in rehearsal, in the last years of his life, intent on awakening the scenic *bios* of an actor who already has a great deal of professional experience.

Stanislavski helps him by using the word 'rhythm', which belongs to their common working language. But he places the word in the context of a sentence which makes it unrecognizable:

'You are not standing in the correct rhythm!'

Vassili Toporkov, the actor, thinks:

'To stand in rhythm! *How* to stand in rhythm?
To walk, to dance, to sing in rhythm, this I could understand, but *to stand*!'

And he asks:

'Pardon me, Konstantin Sergeyevitch, but I have no idea whatsoever what rhythm is.'

Stanislavski is in fact working on the *sats*, or rather, on that which in the working language adopted in this book we call *sats*[20]:

That is not important. Around that corner is a mouse. Take a stick and lie in wait for it; kill it as soon as it jumps out . . . No, that way you will let it escape. Watch more attentively – *more attentively*. As soon as I clap my hands, beat it with the stick . . . Ah, see how late you are! Once more. Concentrate more. Try to make the stroke of the stick almost simultaneous with the clap. Well then, do you see that now you are standing in a completely different rhythm than before? Do you feel the difference? To stand and watch for a mouse – that is one rhythm; to watch a tiger that is creeping up on you is quite another one.[21]

If we removed the word 'rhythm' from Konstantin Sergeyevitch Stanislavski's words above and substituted for it the word 'emotion', the essential meaning of his instructions would not change. The most interesting fact for us, however, would remain concealed: that the effectiveness of the 'magic if' or the 'emotional memory' is stimulated from the outside, by working on the *sats*. By this means, the performer is freed from the fetters of having 'to decide to act'. S/he reacts, *is decided*.

It is work on *sats* and on immobility in motion which Stanislavski is drawing attention to in the list of the twenty-five phases which make up the Method of Physical Actions during rehearsals. Phases eighteen and nineteen are:

18. Seated around the table, the actors should now read the playscript to each other. At the same time, but without moving, they should attempt to convey their Physical Actions.
19. This time, moving only their heads and hands to demonstrate their activities, the actors read the play again at the table.[22]

Intermezzo: the bear who reads the thought, or rather, deciphers the sats

'Now', says Mr. C. politely, 'I must tell you a story. While travelling in Russia, I spent some time on the property belonging to Mr. G., a gentleman, whose sons were at that time assiduously practising fencing. The elder son in particular had become quite expert and, one morning when I was in his room, he handed me a foil. We fenced, but it so happened that I was better than he and, moreover, had the urge to unsettle him. Nearly all my thrusts hit the mark and, finally, his foil flew into a corner. As he retrieved it he remarked, half in jest, but also slightly resentfully, that he had met his match. He then added that each and every one of us has his match somewhere in the world, and that he could even take me to mine. His brothers burst out laughing and exclaimed: "Yes! Let's go! Down to the woodshed!" And they took me by the hand and led me to a bear which their father, Mr. G., was having raised on the estate.'

'In quite a state of shock, I approached the bear, who was standing

60

on his hind legs, his back up against the stake to which he was tied. His right paw was raised, ready to strike, and he was looking straight into my eyes. This was his fencer's stance. Finding myself faced with such an adversary, I felt as though I was dreaming, but: "Strike! strike!", said Mr. G., "see if you can hit him!"'

'Recovering my senses somewhat, I attacked with my foil; the bear made a slight movement with his paw and parried. I tried to confuse him with feints; the bear didn't move. I attacked again, quickly – had my opponent been another man, I would certainly have struck his chest. The bear made another slight movement with his paw and parried. I was reduced almost to the state of the young Mr.G. The bear's serious manner contributed to my growing nervousness, thrusts and feints followed one after another, I was covered with sweat – in vain!'

'The bear did not only parry my thrusts like the best fencer in the world, but ignored my feints, in a way which no fencer in the world would have been able to imitate. He was simply there, eye to eye with me, as if he could read my soul, his paw raised and ready to strike, and when my thrusts were not real, he didn't move.'

'Do you believe this story?'

'Completely!', I exclaimed enthusiastically. 'It is so convincing, I would believe it even if a stranger told it to me; I believe it even more coming from you.'[23]

Animus *and* Anima – *the temperatures of the energy*

I have already said that energy in the theatre is a *how*, but for the performer it is useful to think of it as if it were a *what*. By so doing, s/he does not lie to her/himself about the nature of biological processes, but invents her/his own scenic biology.

The ability to identify and distinguish between the various facets of energy is part of this professional strategy.

The first step consists of the perception of the existence of two poles, one vigorous, strong (*Animus*), the other soft, delicate (*Anima*); two different temperatures, which one is tempted to confuse with the polarity of the sexes. This tendency, which seems innocuous on the abstract level of classifications, has, however, damaging consequences on the practical level.

Interest in male performers who play female roles and female performers who play male roles is periodically rekindled. At such times, one might almost suspect that behind these disguises, these contrasts between reality and fiction, lies hidden one of the theatre's secret potentialities.

In each man there is a woman and in each woman a man. This commonplace does not help the performer become aware of the quality of her/his energy. In many civilizations, it was or is normal that a performer's sex and that of the character s/he is playing were or are not the same.

The question of the performer's natural sex in relationship to the sex of the character s/he is playing is very interesting from an historical point of view, as an indication of the customs of an era, in the context of the principles and preconceptions of different cultures, their respective tastes and aesthetics, their intolerances. But it is of no help when one is faced with an elementary professional problem: the nature of the performer's energy and the existence of an Anima-energy and an Animus-energy.

Anima-energy (soft) and Animus-energy (vigorous) are terms which have nothing to do with the distinction between masculine and feminine, nor with Jungian archetypes. They refer to a polarity, pertinent to the anatomy of the theatre, difficult to define with words, and therefore difficult to analyse, develop and transmit. And yet, any possibilities which the performer may have to avoid becoming crystallized in a technique stronger than her/himself depend upon this polarity and the way in which the performer succeeds in dilating its territory.

Performers are targets in front of the spectator. They therefore try to make themselves invulnerable. They build a cuirass; by means of techniques passed on to them by tradition, or by means of the building up of a character, they arrive at an artificial, extra-daily form of behaviour. They dilate their presence and consequently also dilate the spectator's perception. They are a *body-in-life* in the fiction of the theatre. Or aspire to be so. To this end, they have worked for years and years, in some cases since childhood. To this end, they have repeated the same actions over and over again, have trained assiduously. To this end, they make use of mental processes, 'magic ifs', subtexts, 'subscores', personal points of support invisible to the spectator. To this end, they imagine their bodies at the centre of a network of physical tensions and resistances, unreal but effective. They use a 'paradoxical way of thinking', an extra-daily body and mind technique which helps them become invulnerable.

On the perceptible level, it seems that they are working on the body and the voice. In fact, they are working on something invisible: energy. The experienced performer learns not to associate energy mechanically with an excess of muscular and nervous activity, with impetuousness and shouting, but with something intimate, something which pulsates in immobility and silence, a retained power-thought which grows in time without manifesting itself in space.

'Energy' is a personal temperature-intensity which the performer can determine, awaken, model.

The performer's extra-daily body technique dilates the body's dynamics. The body is re-formed, re-built for the theatrical fiction. This 'art body' – and thus, 'non-natural body' – is neither male nor female *in and of itself*. On the stage, it has the sex it has decided to represent.

The performer's task is to discover the individual propensities of her/his own energy and to protect its uniqueness.

The first days of work leave an indelible imprint. The performer, in the first days of apprenticeship, has all her/his potentialities intact: s/he begins to make choices, to eliminate some potentialities in order to develop others. S/he can enrich her/his work only by diminishing the territory of her/his experiences, in order to be able to mine more deeply into a narrow vein.

Any possibilities the performer may have to safeguard and reinforce the double profile of her/his energy are decided in this initial phase of the profession. Otherwise, there prevails a unilateral tendency which makes her/him more secure, stronger, prematurely invulnerable.

It is the acquisition of an *ethos* which first characterizes every performer. *Ethos* understood as scenic behaviour, that is, physical and mental technique; *ethos* understood as a work ethic, as a mentality modelled by the human environment in which the apprenticeship takes place.

The nature of the relationship between master and student, between student and student, between men and women, between old and young, the degree of rigidity or elasticity of the hierarchy, of the norms, of the demands and limits which are imposed on the student, influence her/his artistic future. All of these factors act upon the balance between two opposing necessities: on the one hand, selection and crystallization; on the other hand, safeguarding what is essential in the potential richness of the beginning.

In other words, to select without suffocating.

This apprenticeship dialectic is constant, whether in theatre schools or in the face-to-face teaching between master and student, in the performer's practical initiation, from when s/he first starts to 'rise from the ranks', or in autodidactic situations.

Serious amputations, which risk suffocating the performer's future development, sometimes occur for unnoticed reasons.

In the period of apprenticeship, performers (unconsciously or in order to be expedient) often arbitrarily limit the territory in which they explore the individual propensities of their own energies. The range of the orbit whose poles are Animus-energy and Anima-energy are thus reduced. Some choices, apparently 'natural', turn out to be a prison.

When the male student adapts himself from the beginning exclusively to male roles, and the female student exclusively to female roles, he or she undermines the exploration of her/his own energy on the pre-expressive level.

To learn to act according to two clear perspectives which trace the distinction between the sexes is an apparently inoffensive point of departure. There is a consequence, however: the introduction of mental rules and habits from daily reality into the extra-daily territory of the theatre.

On the final level, that of results and of the performance, the performer's presence becomes a scenic figure, a character, and masculine or feminine characterization is inevitable and necessary. It is, however, damaging when this masculine or feminine characterization is also dominant on a level where it does not belong: the pre-expressive level.

During apprenticeship, individual differentiation passes through the negation of the differentiation of the sexes. The field of complementarity dilates. This is noticeable when the work on the pre-expressive level takes no account of what is masculine and what is feminine (as in modern dance or the training of many theatre groups) or when a performer explores masculine and feminine roles indiscriminately (as in classical Asian theatre). The double-edged nature of her/his particular energy becomes tangibly evident. The balance between the two poles, Animus-energy and Anima-energy, is preserved.

Also in the Indian tradition, performers work within the polarity of the energy and not according to the correspondence between the character and the performer's sex. The styles of Indian dance are divided into two categories, *lasya* (delicate) and *tandava* (vigorous), depending on the way the movements are executed and not on the sex of the performer.

The world of Indian dance develops between these two sides of a single unity; not only the styles but also each element of a single style (movement, rhythm, costume, music), is defined as *tandava* if it is strong, vigorous, exuberant, while, if it is light, delicate, gentle, it is defined as *lasya*.

For the Balinese, *bayu* ('wind', 'breath'), normally indicates the performer's energy and the expression *pengunda bayu* refers to a well-distributed energy. The Balinese *bayu* is a literal interpretation of the increase and decrease of a force which lifts the whole body and whose complementary aspects (*keras*/vigorous and *manis*/soft) reconstruct the variations and nuances of life.

In the terminology used in this book, Animus and Anima refer to a *concordia discors*, an interaction between opposites which brings to mind the poles of a magnetic field, or the tension between body and shadow. It would be arbitrary to give them sexual connotations.

Keras and *manis*, *tandava* and *lasya*, Animus and Anima, do not refer to concepts which are completely equivalent. What is similar, however, in different cultures, is the necessity to specify, by means of an opposition, the extreme poles of the range in which the performer mentally and practically breaks down the energy of her/his natural *bios* modulating it into scenic *bios*, that which enlivens, from the inside, her/his technique. These terms do not refer to women or men or to feminine or masculine qualities, but to softness and vigour as flavours of the energy. The warrior god, Rama, for example, is often represented in the *lasya*, 'soft', way. The alternation of Anima-energy and Animus-energy is clearly perceptible in Indian, Balinese and Japanese performers who tell and dance the stories of several characters; or in Western performers who, from the beginning, have been formed by a training which does not take sexual differences into consideration.

One form of essential research, common both to Theatre Anthropology and to our craft's empiricism, is research into the constant polarities hidden beneath the variety and fluctuation of styles, traditions, genres, and different work practices. To give a name to the flavours, to the performer's experiences, to the spectator's perceptions, even the most subtle of them, seems a futile abstraction. But it is a premise for leaping from a situation in which we are immersed and which dominates us, to a real experience, that is, something which we are able to analyse, to develop consciously and to transmit.

It is the leap from experiencing to having experience.

Before being thought of as a purely spiritual entity – platonic or Christian – the word 'soul' meant a wind, a continuous flow which animated the motion and life of animals and human beings. In many cultures, the body is compared to a percussion instrument; its soul is the beat, the vibration, the rhythm.

This wind which is vibration and rhythm can change face, while remaining itself, by means of a subtle mutation of its internal tension. Boccaccio, commenting on Dante and summarizing the attitudes of a millenarian culture, said that when Anima, the living and intimate wind, is drawn towards something external, it turns into Animus.

In the course of her/his career, the performer comes to realize that the most insidious obstacle is not difficulty in learning, but having learned so much that s/he has become invulnerable. S/he senses that her/his technical cuirass creates interest, commands respect, dazzles. S/he becomes, for the observer, a deforming and revealing mirror.

But because s/he is invulnerable, her/his shadow has withdrawn into its shell.

The shadow can emerge only from a fracture, when the performer is able to open a vent in the cuirass of technique and seduction which s/he has built and dominating it, abandons it, exposing her/himself, undefended, like the warrior who fights with bare hands. Vulnerability becomes strength.

This takes us back to the performer's origins, to the first day of apprenticeship, when the gamut of unrealized and invisible potentialities collided with the tangible work of selection and crystallization. Here, energy, the wind which blows through the cuirass of technique and which animates it from inside, risks becoming tamed by the dominant models of scenic behaviour and performing. The dynamic relationship between the Animus and Anima potentialities, their consonance and dissonance, tend, with time, to become stabilized in a consolidated technique.

But the fracture through which the shadow can filter is determined by the simultaneous presence of Animus and Anima, by the performer's ability to explore the range between one pole and the other, to show the dominant profile of her/his energy and to reveal its double nature – vigour and tenderness, vehemence and grace, ice and snow, sun and flame.

And thus the spectator discovers the invisible life which animates the theatre and experiences an experience.

The double profile of the wind in the cuirass, the dual tension which characterizes energy on the theatre's cellular level, is the material source of this spiritual experience.

In a short, recondite treatise written around 1420, when he was almost sixty years old, Zeami laid out a scale of nine steps corresponding to the nine degrees of perfection of the performer's art (*Kyui*, 'The Nine Steps'). For each of the nine steps he chose a poetic image drawn from the literature of Zen monks. Here are the first three images:

> In Silla, in the dead of night,
> the sun shines brightly.
>
> Snow covers a thousand mountains;
> why is there one peak that is not white?
>
> Piling up snow
> in a silver bowl.[24]

Reading three verses one after another as if they were a poem, I am struck by the difference between the first two verses and the third. I will not try to interpret them but to comment on them freely within the context of our argument, not Zeami's.

In the first and second verses, the complementarity or correspondence between the opposites is very obvious, while in the third verse it is veiled by a fundamentally monochromatic image brought alive by the different gradations between the brilliant whiteness of the snow and the dazzling yet warm luminosity of the silver. I emphasize 'warm'; in a subsequent verse appears another gleam of metal in which a cold quality is explicitly referred to ('The shadow of the metal hammer moving; the cold gleam of the sacred sword'). The image of the snow in the silver bowl, however, transforms the natural notion of cold into serene, clear light. One could say that the impression created is one of spring in the heart of winter. Here as well, then, there is a complementarity but now it is dissimulated by the absolute absence of dissonance.

Zeami goes on to use the image of the snow and the silver to discuss the imperturbable presence of the performer who achieves the *unusual* without any visible dramatic effect. We will use it, however, to conclude these reflections on the various temperatures of energy.

One of the most insidious pitfalls which lie in wait in books dedicated to the procedures of art derives from the radical difference between the tactics which guide conceptual comprehension and those which, on the other hand, guide practical comprehension through experience of action.

In order to understand rationally the existence of a gamut of different possibilities, it is helpful to emphasize extreme points (as we have just done with Animus and Anima; and as we have done from the beginning of this book with North Pole and South Pole performers). But we must remember that the purpose of this insistence on extremes is the clarity of the discussion and not practical effectiveness. If, in a work situation, one concentrates on extreme poles, what one attains is only technique gone mad. In order to understand the criteria which can lead us towards a conscious modelling of energy, it is important to insist on polarities like *keras* and *manis*, Animus and Anima, sun and midnight, *lasya* and *tandava*, black and white, flame and ice. But in order to translate those criteria into artistic practice, one must work not on the extremes, but on the gamut of nuances which lie between them. If this does not happen, instead of artificially composing the energy in order to reconstruct the organicity of a body-in-life, one produces only *the image of artificiality*.

The couplet

> Piling up snow
> in a silver bowl

can represent, in our context, an antidote to the tendency towards extremes. It reminds us that making the *bios* visible depends on the imperceptible nuances of rhythm, of single waves, each one different from the other, which make up the living current between the banks.

But we must not forget that the softness of the snow and the hardness of the silver in which it is contained are also themselves two extremes which condense, in an oxymoron, the simultaneous action of two divergent forces. For Zeami, the secret of the *unusual*, the performer's 'flower', her/his scenic *bios*, lies in this ability to give life to an opposition.

In the treatise, *Fushikaden*, we read:

> When performing *nō*, there are endless matters that must be kept in mind. For example, when an actor plans to express the emotion of anger, he must not fail to retain a tender heart. Such is his only means to prevent his acting from developing roughness, no matter what sort of anger is expressed. To appear angry while possessing a tender heart gives rise to the principle of novelty. On the other hand, in a performance requiring grace, an actor must not forget to remain strong. Thus all aspects of his performance – dance, movement, role playing – will be genuine and lifelike.
>
> Then, too, there are various concerns in connection with using the actor's body on stage. When he moves himself about in a powerful way, he must stamp his foot in a gentle way. And when he stamps his feet strongly, he must hold the upper part of his body quiet. This matter is difficult to describe in words. It is better to learn this directly from a teacher.[25]

Another treatise by Zeami, *Shikado* ('The true path for the flower'), introduces us to the nuances found between extremes. This text should be read in conjunction with another treatise: *Nikyoku Santai Ezu* ('Two arts and three illustrated types').

Zeami draws the performer's attention to the importance of three figures: the Woman, the Warrior, and the Old Man. Three apparently different roles. He writes:

> An actor who is beginning his training must not overlook the Two Arts

(*Nikyoku*) and Three Types (*Santai*). By the Two Arts, I mean dancing and chanting. By the Three Types, I refer to the human forms that constitute the basis of role impersonation: an old person (*rotai*), a woman (*nyotai*), a warrior (*guntai*).[26]

The three basic types of which Zeami is speaking are not, however, roles. They are not actual 'types', as they are usually understood to be, but *tai*, that is, bodies guided by a particular quality of energy which has to do neither with sex nor with age. Zeami's three basic *tai* are distinct ways of carrying the same body, giving it a different scenic life by means of specific qualities of energy. One of the other meanings of *tai* is, in fact, *semblance*.

It is particularly important to look not at the extremes – the woman and the warrior – but at the body, the *tai*, of the old person such as it is described and drawn in the essay *Nikyoku Santai Ezu*.[27]

Zeami defines the three types as follows:

Old Man Type: serenity of spirit, distant gaze.
Woman Type: her nature is spiritual. She has no violence.
Warrior Type: his nature is violent. The spirit is applied to detail (delicacy in force).

Alongside these definitions, Zeami places the drawings of the three *tai*: three naked figures in whose bodies the architecture of the three *semblances* is clearly recognizable.

In the sketch of the Old Man, who is leaning on a cane, Zeami has drawn a line to indicate the direction of the Old Man's gaze, upwards, which contrasts with the bent posture of an individual who is so weak that he must support himself with a cane. A tension is created between the nape of the neck and the upper part of the spinal column.

This drawing reveals the secret of the *three bodies*; through the body of an old man, the performer consciously manipulates the two faces of the energy – Animus/Anima – which co-exist within him. In this way, the performer makes the authentic *hana*, the flower, blossom, which, according to Zeami, characterizes the great actor:

Playing the role of an old man represents the very pinnacle of our art. These roles are crucial, since the spectators who watch can gauge immediately the real skills of the actor [. . .]

In terms of stage deportment, most actors, thinking to appear old, bend their loins and hips, shrink their bodies, lose their Flower, and give a withered, uninteresting performance. It is particularly important that the actor refrain from performing in a limp or weak manner, but bears himself with grace and dignity. Most crucial of all is the dancing posture chosen for the *tai* of an old man. One must study assiduously the precept: portray an old man while still possessing the Flower. The results should resemble an old tree that puts forth flowers.[28]

Thought in action – the paths of energy

Let us return to the *jo-ha-kyu*, which is one of the criteria – or paths of thought – which in Japan regulate the arts and therefore also the various forms of classical theatre.

Three phases:

-*jo*: the initial phase, when the force is put in motion as if overcoming a resistance;
-*ha*: the transition phase, rupture of the resistance, increase of the motion;
-*kyu*: the rapid phase, an unbridled crescendo ending in the sudden stop.

Let us translate literally: resistance, rupture, acceleration.

But we have not yet even begun to understand this regulatory principle. One of the impediments to our understanding is the fact that this principle is applied to all levels of the theatre, from performing to dramaturgy, from the composition of the programme of a *nō* day to the music. We will focus only on the performer's physical action.

The third moment is characterized by a sudden stop. The impression given to the spectator by the performer is that of someone who comes to an abrupt halt at the edge of a ravine. The performer's feet suddenly stop, the trunk sways slightly forward while the spine extends and the performer seems to increase in size. In fact, the moment of the stop is a transitional phase. Some performers say that in the *kyu*, they do not exhale completely and keep enough breath to start the action again without having to inhale. The movement is interrupted but the energy is suspended. The Peking Opera performer could repeat here his synthetic and effective remark: *movement stop, inside no stop*. In other words, the final moment of the phase in which the performer stops is a *sats*, the point of departure for a new *jo*. The *jo-ha-kyu*, in short, is cyclical.

We have made a step forward in our understanding, but we are still a long way off.

One might think that *jo-ha-kyu* works like the 'infinite' or 'perpetual canon' of traditional Western music. This is not the case. When referred to in books, it can seem to be a metre based on three phases, each with a different speed. In fact, each of the three phases is in turn subdivided into *jo-ha-kyu*. If the classical Japanese performer, after having first explained the rudiments of *jo-ha-kyu*, then goes on to analyse the structure of her/his action, s/he begins to speak of a *jo* of the *ha*, of a *ha* of the *kyu* of a *kyu* of the *jo*, and so on. The performer can carry out an entire dance while explaining the different phases, and the sub-phases of each phase, to those who are watching.

The observer then begins to get lost. Trying to find a *fixed point* on which to focus, he pushes the question to the absurd: 'But does that mean that there is also a *kyu* of the *jo* of the *ha*?' 'Exactly', the performer replies. Beyond a certain limit, s/he also begins to get lost. We realize that *jo-ha-kyu* is not really a rhythmic structure but a pattern of thought and action. On the macroscopic level, it is a clear technical articulation, but once a certain threshold has been passed, it becomes a rhythm of thinking.

Does it then cease to be something which is relevant to practise?

The Japanese performer who is demonstrating the basic techniques of her/his art cannot continue to indicate to us the infinitesimal sub-phases of each action. They are no longer actual segments of a score. This does not exclude them from being accents of the thought, mental behaviour which makes it possible for the performer always to vary, in an imperceptible way, her/his way of being in the action. It is thought which etches and sculpts time, thus becoming rhythm. The action is rigorously codified in its detailed score but there is a kind of sub-score along which the performer improvises. S/he does not change the form; the same design of movements is executed, while the performer invents innumerable *jo-ha-kyu* relationships, each time as if it was the first time.

'I first heard the term *jo-ha-kyu* when I was an adult. When I learned the word, I already knew what it was', says *kyōgen* actor Kosuke Nomura during a demonstration at the Blois ISTA in April, 1985. Kosuke was twenty-five years old and already had twenty-three years of theatrical experience. He began to work with his grandfather at the age of two-and-a-half, for fifteen minutes a day. He can already perform three hundred of the one thousand roles which make up the repertoire of a *kyōgen* actor. *Jo-ha-kyu* is not only an important quality of his style. It has marked his identity as a performer.

Let us return to that beginner's class at the Ballet School of the Royal Theatre of Copenhagen where we have already been, to observe how the luxury balance of the ballet dancer is constructed. The teacher points out one young girl from among the other students. It seems to me that her way of doing the exercises is just like that of all the other students. The teacher explains to me that it is not a question of technical ability but of the quality of her phrasing. This means that the child is following the music without abandoning herself to it. In spite of the elementary level of the exercises, she already shows an ability to withhold and model her own rhythm – her own energies – in a personal dialogue with the music. Even though her dancing is inexpert, the way in which *she thinks it with her whole body* is not mechanical.

We have several times repeated that the performer's energy is not impetuosity, over-excitement, violence. Neither is it, however, an abstraction or a metaphor, with which one cannot work.

In its basic, material form, energy is muscular and nervous force. But it is not the pure and simple existence of this force, present by definition in every living being, which is of interest to us. Nor is it enough that this force undergoes change; every moment of our lives, consciously or unconsciously, we are modelling our physical energy.

What must be of interest to us is the way in which this biological process becomes thought, is re-modelled, made visible to the spectator.

In order to re-shape her/his own energy artificially, the performer must think of it in tangible, visible, audible forms, must picture it, divide it into a scale, withhold it, suspend it in an immobility which acts, guide it, with varying intensities and velocities, through the design of movements, as if through a slalom course.

We note, therefore, that what we call energy is in fact *leaps of energy*. The principle of the absorption of the action, the *sats*, the ability to compose the transition from one temperature to another (Animus and Anima, *keras* and *manis* . . .) are different stratagems for the production and control of the leaps of energy which enliven the performer's *bios*. These leaps are variations in a series of details which, intelligently assembled in sequence, are called in the various working languages 'physical actions', 'design of movements', 'score', *kata*.

It does not matter what names the performer uses, whether s/he resorts to scientific metaphors or poetic images, follows the dictates of a tradition or a personal way of thinking. What is important is that in the practice of the apprenticeship and in the experience of her/his thinking, s/he knows how to construct and subdivide a precise route which makes it possible for the energy *to leap*. This verb is used in scientific language to describe the behaviour of 'quanta' of energy. In Latin, it means *to dance*.

Let us again listen to Toporkov, who we last saw working with Stanislavski. He is now the spectator, while Konstantin Sergeyevitch Stanislavski is doing the exercise of a man at a news-stand:

> He would buy a paper when there is a whole hour before the departure of the train and he doesn't know how to kill the time, or when the first or second bell has rung, or when the train has already started. The actions are all the same but in completely different rhythms, and Konstantin Sergeyevitch was able to carry out these exercises in any order by increasing the rhythm, by diminishing the rhythm, by sudden change.[29]

The exactness with which the action is designed in space, the precision of each of its characteristics, a series of exactly fixed points of departure and arrival, of impulses and counterimpulses, of changes of direction, of *sats*: these are the preliminary conditions for the dance of energy.

Natsu Nakajima, direct heir of Tatsumi Hijikata who, with Kazuo Ohno, founded *butō* dance, is explaining and demonstrating her way of working (Bologna, ISTA, July 1990). She chooses a series of images for each of which she establishes an *attitude*, a figure for her dance. She thus has available a series of immobile poses sculpted into her body. She now assembles the individual poses one after another, passing from one to another without interruption. She obtains a precise design of movements. She repeats the same sequence as if meeting three different types of resistance, which must be overcome with three different types of energy: it is as if she was moving in a space as solid as stone; in a liquid space; and in the air. She is constructing, on the basis of a limited number of poses, a universe of images, a choreography.

Up to this point, watching her demonstration, we have seen a rigorous work of combination characterized by precision and by the recognizability of every individual fragment. But when Natsu goes through this combination of fragments again, without varying the order of the pattern, all of us who had previously watched the long and passionless preliminary anatomy, now have the impression that she is improvising her dance.

And Natsu is actually improvising, just as Stanislavski was improvising in his scene at the news-stand. Natsu has a completely different culture, tradition, aesthetic ideals, repertoire of images and concepts, but the basic principles which she is using (not her *technique*, but *the technique of her technique*) are no different than those used by Stanislavski.

Let us consider, for a moment, how misleading is the ghost of the word 'improvisation', which often crops up in professional discussions, sometimes to indicate an ideal to be achieved, sometimes to warn one about a form of decay to be avoided. When the word improvisation does not mean a lack of precision, when it is used in a positive sense, it denotes a quality of the performer which derives from a refined work on the various levels of scenic *bios*. It is thought/action on the riverbed of a physical score. It does not matter if this score is constructed by the performer during the long and patient work of rehearsal, if it has been fixed by tradition, or if, on the other hand, the performer, carried by the second nature of her/his extra-daily body, composes it at the same time as executing it.[30]

The return home

One of the best practical manuals for the training of the 'realistic' actor is *To the Actor*, by Michael Chekhov, published by Harper and Row in New York in 1953. It is subtitled: *On the technique of acting* and is furnished with explanatory drawings by Nikolai Remisov.

It is a typical manual for South Pole performers. Thus, while Theatre Anthropology often carries us far away, with Michael Chekhov we find ourselves very close to home: the actor to whom he is speaking is the kind most commonly found in theatre, cinema and television today. The traditions of codified theatre, whether Asian or Euro-American, are not mentioned in his book.

In Russia in the twenties, Michael Chekhov was considered the most original actor of his generation. His interpretation of Hamlet had shaken the public and annoyed Stanislavski because of what appeared, in the eyes of the old master, to be an excess of artificiality and the grotesque. His interpretation of Khlestakov, in Gogol's *The Government Inspector*, had enraptured Meyerhold. It is 1921; five years later, Meyerhold will create 'his' version of

The Government Inspector, one of the most significant productions of the twentieth century. He acknowledges that his ideas developed from the seed of Michael Chekhov's acting, and recommends to his actors that they must not imitate him, but compete with him.[31]

In 1928, Michael Chekhov emigrated from Russia but did not succeed in any foreign theatre. Both Stanislavski and Meyerhold tried to convince him to return to Russia. He, on his part, attempted to persuade Meyerhold to emigrate to the West. But Meyerhold remained in his homeland and was tortured and shot in one of Stalin's prisons on 2 February 1940. Michael Chekhov lived a double exile, separated from his homeland and from his theatre. He published *To the Actor* at the age of fifty. He began it with these words:

> This book is the result of prying behind the curtain of the Creative Process – prying that began many years ago in Russia at the Moscow Art Theatre, with which I was associated for sixteen years. During that time I worked with Stanislavski, Nemirovich-Danchenko, Vachtangov and Sulerjitsky.[32]

The Second World War had made survival impossible for the small art theatres. Michael Chekhov was obliged to put his knowledge at the disposal of Hollywood and Broadway actors. When he published his book, he was obliged, for the umpteenth time, to present his own credentials, and he reminded his readers that he had worked with artists like Chaliapin, Moissi, Jouvet, Gielgud. Among his students – in addition to Gregory Peck – was Yul Brynner who, just around that time, nearly forty years old, had become a star. For this reason, Michael Chekhov asked him to write the preface to his book.

It is one of the best actor's manuals. It should be read and re-read, reflected upon, pried into.

I began my investigations into Theatre Anthropology by reflecting on my first days of work, and, going back in time, by 'prying into' the first days of work of masters like Sanjukta Panigrahi, Hideo Kanze, Katsuko Azuma, I Made Pasek Tempo, Pei Yanling, I Made Bandem. We exchanged questions and answers. We realized that the first days of work were the days of the roots. And the different roots were much more similar than were the plants which grew from them. The same considerations applied for Ingemar Lindh, formed in Decroux' school, for Dario Fo, for Ryszard Cieslak from Grotowski's Teatr-Laboratorium, and for the actors of Odin Teatret.

The first days of apprenticeship of classical ballet dancers, the first days of a *butō* dancer, the first days of a clown ... It is on this threshold that the recurring principles meet.

Let us look at Michael Chekhov and his book from the same point of view. The book begins with seven basic exercises (the italics are Chekhov's own):

Exercise 1 Do a series of wide, broad but simple movements, using a maximum of space around you. Involve and utilize your whole body.

Make the movements with sufficient strength, but without straining your muscles unnecessarily. Movements can be made that will 'enact' the following:

Open yourself completely, spreading wide your arms and hands, your legs far apart. Remain in this expanded position for a few seconds. Imagine that you are becoming larger and larger. Come back to the original position. Repeat the same movement several times. Keep in mind the aim of the exercise, saying to yourself, 'I am going to awaken the sleeping muscles of my body; I am going to revivify and use them.'

Now *close* yourself by crossing your arms upon your chest, putting your hands on your shoulders. Kneel on one or both knees, bending your head low. Imagine that you are becoming smaller and smaller, curling up, contracting as though you wanted to disappear bodily within yourself, and that the space around you is shrinking. Another set of your muscles will be awakened by this contracting movement.

Resume a standing position, then *thrust* your body forward on one leg, stretching out one or both arms. Do the same *stretching* movement sideways to the right, to the left, using as much space around you as you can.

Do a movement that resembles a blacksmith *beating* his hammer upon the anvil.

Do different wide, well-shaped, full movements – as though you were in turn *throwing* something in different directions, *lifting* some object from the ground, *holding* it high above your head, or *dragging*, *pushing* and *tossing* it. Make your movements complete, with sufficient strength, and in moderate tempo. Avoid dancing movements. Do not hold your breath while moving. Do not hurry. Pause after each movement.

This exercise will gradually give you a glimmer of the sensations of *freedom* and *increased life*. Let these sensations sink into your body as the first psychological qualities to be absorbed.[33]

Notice how the action of physical extension and the action of closing, once they have reached their limits, continue internally (*movement stop, inside no stop*). This internal echo can be called, according to the terminology preferred, 'feeling', 'state of the soul', '*io-in*', but it is basically a way of experiencing energy. Or rather, *a way of canalizing it and therefore of experiencing it* by means of a particular use of the pauses, of a luxury balance, of actions which, beginning in the trunk, involve the entire body.

Exercise 2 Imagine that within your chest there is a *center* from which flow the actual impulses for all your movements. Think of this imaginary center as a source for all your movements. Think of this imaginary center as a source of inner activity and power within your body. Send this power into your head, arms, hands, torso, legs and feet. Let the sensation of strength, harmony and well-being penetrate the whole body. See to it that neither your shoulders, elbows, wrists, hips nor knees staunch the flow of this energy from the imaginary center, but let it course freely. Realize that the joints are not given you to make your body stiff but, on the contrary, to enable you to use your limbs with utmost freedom and flexibility.

Imagining that your arms and legs originate from this center within your chest (not from the shoulders and hips), try a series of natural movements: lift your arms and lower them, stretch them in different directions, walk, sit down, get up, lie down; move different objects; put on your overcoat, gloves, hat; take them off, and so on. See that all the movements you make are actually instigated by that power which flows from the imaginary center within your chest.[34]

Every tradition and every performer locates the centre from which energy radiates in a different part of the body.[35] It serves no purpose to debate about who is right nor to ask where the centre of energy really is. What is important is that every performer selects a very precise place, not arbitrarily chosen, mentally and therefore physically effective, different from the points at which, in daily action, movements seem to begin (joints, muscles). It is often useful to have someone on the outside indicate the origin of the energy, thus giving the choice an aura of prestige or objectivity.

In other words, it is not the energy itself which helps us discover its source, but, on the contrary, it is by *imagining* the place in the body in which the source is situated that we are able to think of the energy, to experience it as something material, to divert it through subtle variations, to intensify it by means of a slalom which moulds it into scenic *bios*.

The phrase 'that power which flows from the imaginary centre' makes one think of a spontaneous force which originates on its own. In reality, to imagine the precise source from which energy radiates means creating a resistance. The performer is obliged to destroy automatic (daily) movements and reactions and to create an architecture of tensions and a dynamism which belong to the extra-daily reality of the theatre.

The exercises which follow draw attention to yet more ways of faceting energy, exploring the gamut of its various nuances.

Exercise 3 As before, make strong and broad movements with your whole body. But now say to yourself: 'Like a sculptor, I *mould* the space surrounding me. In the air around me I leave forms which appear to be chiselled by the movements of my body.'

Create strong and definite *forms*. To be able to do this, think of the beginning and the end of each movement you make. Again say to yourself: 'Now I *begin* my movement which creates a form', and after completing it: 'Now I *finished* it; the form is there.' Along with this, think and feel your body itself as a *movable form.* Repeat each movement several times until it becomes free and most enjoyable to fulfill. Your efforts will resemble the work of a designer who, again and again, draws the same line, striving for a better, clearer and more expressive form. But in order not to lose the moulding quality of your movement imagine the air around you as a medium which resists you. Also try the same movements in different tempos.

Then try to reproduce these movements by using only different parts of your body: mould the air around you with only your shoulders and shoulder blades, then with your back, your elbows, knees, forehead, hands, fingers, etc. In all these movements preserve the sensation of strength and inner power flowing through and out of your body.[36]

Exercise 4 [. . .] In the exercise imagine the air around you as a surface of water which supports you and over which your movements lightly skim. Change tempos. Pause from time to time.[37]

Exercise 5 Imagine your whole body flying through space. As in the previous exercises, your movements must merge into each other without becoming shapeless. In this exercise the physical strength of your movements may increase or diminish according to your desire, but it must never disappear altogether. Psychologically you must constantly maintain your strength. You may come to a static position outwardly, but inwardly you must continue your feeling of still soaring aloft. Imagine the air around you as a medium which instigates your flying movements. Your desire must be to overcome the weight of your body, to fight the law of gravity. While moving, change tempos.[38]

The way in which Michael Chekhov insists on the 'punctuation', on how to 'pause from time to time', how to 'think of the beginning and the end of each movement', how to 'change tempos', stressing that 'your movements must merge into each other without becoming shapeless', reveals the desire to safeguard the secret pulsation of scenic life, the impulses and counter-impulses, the *sats.* 'Not forms, but the marrow of forms', as Garcia Lorca says. 'And that which seems to be a flower is in fact honey.'

Exercise 6 Begin this exercise, as always, with the broad, wide movements of the previous exercises, then go into the simple, natural movements next suggested. Lift your arm, lower it, stretch it forward, sideways; walk around the room, lie down, sit down, get up, etc.; but continuously and in advance send the *rays* from your body into the space around you, in the direction of the movement you make, and after the movement is made.

You may wonder perhaps how you can continue, for instance, sitting down after you have actually sat down. The answer is simple if you remember yourself as having sat down, tired and worn out. True, your *physical body* has taken this final position, but *psychologically* you still continue to 'sit down' by *radiating* that you *are sitting*. The same with getting up while imagining yourself tired and worn-out: your body resists it, and long before you really get up you are already doing it inwardly: you are radiating 'getting up' and you continue to get up when you are already standing.[39]

Exercise 7 When you are thoroughly familiar with these four kinds of movements (moulding, floating, flying and radiating), and you are able to fulfill them easily, try to reproduce them in your imagination only. Repeat this until you can easily duplicate the same psychological and physical sensations you experienced while actually moving.[40]

We seem to have returned to Japan, almost as if Michael Chekhov had inspired Hijikata (the founder of *butō*, Natsu's master) to establish distinct types of resistance by means of which the same design of movements acquires different energy temperatures (moving in a space of stone, of water or air, for Hijikata and Natsu; moulding, floating, flying, radiating, for Michael Chekhov). But we are faced with a way of thinking which is so diffuse that it would be futile to attempt to trace direct influences.

The exploration of the different temperatures of energy is a recurring principle found not only in mental techniques based on personal images but also in codified distinctions like *keras* and *manis*, *tandava* and *lasya*.

Michael Chekhov's *Exercise 7*, with its four variations (moulding, floating, flying and radiating) not only recapitulates the procedures for 'embroidering' one's own energy but suggests absorbing the actions until the visible energy is distilled into thought: 'When you are [. . .] able to fulfill [these movements] easily, try to reproduce them in your imagination only. Repeat this until you can easily duplicate the same psychological and physical sensations you experienced while actually moving.' We are irresistibly reminded of Decroux and his 'passionate act', his immobility. Or of Hisao Kanze who danced his *i-guse* as stillness in motion.

At the beginning of this chapter, I called attention to the risks inherent in understanding 'energy' as impetus, violence, speed. It is now necessary to warn against the opposite risks. In *My Life in Art*, Stanislavski refers to how he had himself experienced the pernicious consequences which can result from research into the actor's immobility.[41]

When the performer decides to eliminate movements and searches for immobility, her/his first tendency is to concentrate on facial mimicry, on the eyes. The performer, to use theatrical jargon, 'pumps' feeling, the mood, forces the breathing, stiffens in inorganic tenseness. Immobility in motion is exactly the opposite, it is *firm suppleness*. It is the arrival point. If one runs to this goal by shortening the route, without long experience of the logic of physical actions, one ends up with a parody. Immobility in motion cannot be achieved directly. One must arrive at it in an indirect way, by means of the construction of an elaborate and detailed physical score. All those who speak of the performer's immobility insist on this point: it *is not absence* of the movement, *but miniaturization* of the movement, the dance, the score. The more the movement (that which one allows to filter through to the outside) is reduced, the more the thread of the dance or the score which the performer has absorbed must be refined, subdivided into detailed segments. These segments must then be fused together by a precise variety of *sats* which define and interweave the individual actions.

Michael Chekhov attaches great importance to the performer's interior life. His 'first days' show, however, that everything that he calls 'sensation', 'feeling' or 'psychological state' is innervated through precise physical attitudes. For Chekhov as well, the work on the body-in-life and the thought-in-life are two sides of the same coin.

In the fifth chapter of the book, devoted to the 'psychological gesture', Michael Chekhov explains how the rhythm of the energy, or rather, of the thought, in its macroscopic manifestation (physical aciton) and in its microscopic manifestation (internal action) gives rise to counterpoints and contrasts:

Our usual conception of tempo on the stage fails to distinguish between the *inner* and *outer* varieties. The inner tempo can be defined as a quick or slow change of thoughts, images, feelings, will, impulses, etc. The outer tempo expresses itself in quick or slow actions or speech. Contrasting outer and inner tempos can run simultaneously on the stage. For instance, a person can expect something or somebody impatiently; the images in his mind follow each other in quick succession, thoughts and desires flare up in his mind, chasing one another, appearing and disappearing; his will is stirred to a high pitch; and yet, at the same time, the person can control himself so that his outer behaviour, his movements and speech, will remain calm and slow in tempo. An outer slow tempo can run concurrently with a quick inner tempo, or vice versa. The effect of two contrasting tempos running simultaneously on the stage unfailingly makes a strong impression on an audience.

You should not confuse slow tempo with *passiveness* or a lack of energy in the actor himself. Whatever slow tempo you use on the stage, you as an artist must always be *active*. On the other hand, the quick tempo of your performance must not become an obvious *haste* or an unnecessary psychological and physical tension. A flexible, well-trained and obedient body and a good technique of speech will help you to avoid this mistake and make possible the correction and simultaneous usage of two contrasting tempos.[42]

It is the development of a similar way of thinking which Stanislavski, as we have seen, made Toporkov discover when he asked him to 'stand with the correct rhythm', even in immobility.

The banal realism of the scene proposed by Stanislavski (to be ready to catch a mouse as it comes around a corner) concealed a refined activity just as intense as the *i-guse*. The apparently conventional hotel scene proposed by Michael Chekhov in his *Exercise 17* is no less significant:

> Do a series of improvisations with contrasting inner and outer tempos.
>
> For example: A big hotel at night. Porters with quick, skilful, habitual movements carry the luggage from the elevator, sort it out and put it into waiting automobiles that must hurry to catch the train. The *outer tempo* of the servants is quick, but they are indifferent to the excitement of the guests who are checking out. The *inner tempo* of the porters is slow. The departing guests, on the contrary, trying to preserve an outer calm, are inwardly excited, fearing they will miss the train; their *outer tempo* is slow, their *inner tempo* is quick.[43]

The elementary principles which govern scenic *bios* on the cellular level are never present in the pure state, but always appear in the guise of a style or a theatrical tradition. The pre-expressive is suggested by means of the expressive level. When the guises belong to styles and traditions which are foreign to us, there is the danger that those elementary principles can remain hidden from us because of the strangeness of the form which contains them. When the guises are familiar to us, it is this very familiarity which makes our attention slip. For example something urges us to pass over, almost as if it bothered us, the contents of Michael Chekhov's *Exercise 17* quoted above. Is it not perhaps a scene with which we are all too familiar? Is it not a typical fragment from a Feydeau farce or from *Grand Hotel* with Greta Garbo and John Barrymore?

Thus, when in the eighth chapter of *To the Actor*, Michael Chekhov speaks of the 'composition of the performance', it is difficult to discover at first glance, beneath the good sense and the advice for constructing a correct *mise en scène*, the alternation of the *sats*, the dance of energy, or rather, the thought.

> Life, in all its manifestations, does not always follow a straight line. It undulates like waves, it breathes rhythmically. Thus *rhythmical waves* assume various characters with different phenomena; they flourish and fade, appear and disappear, expand and contract, circumfuse and centralize, ad infinitum. In application to dramatic art we can consider these waves as expressing only *inner* and *outer action*.
>
> Imagine a beautiful stage pause radiant with power, inwardly active, creating a strong atmosphere and holding the audience in suspense. It is not unusual to find a pause so pregnant, for a pause is never a complete vacuum, gap, or a psychological void space. Empty pauses do not, and should not, exist on the stage.

Every pause must have a purpose. A real, well-prepared and perfectly executed pause (long or short) is what we might call *inner action*, since its significance is implied by silence. Its antithesis is *outer action*, which we can define as a moment when all visible and audible means of expression are used to the fullest extent; when speech, voices, gestures, business, and even lighting and sound effects, ascend to their climactic point. Between these two extremes there is a spectrum of outer action that increases or decreases in varying degrees. A veiled, muted, almost imperceptible action often resembles a 'pause'. The very beginning of the tragedy, before Lear's entrance, may be described as such a muted-action pause, and so may the pause after his death at the end of the performance. Ebb and flow of inner and outer action, these are the rhythmical waves of a performance's composition.[44]

We could conclude by saying that by these ways and means, irrespective of the presence or absence of a codification, the South Pole performer meets the North Pole performer. The different genres of performance for which both train cannot hide the presence of similar principles.

We might well ask ourselves if it really was worthwhile to travel so far from home, when the essential fruits gathered during the journey were already there, a step away from our point of departure.

It would have been enough to follow the study programme of Meyerhold's Studio in 1922, which starts with

Movement centred on a conscious point, balance, transition from ample to small movements, awareness of the gesture as the result of a movement, even in static situations.[45]

But only the length of the voyage makes it possible for us to discover the riches of home upon our return.

The method and the goal of Theatre Anthropology are contained in this paradox.

6

THE DILATED BODY
Notes on the Search for Meaning

[handwritten marginalia: society in which spectacle defines who we are. who i am is what i present. perception is reality]

[handwritten marginalia: to be open + willing to react completely = dilation]

At the theatre with my mother – I was fifteen years old when I went to the theatre for the first time, in Rome. My mother took me to see *Cyrano de Bergerac*. The hero was played by Gino Cervi, a very popular Italian actor. But it was neither he nor the other actors who impressed me, nor the story which I followed with interest but without amazement. What impressed me was a horse. A real horse. It appeared pulling a carriage, according to the most reasonable rules of scenic realism. Its presence suddenly exploded all the dimensions which until then had reigned on that stage. Because of this sudden interference from another world, the scene was torn asunder before my very eyes.

In later years, I searched in theatre for that disorientation which had made me feel alive, for that sudden dilation of my senses. In vain.

No more horses appeared. Until I arrived in Opole, Poland and Cheruthuruthy, India.

That horse was the first verse of a song that I did not then know I would sing.

*   *   *

One day you meet a little girl again – Memory is the song which we sing to ourselves, a path of hieroglyphs and perfumes with which we draw nearer to ourselves.

The horse is set free, to fly and prance, chasing its visions.

[handwritten marginalia: only one logic]

Sometimes, when you go away, you leave behind a little girl who is vivacious and graceful. Then, a few years later, you meet her again, and it is a mystery how that little girl could have disappeared into a woman who has found her destiny, with fullness and shadows, with a *eros* which ensnares us and unleashes our fantasy.

When I left Grotowski's theatre, in 1964, Ryszard Cieslak was a good actor. He wanted to be an intellectual. It was as if his body, full of life, was encumbered by a huge brain, as if he was trapped in a two dimensional reality.

[handwritten marginalia: point of dilation. mind + body connection]

I saw him again two years later, when he presented *The Constant Prince* in Oslo. From the moment the performance began, it was as if all my memories, the categories on which I depended, had been swept away and I saw another being, I saw a man who had found his fullness, his destiny, his vulnerability. That brain which before had been like a jelly blurring his actions, now imbued his entire body with phosphorescent cells.

The power of a hurricane. 'Surely he can't do any more.' And yet, a stronger, even higher wave surged out of his body and hurtled around him.

He was an actor, but I never asked myself, at any time during the performance, how he had arrived at such a peak. Only afterwards, sheltered from the fury of the elements, did I reflect. An entire horizon which up until then had circumscribed my professional borders had now been moved for miles and miles, revealing a land that was as yet difficult to scrutinize, but which existed and which could bear fruit.

* * *

Meaning and theories – The theatre can be an anthropological expedition. This is a contradiction in terms, because the anthropologist chooses a place, settles there and does research in the field.

I left Norway and went to the Warsaw Theatre School to become a director. I left the school. But I stayed in Poland, in Opole, a town of 60,000 people, with Grotowski, in his small 'Theatre of the Thirteen Rows'. There, one of my longest and most unforeseeable journeys took place. The other happened in Holstebro, Denmark.

The theatre can be a kind of anthropological expedition which leaves the obvious territories behind, abandons recognized values, the places where offering one's hand is a sign of greeting, where raising one's voice is a symptom of irritation, where a comedy is a cheerful performance, and where a tragedy is a poignant one.

In Poland in the early sixties, the authorities imposed production norms, a pre-established number of performances and openings for each season. One's work was recognized, and deemed to be socially and artistically healthy, on the basis of quantity. This frenzy of production and quantity, this illusion of numbers and statistics was called 'cultural politics', 'democratic culture', 'popular theatre'.

Grotowski did not want to make eight, seven, three new productions a year. He wanted to prepare just one, but well. To give the maximum. To present it to a limited number of spectators in order to deepen the communication. With these few spectators, he wanted to establish spatial and emotional relationships which constituted an encounter, a dialogue with themselves, a meditation on the times. In order to fulfill this personal necessity of his, he had to fight against his times. In 1961, 1962, 1963, sometimes only three or four people came to his performances. During the three years I stayed with him, I witnessed his resistance, practised for only a handful of spectators. He did his work for each of them, for their individual uniqueness, not for the public. Grotowski's 'poor theatre' was not a theory, not a technique, not a *how* to make theatre. It was *why* he was doing theatre.

In 1960, when I was twenty-four years old, I arrived in that town of Opole, by accident, and there I met Grotowski, a young man a couple of years older than myself who looked at me with smiling eyes (were they ironic or understanding?) when I spoke to him of theatre for the people, of political theatre, of theatre's social function. His theatre consisted of a room eighty metres square, only six or seven actors, and about as many loyal and motivated spectators.

He had been one of the leaders of the rebellious, anti-Stalinist youth. In 1956, the workers of Poznan revolted and the university students took a stand for Gomulka, who then came to power and began the famous Polish October. For the first time, there was a feeling that change was possible in a socialist country. But in 1957 and 1958 began what the Poles called 'sausage politics': the cutting away, slice by slice, of what had been conceded. Grotowski was no longer on the political scene. He had disappeared into a tiny theatre in Opole.

I talked to him about Brecht and his theories. He listened, smiling in a way that invited me to keep on talking.

My first meeting with Brecht happened right about that time, five years after his death and five years after the Polish October.

I had arrived in Poland in 1960, my head full of Brechtian theories, and began to study directing at the Warsaw Theatre School. There I met Tadeusz Kulisiewicz, a graphic artist who had worked with Brecht. He had designed the poster for *The Life of Galileo* in which the delicately drawn figure of Galileo is shown stooping, as if shut up in his own world, ready to explode, like a steel spring. Kuliesiewicz gave me a letter of introduction to Helene Weigel, Brecht's wife, and with this letter in my pocket, I left for Berlin.

It was hard to arrive in Berlin (West Berlin), from Warsaw. Warsaw still bore the scars of the war. Polish reconstruction was proceeding slowly, but in certain circles, at night, there were outbursts of joie-de-vivre. After their performances, actors went to the Spatif Club, open until two in the morning. Vodka, food, and that special post-performance exhilaration made them exuberant. Often they wanted to keep going all night long and so made their way to the Bristol, the only place in Warsaw open until dawn. An old woman sat on a step at the entrance, selling paper flowers. The actors willingly gave her a little of their change and offered artificial flowers to their companions.

At night, the streetlights were outshone by hundreds and hundreds of little lamps lit by women amid the bombed-out ruins of the city. In the glow of these tiny flames one could read on the walls the names of the Poles shot by the Germans during the Occupation.

Warsaw was gloomy, with long queues outside the food shops. Bulldozers clearing away the ruins uncovered human bones. Trucks carried them away, load after load.

From this Warsaw I travelled to West Berlin. When I saw all its neon, its shops overflowing with flowers and fruit, with chocolate and coloured plastic, I had a sudden urge to vomit. And with this feeling of nausea, I crossed the Wall, which had just been built, and entered East Berlin.

At the end of the performance by the Berliner Ensemble, I realized that I was crying. I was at *The Mother*. If it is true that at the end of one's life the images that have touched one's soul pass before one's eyes, I believe that for me among those images will be Helene Weigel with her red flag, in the last scene of *The Mother*.

I returned to Warsaw confused: how could I have let myself be drawn into sentimentality? After all, Poland was a good school of cynicism. If I had been ingenuous enough to cry, what was it, either in the performance or in me, the spectator, that had not worked? What had happened to the 'effect' sought by Brecht and which was so scientifically described in his writings?

I was not merely confused, but shaken. My theatrical theories became blurred. And others as well.

Poland acted like a corrosive acid. My student hostel faced the Ghetto Heroes' Square. The ruins here had not been cleared away, just levelled out. There was a monument in the centre. Every day big buses arrived from East Germany. Germans – good, socialist Germans, these – got out, and the guide showed them around. They were nearly all the right age to have fought in the war.

One of my friends was a promising young Communist Party official. 'Trying to change something in this country', he said to me, 'is like sticking your prick in a block of ice. You end up castrated and you don't make anything melt.' He accepted the rules of the game. What hurt me the most was that he did so in spite of his intelligence.

Brecht and the theatre were no longer real problems. The real problem was bewilderment.

Groping, I arrived in Opole, where I met Grotowski.

In 1978, I returned to East Berlin for the celebration of the anniversary of Brecht's birth. He would have been eighty years old. The international cream of the Brechtian intelligentsia was there, professors who had built careers writing about Brecht and who for years had been imposing his theories as a new orthodoxy. Now they were saying that the Berliner Ensemble was the museum of another age.

A new production had just opened at the Berliner, the first version of *The Life of Galileo*, which shows how an intellectual can make his voice heard in spite of a regime which is trying to muzzle it.

Once again, I was overwhelmed with emotion. But even stronger was my astonishment: how had they dared to present this production *here*? The last scene was glacial and terrible. Galileo is blind and is being spied upon by his daughter. Believing that no-one is watching him, he reaches under his stool, and, with the rapid gestures of a conspirator, with the greedy hands of a thief, he pulls out some paper. He writes, writes furiously, then immediately hides what he has just written.

I felt rage towards all those intellectuals from the 'free' countries seated around me, whispering, as if they didn't understand what the performance was crying out to them: 'How boring! The Berliner is dying! We've seen this already. They are repeating themselves! It doesn't mean anything anymore!'

Today, the Wall has fallen. Freedom, Penury and Supermarket dance together. Many still ask themselves: 'What is the meaning, today, of making theatre?'

* * *

An empty and ineffective ritual – One of the most moving and ambiguous myths of Western civilization tells the story of a man who is searching for his origins. On the path towards his identity he kills his father, sires sons-brothers with his mother, brings the plague upon an entire population. He goes into exile, alone. But a young girl follows him. Years later, when she goes back to her city, Thebans are fighting Thebans. Brothers take delight in torturing brothers. Children carry arms and have learned to slaughter. Violence and horror, Thebes is the heart of darkness.

Confronted with the civil war in which her brothers have killed each other, Antigone takes a stand. She does not defend her uncle Creon and the law of the state which he represents. Neither does she take to the hills to join her brother's army in the war against the state. She knows the role she has chosen. And she acts in a way that is loyal to this role. She leaves the city by night and goes to the battlefield, takes a handful of dust and scatters it over her brother's corpse, to which Creon has refused burial. A symbolic ritual, empty and ineffective against horror. But she carries it out through personal necessity. And pays with her life.

This is the theatre: an empty and ineffective ritual which we fill with our 'why', with our personal necessity. Which in some countries on our planet is celebrated with general indifference. And in others can cost the lives of those who do it.

* * *

The sleeping spectators – Cheruthuruthy, India, September 1963; at nightfall, incessant drums announce a *kathakali* performance. The spectators arrive and sit on the ground. Two young performers, without costume or makeup, dance for Shiva Nataraja. The performance can begin. Two boys unfurl a brightly coloured silk curtain. Two hands grasp it from behind and shake it: the hidden performer is making his presence known. One of the hands is deformed by long silver nails. The drum rolls increase. Beneath the little curtain, one sees the performer's feet dancing frenetically on the spot. One

85

hears his voice, elaborate yells, hoarse and sharp tones. For a split second, the actor abruptly pulls down the curtain. The spectators see a face whose human aspect has been obliterated by makeup. This first lightning contact is repeated. Then the curtain is folded up and the performer appears in all of his majesty.

Children cry and run between the men and women crouched on mats, while vendors hawking tea, coffee, betel and spicy fritters pass by me. While the drums pound ceaselessly, one after another the singers take up the verses of the story and the *kathakali* performers seem to float in the air, with the same vigour as the oil lamp in the centre of the stage. The hundreds of silver paillettes hanging from their impressive headpieces flash in the light of the flame, lighting up the performer's green-painted faces. Huge white eyes, injected with red dye. Stiff beards, like collars. Faces glittering with sweat and the oil of the make-up. The Konorak statues are dancing. You want to touch them, caress them, lick them. It is impossible to discern, behind these monumental beings, those boys I saw this morning, their loins wrapped in white cloth, their torsos frail, like urchins who never get enough to eat, their stick-like legs that seemed unable to withstand the exertion.

The butterflies skimming around the flames are indifferent to the crying children, to the men and women chatting, to the sound of the peasants who now, the night well advanced, are stretching out to rest and sleep. And, after five or six hours, I feel empty, dazed by the indifference of the spectators, by the increasing obstinacy of the performers, by this night I have become accustomed to and during which every charm of the exotic has been pulverized.

And yet, at certain moments, *something occurs* which awakens my senses once again. The spectators fall silent and lean forwards, toward the performers. Something happens, an action, which all the preceding monotony has been leading up to: now, Bhima and Dushasana, Nala and Damayanti ... In the sudden silence, the spectators' satisfaction can be heard. Then it all begins again, the singing, the performers fighting battles, confronting demons, crossing mountains, people stretching out and sleeping on the ground, children whimpering, and women, gathering their saris around them, chatting away.

Humility and power of the performer who accepts that he is not the *omphalos* of the people around him.

* * *

The body-mind – There is a physical aspect to thought: its way of moving, of changing direction, of *leaping*, its 'behaviour'. The dilation does not belong to the physical but to the body-mind. The thought must tangibly cross through matter, not only manifest itself through the body in action, but pass through the *obvious*, the inertia, that which first presents itself when we imagine, reflect, act.

One of the clearest descriptions of this mental behaviour is contained in the book by Arthur Koestler[1] which is dedicated to 'the history of the changes in man's vision of the universe'. Koestler shows how every creative act – in science, in art or in religion – is accomplished through a preliminary regression to a more primitive level, a *reculer pour mieux sauter*, a process of negation or disintegration which prepares the leap towards the result. Koestler calls this moment a creative 'pre-condition'.

It is a moment which seems to negate all that which characterizes the search for results. It does not determine a new orientation, but is rather a voluntary disorientation which demands that all the energy of the researcher be put in motion, sharpening his senses, like when one advances in the dark. This dilation of one's potentialities has a high price: one loses control of the meaning of one's own action. It is a negation which has not yet discovered the new entity which it affirms.

The performer, the director, the researcher, the artist, all often ask themselves: 'what is the meaning of what I am doing?' But at the moment of the negation of the action, or of the creative 'pre-condition', this is not a fruitful question. At this point it is not yet the meaning of what one is doing that is essential, but rather the precision of the action which prepares the void in which an unexpected meaning can be captured.

Theatre artists, obliged to create in a way which nearly always involves the collaboration of many individuals, are often impeded by a fetishism for meanings, by the need to agree at the outset on the results to be achieved.

A performer, for example, executes a certain action which is the result of an improvisation or of a personal interpretation of a character. It is natural that s/he gives this action a very precise value, that s/he associates it with specific images, intentions, objectives. If, however, the context into which the action is introduced makes the original meaning which it had for the performer inappropriate, then s/he thinks that it should be dropped and forgotten. S/he believes, in short, that the marriage between the action and the meaning associated to it is indissoluble.

In general, if one says to a performer that her/his action can remain intact while its context (and therefore its meaning) is completely changed, then s/he thinks that s/he is being treated as inert matter, manipulated by the director. As if it was the sense that made the action *real* and not the quality of the action's energy.

Many directors have the same preconception. They tend to believe that a specific image or sequence of images can only transmit a particular meaning.

In the course of work on a production, a performer's actions sometimes begin to come alive, even if one doesn't understand why s/he is acting in that way. It can happen that the director, who is the performer's first spectator, does not know how, on the basis of their common interpretation of the performance, to explain rationally the meaning of what the performer is doing. The director can fall into the trap, show the difficulty s/he has in accepting this spark of unknown life, ask for explanations and demand

87

coherence from the performer. The collaboration is thereby jeopardized as the director seeks to eliminate the distance which separates her/him from the performer. The director demands too much, and in reality, too little. S/he demands a consensus, an agreement about intentions, a meeting on the surface.

Creative thought is actually distinguished by the fact that it proceeds by leaps, by means of a sudden disorientation which obliges it to reorganize itself in new ways, abandoning its well-ordered shell. It is *thought-in-life*, not rectilinear, not univocal.

The growth of unexpected meanings is made possible by a disposition of all of our energies, both physical and mental: perching on the edge of a cliff just before taking off in flight – a *sats*. A disposition which one can distil through training.

The physical training exercises make it possible for the performer to develop a new behaviour, a different way of moving, of acting and reacting, a specific skill. But this skill stagnates into a one-dimensional reality if it does not reach down into the depths of the individual.

The physical exercises are always spiritual exercises.

In the course of my experience as a director, I have observed an analogous process occurring in me and in some of my companions: the long daily work of training, transformed over the years, slowly distilled internal patterns of energy which could be applied to the way of conceiving and composing a dramatic action, of speaking in public, of writing.

*   *   *

Thought and thoughts – John Blacking, during the seminar 'Theatre, Anthropology, and Theatre Anthropology', organized by the Centre for Performance Research in Leicester, in the autumn of 1988, speaks about a thought which does not become a concept. A world-famous anthropologist and ethnomusicologist, Blacking explains how the circular system mind–hand–stone–mind of a 'primitive' man who is splintering a piece of flint to make an arrowhead 'thinks' with detailed precision. He describes as 'thought' the actions of the hands which are rotating a stick to start a fire, or playing a drum. He speaks of the body which 'thinks' when dancing. At first, Blacking's formulas seem to be only suggestive ways of speaking. But then the idea that they are something more takes hold. A way of speaking 'literally'.

Blacking concludes by proposing a *thinking in motion–thinking in concepts* polarity.

I ask myself whether *thinking in motion* might not be the best way to define the teaching of 'physical actions' which Stanislavski tried to pass on to the actor, the teaching of which Grotowski is now the true master.

But conceptual and analytical thought can also contain polarities, tensions, positions and oppositions which oblige it to be *in motion*, outside its orbit.

During the years of my work with Grotowski, I spoke about the *wishful thinking–concrete thinking* polarity. *Wishful thinking* indicates a particular phase in the process of planning a production: giving free rein to the vision which obsesses us, dreaming with open eyes, believing in and letting oneself be magnetized by the suggestivity of the theme of the performance, letting the *mythos* triumph. *Concrete thinking* implies: profaning the fascination of the theme with cold analysis, vivisecting it with scepticism and a caustic attitude, transfixing it with our experience of reality, not what *is known*, but what *I know*.

At the second session of ISTA, in Volterra in 1981, we worked on Edward Bond's *Narrow Road to the Deep North*. For pedagogical reasons, I divided the process into two phases. I did the first part on the text itself: cuts, reconstruction and interpretation. The second part was a *mise en scène*. I had difficulty making it understood why the work on the stage consisted of a continuous polemic with the work which I myself had done seated at a table. *Thinking in concepts–thinking in motion*; *wishful thinking–concrete thinking*.

The word 'concrete' comes from *con-*, together, and *crescere*, to grow, that is, to let oneself change. But this is never agreeable, either for our way of thinking or for our intellectual identity.

*　*　*

The Flying Dutchman – Leaps of thought can be defined as peripeteias. A peripeteia is an interweaving of events which causes an action to develop in an unforeseeable way, or causes it to conclude in a way opposite to how it began.

[handwritten margin note: constant movement of frenetic]

[handwritten margin note: reversal in order to do something you ensure the exact opposite]

A peripeteia acts through negation: this has been known since at least the time of Aristotle.

The behaviour of thought is visible in the peripeteias of stories, in their unexpected changes as they pass from person to person, from one mind to another. Just as happens in the theatrical creative process, so in this case the unexpected changes do not take place in the mind of a solitary artist, but are the work of various interacting individuals sharing the same point of departure.

The Flying Dutchman was Captain Van der Decken. In his attempt to round the Cape of Good Hope, Captain Van der Decken cursed God and Hell: he would not yield to the forces of storms and destiny, but would continue in his attempt until his last day. Thus it was that he heard a voice from the heavens repeating his own words, but now they had become a condemnation: 'until the last day . . . the last day'.

And so the seed of a story is sown: a Captain who remains at sea and never dies. A ship which sails on and on. Now, this seed abandons its original context and 'leaps' into other contexts.

Popular imagination superimposes the image of the Captain and his eternal peregrination on that of Ahasuerus, the Wandering Jew, who never found peace. Thus the story of Van der Decken changes; it is told that he was damned because he led such an immoral, atheistic life, that he had given the order to weigh anchor on Good Friday, the day on which the Saviour was killed.

Or, the image of the Captain fades away and in its place in the imagination his ship becomes the protagonist. The Ghost Ship suddenly appears to the sailors, black, and with sails the colour of blood, or yellow, or iridescent, bewitching, changing colour many times an hour.

Time passes and the theme of the Captain and his curse becomes associated with that of a woman who rescues him. This mutation takes place during the same years as the story of two other proverbial adepts of Hell – Don Giovanni and Faust – also changes, and they are saved by the love of a woman.

It was probably Heine who first wove this new motif into the saga of the Flying Dutchman and his Ghost Ship. From time to time Van der Decken docks at a port where he looks for love. He will be rescued from his fate when he finds a woman who will be faithful to him unto death.

In the summer of 1839, Richard Wagner was en route from Riga to London. His wife Minna was with him. Wagner knew the story of the Flying Dutchman, but he understood it only when the boat on which he was travelling was caught in a storm off the Norwegian reefs. The sailors then told the story of the Ghost Ship which always appeared before a shipwreck. They finally managed to anchor between the high cliffs of a fjord at Sandvik, a few miles from Arendal.

When the voyage was over and Wagner reached London and then made his way to Paris, he talked about the storm along the Norwegian coast. He said that the wind was sinister and demonic as it howled in the stays. He told of having seen a sail emerge from the darkness and of believing that he could make out the Dutchman's ship.

It probably occurred – according to lovers of anecdote – that while in Sandvik, Wagner, a guest in the house of a Norwegian captain, became interested in the young girl who was serving at table. He heard the host call her 'jenta' ('girl, servant', in Norwegian) and believed that this was her name.

Later, he changed her name to Senta, a name which is not found in Norway, or only in the Norway imagined by Wagner for *Der Fliegende Holländer*.

Wagner takes the theme of the love which redeemed the Dutchman but turns it around. He accepts Heine's version and at the same time negates its meaning. Senta does in fact love the Dutchman and swears to be faithful to him unto death. But the Dutchman has overheard a conversation between Senta and Erik; Senta had also once sworn to be faithful to Erik unto death. Now, caught by her destiny, irrevocably bound to the Dutchman, she must renege on her promise to Erik. The Dutchman decides to return to sea; salvation seems impossible, impossible that anyone will be faithful to him unto death. He will save Senta, not the other way around; he fears that Senta will betray him just as she has betrayed Erik. And women who betray him are condemned for eternity. The theme of a curse which a woman can redeem turns into one of a new destiny of condemnation which now falls upon women in love.

The Dutchman, then, flees in order to save the woman who should have saved him. He flees, imagining a false love, which is in fact faithful unto death. When the ship sails, Senta throws herself into the sea and, by dying, remains faithful to her promise. The ship then stops sailing, slowly sinks, and as the sun rises, Senta and the Dutchman ascend to Heaven.

And so now a new metamorphosis. The story, as it had been transformed by Heine and developed by Wagner through a series of oppositions, is taken up by Strindberg. He releases all the potential energy contained in the final variations introduced by Wagner. And as this potential energy is revealed, it inverts the meaning of the story. Now the central theme is one of infidelity, of the pain which a woman inflicts on the man who loves her. It is a theme to which Strindberg returns continuously in his work and which he confronts here using the plot he inherits from Wagner. He also uses it by negating it, by turning it inside out: every seven years, the Dutchman must meet and love a woman. This is the condition for his salvation, not because the woman is to redeem him, but because the redemption must arise from the suffering which women will cause him through their infidelity.

The theme of love, which had been introduced as an opposite pole to the theme of condemnation, the Dutchman's never-ending voyage, now leaps again, to a new opposite, and superimposes itself on the theme of the sea voyage, becoming its spiritual equivalent. The Dutchman's true punishment is the continuous failure of love. Love no longer releases him from punishment, as in Heine and Wagner, but is itself the punishment that redeems, that transforms even the Ghost Ship from a prison to a cross.

Let us recall the story as it was at the beginning. Strindberg seems closer to it than his predecessors. And yet he is very far from it. The core of the story, while maintaining its original value, has acquired a new depth. The torment of the physical wandering is heightened by its spiritual double and the sailor who had become similar to the Wandering Jew, to Faust, to Don Giovanni, returns to being a lonely sailor, abandoned by a woman in every port.

The Flying Dutchman is exemplary. The leaps of thought, the metamorphoses which upset our ways of believing and reasoning, ought to be characteristic of the behaviour of the 'collective mind' of the ensemble working on a performance.

* * *

Square circles and twin logics – A physicist is walking along a beach and sees a five-year old child throwing flat stones onto the sea, trying to make them skip. Each stone makes no more than one or two little hops. The physicist remembers that he, in his childhood, was very good at this game. So he shows the child how it is done. He throws the stones, one after the other, showing how to hold them, at what angle to cast them, at what height over the surface of the water. All the stones thrown by the adult skip many times: seven, eight, even ten times.

'Yes', the child then says, 'they skip many times. But that isn't what I was trying to do. Your stones are making round circles in the water, but I want mine to make square circles.'

We know about this episode because the physicist, Piet Hein, told it to Einstein, at that time an old man, when once visiting him. And because Einstein himself reacted in an unexpected way: 'Give the child my compliments and tell him not to be concerned if the stones don't make square circles in the water. The important thing is to think the thought.'

A dialectic relationship does not exist in and of itself. It is born of the will to control forces which, left to themselves, would only conflict with or degrade each other.

When an adult tries to copy the way in which children draw, s/he generally limits her/himself to drawing badly, tries to renounce the logic of her/his own way of seeing, impoverishes it, abandons her/his hand to chance, avoids precision, imitates childish ways of drawing. And thus becomes infantile.

To the adult, indeed, children's drawings appear to be free, fanciful, but inadequate, often clumsy, scrawls. But they actually adhere to an ironclad logic. A child does not draw what he sees and how he sees it, but what he has experienced. If he experiences an adult as a pair of long legs from which a face suddenly bends over him, he will draw this adult as a circle on top of two sticks. Or else he will paint his own 'portrait', giving himself enormous feet because he is happy with his new shoes. If his mother is more important to him than his father, when he draws his parents he will make his mother bigger than his father. He will draw a rectangle with a pole sticking out from each corner because a table is a flat surface with four legs.

For those who study children's drawings, the scribblings which very small children make are also the result of direct experience. They are not representations, but rather traces of actions of the hand in relationship to a mental image: 'Here is a running dog.'

What makes children's drawings 'infantile' is not their approximate or 'primitive' nature, but the presence of *only one logic*. However, many 'good' drawings made by older children or adults also adhere to only one logic. The fact that they are more recognizable, that they demonstrate the possession of shared rules, does not make them less banal. The same thing happens with performances. There are performances of which one understands *nothing*, others of which one understands *everything*. Both are inert.

In the works of a good painter, *numerous logics* act contemporaneously. The artist is part of a tradition, whose rules s/he uses or consciously breaks, causing surprise. In addition to transmitting a way of seeing, s/he also represents a way of experiencing the world and translates onto the canvas not only the image but also the 'gestus', the quality of motion which has guided the brush. Thus one can say that the painter has 'kept the child in himself', not because he has kept his innocence and ingenuity (oddly enough, we like to think that children are innocent), not because he has not been domesticated by a culture, but because, with the concision of his craft, he has woven together *parallel*, or rather, *twin* logics, without substituting one for the other.

Being-in-life is the negation of the succession of different stages of development; it is simultaneous growth by means of ever more complex interweavings.

One of the most treacherous pitfalls which, unsought for, lies in wait in descriptions of exercises and advice for performers, derives from the fact that in a book, things must be placed one after another. They cannot be interwoven. They are textbooks which refer to one context, the only one which can give them a meaning.

Absurdly, some courses of study at the most mediocre theatre schools are not organized as a context but as if they were textbooks. They set up a time (and sometimes a teacher) for each of the individual 'chapters', separating the various threads from which the experience is to be woven.

Professional experience is formed by means of a quality of time which can be organized, coldly put together, but which cannot be the linear time of writing or of programmes that work well on paper. It is a time made up of intermittances and crossroads, of impulses and counterimpulses. It is organic time, not time fractured by the geometry of schedules and calendars.

The action of thought functions in apprenticeship as it functions in the creative situation and in scenic *bios*: by means of the dialectic between order and disorder. Order without order.

Meyerhold spoke of *pedagogical fiction*. Coming from him, a dedicated theatre innovator, 'fiction' could not mean 'duplicity', but the co-existence of several logics, brought simultaneously into view.

＊　＊　＊

The guru knows nothing – 'The master often cheats. The student makes a mistake and the master nods: "Good". Sometimes the student does an entire dance correctly and the master shakes his head: "It's wrong". The master is fishing. He says only: "This is correct, this isn't". He makes no other comment, gives no explanations. The student tries to understand, to think for himself, to concentrate, to observe more attentively. This is how the master fishes for his student.'

I Made Pasek Tempo accompanies his words with a smile. The bluish light from the neon tube makes his face ashen. The first time I came to Tampaksiring, in the early seventies, there was no electric light. Now, twenty years later, in the corner of the courtyard, the whole family is gathered around a television, watching a *dramagong*. In Bali, electricity and obligatory schooling are corroding the age-old master–student relationship. By day, the children go to school; in the evenings, the images on the flickering screen are more attractive than rehearsals of a *gamelan* or a performance.

I Made Pasek Tempo continues speaking. He tells about the Bhagewan (master) Dhomya and his student Utamaniyu, who looked after the master's cows but was given nothing to eat. It is a long, complicated, obscure story. Everything Utamaniyu does to get food is rebuked by the master. Desperate, he eats some *maduri* leaves, the sap of which is poisonous. He goes blind and falls into a well. The Bhagewan pulls him out, asks him how he happened to fall into an empty well. Utamaniyu replies: 'I asked others for food and you said I was greedy; I licked the cowsmilk that had fallen on the grass and you reprimanded me; I ate *maduri* leaves and I lost my sight.'

Bhagewan Dhomya approves: 'For the first time, you are sincere. Now you may consider yourself my student.'

I don't understand. Stories from distant universes, from epochs long gone.

A few months earlier, in the sophisticated atmosphere of a conference on interculturalism organized by Richard Schechner and funded by the Rockefeller Foundation, Sanjukta Panigrahi had described her decade of work at ISTA and her collaboration, at first apprehensive and prudent, with masters from other cultures and theatrical genres. She had concluded by referring to something of which she had become convinced: 'The buildings are different, but they rest on the same ground.' Then she had described the beginnings of her career. When she was three years old, she became the first daughter of a Brahmin family to study dance. Supported by her mother, who fought doggedly against prejudice. In order to improve her dancing, she had to leave home at the age of eight and go to Madras, more than a thousand kilometres to the south, to another culture with another language. She had described how her mother reacted when people reproached her: 'How could you send your daughter down there?'

'When I began', Sanjukta remembered, 'the teacher did not correct me, did not say anything. He made me sit and work with eye exercises. Day after day. I went home and complained to my mother. "The guru knows nothing".'

I Made Pasek Tempo shows me a copy of the *Adiparwa*, the classic containing the story of Dhomya and Utamaniyu. I ask him if, at his age (sixty-five? seventy?), he still likes to read. He answers:

There are two things which are difficult:

- to become a *pragina pradnian*, a complete performer who knows how to dance, play instruments, who knows the classical texts, how to teach and also how to learn;
- *menjiwai*, to make one's soul and thoughts live, to give life to what one wants to achieve, to make one's own spirit at one with the spirit of the *topeng*, of the mask, so that whatever it is that one wants to

transmit through the characters, the spectators can feel it, appreciate it, and say: 'This is truly the *dalem*, the king, the *panisar*, the clown.'

Then I breathe out, empty my lungs and concentrate in order to let the *kundalini* reach the eye of the *bathin*, the inner force. *Kundalini* is the energy which makes the body and the mind live. I am still learning.

* * *

Shakespeare: Prologue to 'The Life of Henry the Fifth' – The actor enters and asks:

> . . . Can this cock-pit hold
> The vasty fields of France? Or may we cram
> Within this wooden O the very casques
> That did affright the air at Agincourt?

This is one of the most famous perplexities regarding the meaning of the theatre: can the massacres of history be represented in a cock-fighting ring?

How to bring the multiplicity and vehemence of the life of an individual, of a society, into the artificial situation of the theatre?

Even Brecht doubted that the theatre could expose the thick web of forces which move history.

Is it possible to bring into the theatre all the horror, the grandeur, the mystery and the simultaneity of human existence without reducing it to a two-dimensional image? Is it possible to dilate this image, as if under the lens of a microscope, bringing to the foreground the dynamic of every fragment of reality, that which is not perceived in everyday life?

There is no gap between the performer's work to master and model her/his energies and the moment in which the creative process emerges as an objective and social result – the performance.

In the same way that the performer's extra-daily behaviour can reveal the tensions hidden within the design of movements, the performance can be the representation not of the realism of the story, but rather of its *reality*, its muscles and nerves, its skeleton. It can lay bare that which is seen only when the flesh of the story is stripped away: the power relationships, the socially centripetal and centrifugal forces, the tension between freedom and organization, between intention and action, between equality and power.

What the theatre says in words is not really very important. What counts is to disclose the relationships, to show at one and the same time the surface of the actions and their internal parts, the forces which are at work and in opposition, the way in which the actions are divided into their polarities, the way in which they are executed, the ways in which they are endured.

Making it possible for the spectator to decipher a story does not mean making her/him discover its 'true meaning' but creating the conditions within which s/he can *ask her/himself* about its meaning. It is a question of exposing the knots of the story, those points at which extremes embrace. There are spectators for whom the theatre is essential precisely because it does not present them with solutions, but knots.

In past centuries, there existed 'Anatomical Theatres'. Even then, on the tiers of the operating theatres, there mingled together starving and thirsty spectators, and curious and conceited spectators, frowning philosophers and young believers, all drawn by the fascinating and frightening mystery of the open man.

Down below, the surgeon and the open man hid their mystery behind the exposure of the organs and the meticulous work. 'How did he get there?', they wondered of the one. 'Why is he doing it?', they wondered of the other.

Similar to one and the other at the same time, to the opened body and to the knowing and heretical surgeon who opens it, is the presence of the performer and what is, above all, her/his own mystery. Vision of what is hidden under the skin.

Similar to the Anatomical Theatre is the theatre of which I am thinking as I sing to myself the song which is my memory: half-way between performance and science, between didactics and transgression, between horror and wonder.

* * *

You are still very beautiful – Luis says: 'Decroux always sang while we worked. The rhythm of the song guided the speed of the movement while the intensity of his voice regulated the dynamics. Sometimes he sang by himself while directing us, sometimes we sang with him while we did the exercises. He always used his voice. Old, popular French or English songs, which he interpreted ironically, playing with the pronunciation. The exhalation, as opposed to what usually happens, was the active phase upon which he supported and developed the action. The inhalation was quick, he called it the *spasme*. It was the beginning of the action which collided with the resistance obtained by prolonging the exhalation as much as possible. I imagine that the *spasme* corresponds to what you from Odin Teatret call *sats*.'

'He was obsessed with invisible movement, that movement which – he said – could only be discovered if examined through a microscope. He used the example of a violinist: the bow moves imperceptibly, yet there is sound; one doesn't see the movement, yet one hears the music. The echo resounds, even if you don't want it to. He called this the "gong effect", the movement is finished but continues.'

I draw Luis' attention to the fact that the same image is used in *nō*: *io-in*, the vibrations of a bell after it has been struck with the clapper; that Meyerhold spoke of 'braking the rhythm' and used music to gag his actors' spontaneity. Luis gets up, demonstrates the *spasme*, the 'gong effect', in certain *figures*, the exhalation which is like a hiss accompanying the physical action. The consequence of this exhalation, this sonorous echo, is contraction of the muscles of the abdomen. Our fellow passengers stare at us in surprise. Our enthusiasm at discovering points in common among Decroux,

96

Meyerhold, Japanese performers and Odin Teatret actors seems out of place in the departure lounge of Sao Paolo's Congonhas airport.

As he does every time we meet, Luis tells me about his 'master', Etienne Decroux. He worked with Decroux in Paris, for three years, from 1976 to 1978. Luis is an actor, a director and a professor at the University of Campinas in Brazil, where he directs a laboratory of performance research. We are travelling together to the Londrina Festival, which this year has been devoted entirely to Odin Teatret.

Luis continues:

In August of 1990, after the Bologna ISTA, I went to visit Decroux in Paris. Jeannette, who runs the bar on the corner, had the house-keys and let me in. She told me about the state of Decroux' health. And that he was always singing, even at night.

He was seated in an armchair, staring into space. He did not respond to my greeting. I knelt down, took one of his hands and kissed it. He looked at me and began to sing. It was as if an arrow had pierced my breast. His fingers rhythmically squeezed my hand. With his elbow resting on the arm of the chair, his forearm was swaying in time to the music.

I too began to sing. I knew those songs so well. I had repeated them every day, hour after hour, during my years with him. Sometimes he tilted his head to one side, gazing upwards and prolonging the final note of a verse, his mouth wide open . . . the violin effect. The movement had stopped but the sound continued. The tension vibrated inside him. He seemed excited.

We sang together for more than an hour. I got up to take my leave. I tried to recognize, in that deformed skull, in those eyes which were two gaping cavities, in that toothless mouth, the old man I had loved. I would not have recognized him if I had seen him somewhere else. I bent down, kissed him on the forehead, and whispered to him: 'You are still very beautiful'. A broad, pure smile and then, suddenly, a profound sadness covered his face. I left him, asking myself if I had done the right thing, saying those words. Six months later I learned of his death.

He said that the performer is like Christ, the right hand must not know what the left hand is doing. He defined improvisation as a 'muscular erection': one should not think, the muscles are singing, and this melody, like an erection, comes and goes without one knowing why. All those who have studied with him have a refined, extraordinary technique. He had a lion inside him and his technique kept it at bay.

*　*　*

The princess who kept the winds at bay – In Denmark, and in southern Sweden, there are some singular archaeological remains: stones strewn over the ground according to a design which, at first glance, looks like the skeleton of a gigantic or prehistoric animal. Some archeologists maintain that these stones represent the paths of a labyrinth. They trace its origins to the legend of Trella, a Norwegian princess whose boat was sailing towards Denmark and was constantly thrown off course by freezing winds. Trella landed on a deserted coast, built an elaborate palace without walls and managed to trap the winds in its wandering corridors, keeping them at bay. And then she continued on her way. In antiquity, the story of Trella inspired other people to create new trellaborgs – *borg* means fortress – to exorcize the forces of nature.

My theatre is a trellaborg. Stones which I knowingly scattered in order to build a labyrinth–castle, without bastions yet present, vulnerable yet effective, where I confront the winds of the spirit of the times.

My dream is *to transmit how* to build a trellaborg.

Another version of the legend has it that while Trella was trying to resist, the winds of the time captured her in the palace which she had built and made her dance at their will and to their fury.

*   *   *

Shiva's female half, moon and darkness – The performer's dilated body is a hot body, but not in the sentimental or emotional sense. Feeling and emotion are reactions, consequences. It is a red hot body, in the scientific sense of the word. The particles which make up daily behaviour have been excited and produce more energy. They have undergone an increment of motion, they move apart, they attract each other, they oppose each other with more force, more speed, within a larger space.

This is fascinating and sometimes deceptive; one is tempted to believe that it has to do only with 'bodies', with physical and not mental actions.

But a way of moving in space manifests a way of thinking. It is a way of thinking laid bare. Or a way of moving which guides the thought.

Bonn, October 1980, the end of the first session of ISTA. Sanjukta Panigrahi dances *Ardhanarishwara*, Shiva's female half. Immediately afterwards, Iben Nagel Rasmussen presents her professional autobiography: *Moon and Darkness*. For a month, all of us assembled here have obstinately examined the cold, technical pre-expressive bases of the performer's work.

Sanjukta dances:

> I bow before you
> You who are both male and female
> Two gods in one
> You whose female half
> has the vivid colour of a champak flower
> And whose male half
> has the palid colour of the camphor flower

98

The female half jingles with golden arm bracelets
The male half is adorned with bracelets of serpents
The female half has love-eyes
The male half has meditation eyes

The female half has a garland of almond flowers
The male half has a garland of skulls
Dressed in dazzling clothes
Is the female half
Nude, the male half

The female half is capable of all creation
The male half is capable of all destruction

I turn to you
Linked to the God Shiva
Your husband
I turn to you
Linked to the Goddess Shiva
Your wife

Iben Nagel Rasmussen sings a lament, the song of the shaman of a destroyed people. She then reappears as Kattrin, the mute daughter of Mother Courage, a stammering adolescent on the threshold of a world at war. The Indian actress and the Danish actress seem far apart, each deep within her own culture. And yet, they meet. They seem to surpass not only their personas and sex, but even their artistic skill, and reveal something more.

I know how many years of work have led to these moments. And yet it seems as if something is blossoming spontaneously, something neither sought for nor desired. I have nothing to say. I can only watch, as Virginia Woolf watched Orlando. 'A million candles burned in Orlando, without him having thought of lighting even a single one.'

* * *

A fistful of water – My gaze wanders over the candles which are spread everywhere. I have been told that this is not a performance, yet I see 'people who are acting'. If what is happening here is only for them, then why am I here? Why was I invited and why did I come? May 1990; it is thirty years since I first met Grotowski, who is now seated beside me in a converted barn in the Tuscan countryside where Roberto Bacci has provided him with a sanctuary in which to work.

I am here to become a witness, to confirm that 'this' has happened. How does one be a witness? By writing, explaining, justifying, as I had done in 1961 after seeing Grotowski's *Dziady* with a handful of other spectators in that grey Polish town of Opole? What is the duty of the witness: to recount in detail, by allusion, with metaphors, orally, writing for everyone or only for the few who show interest? To be silent? To mask silence with words?

This is how legends are born: there were never any candles in Grotowski's productions; only in the first part of his last one, *Apocalypsis cum figuris*. And yet a performance in which there are candles is defined with a cliché: Grotowskian. Grotowski today is Grotowskian.

What is 'this' that I am watching: a ritual with no content, a celebration of technique, a liturgy without theology or simply a refined montage of physical and vocal actions which the impeccable mastery of a 'director', a 'metteur-en-espace', lifts to the level of ceremony?

What would happen if 'this' had to go in search of witnesses, if it had to move and not remain in its barn?

What would 'this' become in a gymnasium, in a suburban school, in the foyer of a museum, in the warehouse of an abandoned factory?

I watch 'those who are acting'. Some of them are from theatre groups I know. What has made them leave the spotlights to move around here, among the shadows cast by the candles? What will they take with them when they return to the alacrity of theatre work?

I don't know why, but something tightens inside me. Then I am ashamed, I become angry. I think of myself in Opole, when everyone said I was crazy to leave theatre school and spend months and months with Grotowski, a charlatan who was putting on meaningless performances. Everything I have done has been a search for freedom *in* the theatre. Now I am witnessing freedom *from* the theatre.

I am struck by the quality of the work. But I remain outside it, as if a sheet of glass is preventing me from sensing the energy of the bodies in front of me. It is the same feeling I had when I saw *Dziady*. I drown in the mystery, in the non-sense, in my inability to orient myself, to recognize, to connect. 'This' provokes only questions.

The rhythm of 'those who are acting' does not surge, does not quiver, neither accelerates nor slows down. It is a river current which flows implacably, yet seems, to my attentive eyes, to be still. This stillness stirs up thoughts and memories, the torpid life of memory and of the senses. I feel as though I am very far away, within myself, absent from what is happening. An alteration of the normal state of consciousness. Is this the secular *sacrum* to which Grotowski, in *Towards a Poor Theatre*, yearned to give life? It is neither the theatre nor 'this' which is *sacrum*. It is the act, the work which can become it.

The current continues to flow. I immerse my hand in it, to grasp something. My hand comes up empty, again and again. A fistful of water. Why do I imagine, then, that I have seized the meaning?

7

A THEATRE NOT MADE OF
STONES AND BRICKS

What is theatre? A building?

The Alexandrinski, the Dramaten, La Comédie Française? Is it an institution, a name, a statue?

Theatre is the men and women who do it.

And yet, when we visit the theatres of Drottningholm or Versailles, the Teatro Farnese in Parma or the Olimpico in Vicenza, or Epidaurus (built when those who invented Athenian tragedy had already disappeared), or one of those buildings with which the Princes, the Courts and the Academies embellished their small cities, we often experience the same kinaesthetic reactions which a living performance can give us. Those stones and bricks become living space even if nothing is being represented there. They too are a way of thinking and dreaming of the theatre, of materializing it and transmitting it through the centuries.[1]

They are perquisites of wealth. They are usually called 'temples of art'.

Basavanna sang:

> The rich
> will make temples for Shiva.
> What shall I,
> a poor man,
> do?

And he answered:

> My legs are pillars,
> the body the shrine,
> the head a cupola
> of gold.

He concluded:

> Listen, O Lord of the meeting rivers,
> things standing shall fall,
> but the moving ever shall stay.

101

Basavanna was the founder of a rebel religion in India in the twelfth century. Other poor men, rebellious and religious, expressed similar thoughts in other ages and other countries. If we apply these thoughts to the temples of art, the image of Gordon Craig rising to his feet and lecturing to the participants of a congress springs to mind.[2]

Theatre and Drama

We are in Rome, in the autumn of 1934. The Royal Academy of Italy has organized a prestigious world conference on the theatre. Copeau sends a text which is to become famous and in which he speaks of the future of the theatre as a popular art. He foresees that it will be either Marxist or Christian, or else will disappear. Meyerhold is absent, officially because of illness. Almost all the other names of dramatic literature, direction, stage design, architecture and historiography are present: Reinhardt, Yeats, Maeterlinck, Marinetti, Beijer . . . The Congress is presided over by Pirandello.

Gordon Craig was not one of the official delegates. Publicly, he did no more than defend regional Italian actors who performed in their own dialects and who were an embarrassment to fascist solemnity.[3] In discussion with Walter Gropius, he defended the autonomy of the director against the tendencies of a creative but constrictive theatre architecture. Finally, he gave a short lesson to Silvio D'Amico, the leading intellectual of the Italian theatre and the real inspiration behind the Congress.

The idea was circulating at the Congress that in order to overcome the crisis which was crippling world dramaturgy, one could turn to architects for help. Would a new stage architecture be able to produce a new way of writing *for* the stage? The idea was not banal (Copeau had made the same proposal). D'Amico insisted emphatically that it was a misleading idea.

Craig responded:

> Mr. D'Amico has quoted a statement by Mr. Bernard Shaw which probably dates back to about fifty years ago, and which is perhaps one of the most diffuse lies since the world of business began. It has to do with the claim that drama gives birth to theatres but a theatre does not give birth to drama.[4] Mr. D'Amico has reported Shaw's statement and pointed his finger at a little architectural model for a big theatre made of bricks, wood and stone. It is probable that theatre *buildings* have been constructed (with a little help from architects) by the work of dramatists. But the theatre preceding the drama and which is the only theatre that counts was not and is not a building, it is the *sound* of the voice – the expression of the face – the movements of the body – of the person – that is, the actor, *if you please*![5]

The actor of whom Craig is speaking is not a man or woman in his/her naturalness and spontaneity. It is s/he who embodies an architecture in motion: a Form.

Obsession with lost Form had been haunting the frontiers of the theatre since the last decades of the nineteenth century. Eleonora Duse declared that 'the movements, the colours, the "line"' of the actor's craft belonged to an art which had by now become corrupt and suggested that the only solution was a severe 'education in form'. She therefore proposed, along with Gabriele D'Annunzio, a radically new (unrealized) theatre where performances would be collective rituals.[6]

It was a malaise and a vital contradiction; the fixity of the Form seemed irreconcilable with the changeable, living, continuously metamorphosing nature of the performance and of its artists. But, on the other hand, asserting the need for Form was a way of opposing the ephemeral conditions of performance.

This rebellion manifested itself in various ways and nourished disparate dreams. The rise of direction, of the *mise en scène*, was accompanied by the desire to fix on paper, with words and drawings, even the way of directing a text. Chekhov wanted to publish his plays as if they were inseparable from Stanislavski's director's notes. Craig imagined producing Bach's *Saint Matthew Passion* by composing the sequence of the images and movements in such a way that they could be repeated every year during Holy Week. Even Brecht, after the Second World War, attempted in his *Teaterarbeit* to marry dramatic text with production directives, maintaining that it was unjustified that only the words and dialogues of a play were passed on and not also the gestures, the scenic environment, the costumes, the designs of movements for the individual characters and for the actors in relationship to each other.

Meanwhile, on the watershed between theatre and dance, Rudolf Laban had devised a notation system for fixing the design of rhythmic movements on paper. And Emile Jaques-Dalcroze, in his Hellerau school, in collaboration with Adolphe Appia, showed the elite of European theatre how it was possible to create, by means of the physical actions of actor-dancers, a 'poetry in motion' and a 'music for the eyes'.[7]

Great 'modern' performers like Georges Pitoëff and Michael Chekhov challenged both the spectator's taste and the critics' lack of comprehension and composed their interpretations according to a clear, artificial and pre-meditated design, as incisive as if it had been carved. Their fascinating way of performing was sometimes called puppet-like. Critics were appalled because the borders between theatre, dance and pantomime seemed to have been abolished. The same obsession with Form led Nikolai Evreinov, Max Reinhardt, Alexander Tairov and Jacques Copeau to study illustrations of Commedia dell'Arte performers, to work with pantomime, to repudiate the distinction between actor, mime and dancer as a matter of principle.

Georg Fuchs gave the example, as a model of scenic behaviour, of the 'Christ' of the *Oberammergau Passion*, a non-actor who 'never gives in to the temptation to interpret Christ', and who does not *represent* but *presents*, in an impersonal way. He separates himself from the figure which he is showing to the spectators by means of hieratic gestures which precede the evangelical words, and these gestures are 'similar to the chords which, in Bach's *Passion*, introduce Christ's words'.[8]

It is not the form of inanimate matter which cannot be metamorphosed; it is the Form of a living but re-invented body, of a behaviour which has been separated from the behaviour of every day, of a naturalness which is the fruit of artificiality.[9] This is the Theatre which comes before the Drama and before any theatre building. It is the *architecture in motion* in which the performer lives his own autonomy: a theatre not made of stones and bricks. In less figurative and more concrete terms, it is the performer's pre-expressive level of organization.

Pre-expressivity and levels of organization

I did not invent pre-expressivity, nor did Craig. The only thing I invented was a belief in it.

The recurring principles, the dance of the *sats*, the ways of canalizing and modelling the performer's energy, all are descriptions at the pre-expressive level. The performer's work on her/himself and Stanislavski's method of physical actions, Meyerhold's bio-mechanics, Decroux' mime system, all furnish ample material for analysis. The traditional forms of apprenticeship and training of North Pole performers, styles and genres like classical ballet, like the other numerous theatres which have served as points of reference in the preceding pages, all provide material for analysis. But it is above all the practical work and empirical research with performers of different traditions which suggest the validity of thinking of the pre-expressive as a level of organization which is virtually separable from the expressive level.

Obviously, the pre-expressive does not exist in and of itself. Similarly, the nervous system, for example, cannot be materially separated from the entirety of a living organism, but it can be *thought* of as a separate entity. This cognitive fiction makes effective interventions possible. It is an abstraction, but is extremely useful for work on the practical level.

How and why? I will try to answer these questions. First, however, it is necessary to clear up certain misunderstandings.

When one speaks of the performer's pre-expressive level, the following objection is often made: it is impossible for a performer to act in front of a spectator without meanings being produced. This is true. It is materially impossible to prevent the spectator from attributing meanings and from imagining stories when seeing a performer's actions, even when *it is not intended* that these actions represent anything. This is valid, however, from the spectator's point of view: that is, when one sees the results.

But, let us be careful. It is not the action itself which has *its* own meaning. Meaning is always the fruit of a convention, a relationship. The very fact that the performer–spectator relationship exists implies that meanings will be produced. The point is whether or not one wishes to programme *which specific meanings* must germinate in the spectator's mind.

Let us now take the point of view complementary to that of the result, that is, the point of view of the performer's creative process. It is obvious that the performer can work on her/his actions (diction, tonality, volume, bearing, stance, intensity) without thinking about what s/he will want to transmit to the spectator once the process is completed. We would say, then, that s/he is working on the pre-expressive level. It is equally true that there also exist moments or situations based on a tacit agreement between performer and spectator where the absence of consensus regarding the meaning to be attributed to the action is accepted. It suffices to think of so-called pure or abstract dance (the Indian *nritta*, for example).

The condition for the germination of meanings is the existence of a performer–spectator relationship. But before representing anything at all the performer must *be*, as a performer.

For performers, working on the pre-expressive level means modelling the quality of their scenic existence. If they are not effective on the pre-expressive level, they are not performers. They can be used within a particular performance but are no more than functional material in the hands of a director or choreographer. They can put on the clothing, the gestures, the words, the movements of a character, but without an accomplished scenic presence, they are only clothing, gestures, words, movements. What they are doing means only what it *must* mean and nothing else. Linguists would say: they denote but do not connote. The effectiveness of a performer's pre-expressive level is the measure of her/his autonomy as an individual and as an artist.

For those who investigate the secrets of scenic life, to distinguish a pre-expressive level from the expressive level does not mean that one is forgetting that the value of theatre lies in the meaning which the performance in its entirety assumes and reveals. It means following the normal criteria of every scientist and every empirical researcher: to choose one's field of research; to treat it *as if* it was autonomous; to establish operatively useful limits, to concentrate on these limits and to make an inventory of them; to compare, find and specify certain functional logics; and then to reconnect that field to the whole from which it was separated for cognitive purposes only.

Goethe wrote a number of essays 'in honour and memory of Howard', who classified and named the various types of clouds and, so doing, taught a way of looking at the sky. That is, to see differences, to *distinguish*, because without distinguishing one does not see. Goethe begins the elegy to Howard by recalling the Indian god Camarupa who 'enjoys the changing of forms' and after having dedicated verses to stratus, cumulus, cirrus and nimbus clouds he adds:

Und wenn wir unterschieden haben
Dann müssen wir lebendige Gaben
Dem Abgesonderten wieder verleihn
Und uns eines Folge-Lebens erfreuen.

[And after we have distinguished, we must again restore the living gifts back to the isolated form, and rejoice in the constant flow of life.]

At this point, an essential question presents itself: how does one connect work on the pre-expressive to the other fields of theatrical work?

There are three historically verifiable answers to this question:

1 It is work which prepares the performer for the creative process of the performance;
2 It is the work by means of which the performer incorporates the way of thinking and rules of the performative genre to which s/he has chosen to belong;
3 It is a value in and of itself – an end, not a means – which finds one of its possible social justifications through theatre.

Obviously, in the reality of theatre history, all three answers co-exist every time technical/artistic research is carried out in depth. This is not a question of contrapositions but of a difference of gradations which emerge only when we observe the facts from a distance. Formulated in this way, these three answers become a schema for developing our reasoning, not for making historical judgments.

As we will see, there is a fourth possibility: to think by levels of organization.

But let us remain a while longer with our schema. In order to make it clearer (without being too concerned about its crudeness), we could personify the three possibilities with as many names – Stanislavski, Decroux, Grotowski – chosen from among those who have investigated with great experience and scientific rigour the territory we call pre-expressive.

Stanislavski explores this territory as a means of access to the character. He invents poetic (*poiein* = to do) procedures for the actor to make it possible for her/him to incarnate the author's poetry.

Decroux, on the other hand, is obsessed with the idea of the distinction between genres. He invents mime, which, in order to be a pure art, must be concentrated into a restricted territory. He endorses the concept according to which every artistic genre, in order to be such, must limit its own means: 'Our mime, which tries to suggest the life of the mind by using only the movement of the body, will be a complete art. [. . .] An art is complete only if it is partial.'[10]

Grotowski, both during his years as a director and later, when no longer creating performances, pursues a coherence different from that of Stanislavski or Decroux. He scrapes away from the actor's technique everything which belongs to the performance, to the work-for-the-spectator's-attention, and concentrates on physical actions as work of the individual on himself. Today Grotowski no longer speaks of the actor but of the Performer (the capitalization is intentional). He explains that the Performer can *also* become an actor. He associates himself more and more explicitly with an initiatory Tradition. He recognizes in theatrical knowledge, particularly in Stanislavski, one of the means of access to this Tradition.

I repeat, it is a question of different gradations, not of contrapositions. For example, we can consider Stanislavski and his students, especially Vakhtangov and Sulerzhitski, who died in 1916 barely more than forty years old, and of whom Stanislavski said that he was the only one to have understood him completely. They discovered that work on oneself as an actor often became work on oneself as an individual. It is impossible to define the border beyond which scenic *ethos* becomes ethics. In the schools of Copeau and Osterwa as well, this border was often so vague that it was difficult to understand what was the end and what was the means.

In the classical traditions of Asian theatres, the contiguity between the theatrical profession and ceremonial or meditative practices is so normal that their respective languages often intermix. Sometimes one wonders: Is Zeami using theatre to talk about Zen or Zen to talk about theatre? If one was not familiar with the author's life and his historical context, the answer to this question would not always be easy to find.

But there is another way of connecting work on the pre-expressive with other fields of theatrical work.

When we see a living organism we know, from anatomy, physiology and biology, that it is organized on various levels. Just as, in the human body, there is a level of organization of the cells, of the organs and of the various systems (nervous, arterial, etc.), so can we think of the totality of the performer's behaviour as being made up of distinct levels of organization.

The spectator sees results: performers expressing feelings, ideas, thoughts, actions, that is, something which has intention and meaning. The spectator therefore believes that a given intention or meaning is present when the process is begun. But it is one thing to analyse the result and another to understand how it was reached, how the body-mind was used in order to achieve it.

The understanding of the *how* belongs to a logic which is complementary to that of the result: the logic of the process. According to this logic, it is possible to distinguish between the result and the process, and to work separately on the levels of organization which constitute the performer's expression.

The pre-expressive substratum is included in the level of the overall expression perceived by the spectator. However, by keeping this substratum separate during the work process, the performer can intervene on the pre-expressive level *as if*, in this phase, the principal objective was the energy, the presence, the *bios* of the actions and not their meaning.

The pre-expressive level is therefore an *operative level*; it is not a level that can be separated from expression, but a pragmatic category, a practice which, during the process, develops and organizes the performer's scenic *bios* and generates new relationships and unexpected possibilities for meaning.

As a level of organization of scenic *bios*, the pre-expressive has a consistency of its own, independent of the consistency of the ulterior level of organization, that of the meaning. Independent does not mean devoid of relationships. It means that this distinction has to do with the logic of the process and not of the result, where the various levels of organization must blend into an organic unity, must reconstruct the believability of life by means of the artifices of art, and where every detail must contribute to the unity of the whole.

The difficulty in realizing the value which the notion of the pre-expressive can assume derives in large part from a reluctance to consider the point of view of the process. When we are discussing artistic products, our conditioned reflexes lead us to be concerned only with the way in which the result works. It is, however, necessary to realize that in order to understand *the way in which the result works*, it is not sufficient to understand which means must be resorted to in order *to arrive at* a result.

I call this reluctance to assume the point of view of the process 'the spectator's ethnocentrism'. Ethnocentrism, unwillingness to change one's point of view, often becomes an exaggerated presumption of knowledge.

But let us be careful. The concept of 'pre-expressive' is useful only when in relationship to the performer, someone who uses an extra-daily body technique *in a situation of organized representation*. The techniques of levitation, the martial arts, ping-pong and *tai-chi* are all extra-daily techniques but have nothing to do with the pre-expressive. Nor is the concept of 'pre-expressive' useful in the comparison of body techniques from different cultures. It becomes something absurd if we seek to parachute it into other fields. When, in daily life, we speak of a person's 'charisma', 'charm', 'sex-appeal', are we then speaking of something which could be called pre-expressive? Does literature have a pre-expressive level? Does painting? Music? Philosophy? What about medicine? No, *if you please*.

It is not, however, particularly interesting to recognize that this level of organization exists in the performer's work. It is relevant to ask oneself what purpose its internal consistency can serve.

The drift of the exercises

The 'drift' of theatrical exercises is one of the singular developments in the history of twentieth century theatre. A slow drift but one in which it is possible to recognize the tendency to move progressively further away from the continent of rehearsals and performances.

From Stanislavski on, exercises began to be considered as a complex of practices whose purpose was to transform the performer's daily body-mind into a scenic body-mind. Until then, exercises were used only as the ABC of the profession, or for learning the skills necessary for certain characters, or for learning fencing, ballet, acrobatics, magic. From Stanislavski on, new exercises began to represent, for some performers, the quintessence of doing theatre.

Exercises sometimes took on a new role and became an end rather than a means. Even though this was never explicitly said, it can be deduced from observation of the facts. The Studios, begun as experimental laboratories parallel to the Moscow Art Theatre, became a model which spread even among young people, half-way between professionalism and auto-didacticism. Sulerzhitski and Stanislavski himself devoted more and more time to these exercises, as if in them they could savour a meaning which they missed in the principal theatre.[11]

The Studios grew out of the need to look for solutions to specific professional problems. For example, how to perform the texts of the symbolists. However, a new vision of the theatre, not yet well defined but nevertheless evoked by numerous artistic and spiritual questions, began to be manifest in the form of 'schools', 'studios', 'laboratories' and not only in the form of performances.

The same thing happened with Copeau.[12]

We will not dwell here on the general aspects of this trend but restrict ourselves to considering certain of its consequences for our theme. If the exercises (those of Stanislavski, Sulerzhitski, Michael Chekhov, Vakhtangov, Meyerhold, Copeau . . .) did not serve to prepare the repertoire but to form the scenic body-mind, one understands why they did not remain only an introduction to the theatre but became, from the performer's point of view, the very heart of the theatre, a synthesis of its values.

This explains the phenomenon, in Russia at the beginning of the twentieth century, of the *studijnost*, the numerous Studios, made up of students and young intellectuals who saw in the theatre an artistic and spiritual school where they could develop their own personalities.

In the second half of the century, a network of 'workshops', 'seminars', 'laboratories', 'stages', 'talleres', 'ateliers', developed. In certain respects, it resembles the custom – common to the cultured classes in both Asia and Western countries – of learning music, song and dance for non-professional purposes. But, as opposed to what happens in those cases, where the student does exercises in order then to be able to perform works which s/he likes, the focus of the new theatrical pedagogy is not the future execution of plays (in their entirety or only scenes from them), but the very teaching of the exercises as an active experience of the theatre. It is one example – on the sociological level – of the paradoxical tendency of exercises to take on their own life. It is paradoxical because it was never affirmed in theoretical terms and was often even opposed and denounced as a form of cultural waste and professional inefficiency.

A different but symptomatic case is that of the life of a master whose name has appeared several times on these pages: Etienne Decroux. Mime, which he defined as a pure art in its own right, was at first a collection of exercises in Jacques Copeau's Vieux Colombier school. Decroux took the exercises out of the laboratory context and, developing them, made them independent as an autonomous artistic genre.

In other cases – the most historically relevant being that of the Living Theatre's *Mysteries and Smaller Pieces* (1964) – actual performances were created through a montage of exercises. Something similar was also done – in different styles and with different objectives – by the Open Theatre and Odin Teatret.

On these exceptional occasions – which never became the rule – the performer's work on the pre-expressive level was made autonomous and transformed into a 'performance in search of a genre': neither theatre in the usual sense of the word, nor dance, nor mime.

At the beginning of a career, training is a way to introduce a young person to a specific theatrical environment. If s/he is sufficiently obstinate, perseverant, not self-indulgent, giving up the exercises which have already been mastered and searching for or inventing others, and if, above all, s/he does not say, 'It's not useful anymore, the important thing is elsewhere!', then, with time, training will carry this young person towards individual independence. The function of the training inverts. At the start, it serves to integrate the beginner into an environment. Later, it serves to protect her/his independence from that very same environment, from the director, from the choreographer, from the spectators. It becomes, as Patrice Pavis said, the performer's 'physical diary'.[13] A diary is not simply a factual account. It can also be a treasure chest of technical, ethical or spiritual riches which can inspire one and upon which one can draw during a creative process.

We could use the word 'training' similarly to the way the Balinese use the word *agem*: 'attitude'. They speak of two *agem*: *agem* of the body and *agem* of the mind. The master I Made Pasek Tempo used the term *agem mati* ('dead *agem*') when he wanted to say that a performer had not succeeded in putting together, matching, the two *agem*. The word comes from *agama*, 'law, religion, Way, that which ties together'. *Agem* has in fact the double meaning of the expression found in many European languages: 'to take a position', from the moral as well as the physical point of view.

Brecht used the word *Haltung* ('attitude, stance') when he demanded a similar intersection of technique and ethics, of physical engagement and ideological taking of position from a performer. Training teaches one *to take positions*, both as extra-daily behaviour on the stage, and with respect to one's profession, the group in which one works, the social context in which one is immersed: with respect to what one accepts and what one refuses.

This is why training can take on an autonomous sense for the performer who practises it. And why it can become *her/his* stage, a 'theatre of one's

110

own' in which s/he can develop the values of the profession without yet producing anything for the eyes and mind of the spectator.

Training is, in other words, one of the ways in which Craig's metaphor takes concrete form: a theatre before the drama, an architecture in motion.

The drift of the exercises; their progressive and never definitive separation from the continent of rehearsals and performance; training as a score of actions, in relationship with a particular moment in the performer's research and experience; its personalization; all of this, and not Asian theatre, constitutes the historical context of the genesis of Theatre Anthropology.

It does not constitute, however, its only objective. Experience of the relative autonomy of exercises with respect to work on performance has led us to think of the pre-expressive as a separate level of organization. And this way of thinking leads elsewhere.

Let us look at what happens with exercises. Each exercise is a complete pattern, a design of movements. One does an exercise, then another, and so on. But once learned, the exercises are repeated, one after the other, in a continuous flow. What is the performer now doing? Dancing? Representing something? Is her/his 'physical diary' becoming an 'intimate diary', a sort of personal confession without words? No, s/he is simply executing a chain of exercises. But the observer cannot avoid interpreting, projecting images, stories, scenes, flashes of supposed inner relevations, onto an action which for the performer is perhaps only practice, similar to that of a pianist or singer who does musical scales to exercise the fingers or the voice. Except that the scales which the performer ascends and descends are living scales. They take on an emotive power, a meaning in the eyes of the observer, independently of the will of the practitioner. This happens because the action is *real*.

I remember an occasion about twenty years ago, in the lecture hall of an Italian university. An Odin Teatret actress was showing her personal training to theatre students and professors for the first time. She went up and down her 'scales', without ever interrupting the passage from one of her exercises to another.

We were simply showing what the technical work of an Odin performer consisted of, what training was. We made a mistake. The observers immediately turned into spectators. They believed that the actress was showing a scene from a performance rather than exercises. Some spoke of tragedy. Others of a kind of immodesty, as if the actress had revealed something intimate in public. At the end of what was intended to be a university lesson, while the actress was taking a shower, some students and professors, who we had unwillingly made into spectators, poured out their reactions to me, discreetly. I listened, and at the same time, a phrase of Diderot's passed through my mind, 'At the end of the performance the actor is tired and the spectator is moved.' It was not a performance we had intended to present in that university hall. I talked this over with the actress and we looked at each other and shook our heads: 'Is it them having hallucinations or us not knowing what we are doing?' We were not yet familiar with the tricks of the pre-expressive.

The actress had shown her personal training. But 'personal' in this case does not mean intimate. It means autonomously elaborated, not following the behaviour dictated by a tradition or genre. But the situation is no different when a classical dancer or a mime of the Decroux school or a performer from one of the Asian traditions executes without interruption a flow of elementary exercises, the design of movements, that kind of physical lexicon or phrase-book which is taught to the student in the first months of apprenticeship.

How can the ABC of the exercises change in front of our very eyes into *real* actions, into a net which captures the images and reflections of the observer, even though the substance of the actions was none other than a movement primer? Because it had become an organic process.

In fact, in these movements, every point of arrival coincides with a point of departure. There are no pauses, only transitions. Every stop is a go, every *kyu* is a *jo*, every point of arrival–departure is a *sats*. The scansion of the *sats*, the tensions of the luxury balance, the play of oppositions model the energy. The energy, the thought-action, darts, slides, leaps, from one of its possible temperatures to another, between Animus and Anima, engages the whole body even when the movement is minuscule, exploits the possibility of not being fully developed in space, of being withheld and absorbed. Its external rhythm can be matched with the internal rhythm in a consonant manner or by discrepancy and contrast, by *hippari hai*.

What we are describing here is an embryonic score in which the golden rule of segmentation is already at work. Stanislavski discovered it, or rather formulated it explicitly, for South Pole performers. For those of the North Pole, it is such an obvious rule that it almost always remains implicit. Every sequence of actions, according to the golden rule, must be subdivisible (for the performer, not in the eyes of the spectator) into smaller sub-units. These must not be simple pieces (if an action is *taken to pieces* it is literally put to death). Every sub-unit is also a design of movements, with its own beginning, its own climax, its own end. The beginnings and ends must be precise and blend together by means of leaps of energy in a score which is experienced as an organic flow.

When a performer behaves in this manner, s/he usually experiences a significant change in the way of perceiving and thinking of what s/he is doing. Some performers say that at this point 'images start to come into' their minds. Others claim that when what they are doing 'works', the distance between the head, which is giving the orders, and the body, which is carrying out those orders, disappears. Others add: 'The body leads and the mind follows after.' Still others say: 'It is the body which is thinking: the shoulders, the elbows, the knees, the spine. . . .'

A perceptive change also takes place in the mind of the observer; s/he no longer sees a body doing exercises, but a human being intervening in space.

These observers feel they must decipher what they are seeing. Some are bold enough to believe that what they are deciphering in the performer's actions is actually the content of something objective. Others are more in doubt: 'Am I projecting my images on what s/he is doing? Or is it s/he who is projecting them?'

There are not many performers who have the strenuous privilege of possessing a personal training. The example therefore has the defect of referring to a work situation which few have experienced, even among professionals. But the usefulness of the example derives from the fact that it draws attention to an intermediate zone, a kind of limbo or dawn, between purely technical exercises and the life of a *real* action.

The performer can move in this territory of potentialities for a long time. The tension-attention of the spectator cannot stay there for as long a time. If the intention which makes it possible for the spectator's demands and imagination to become canalized in a precise, chosen and objective direction does not appear, the observer-performer relationship is enfeebled. Attention disassociates and boredom takes over.

The moon and the city

Four years before his participation in the Rome Congress, Craig had published a book about the great actor-manager Henry Irving.[14] Craig had observed him at first hand, carefully watching the way he composed his characters. Many years later, and long after Irving's death, Craig explained that Irving constructed a role by means of a design of movements, a microscopic dance which pervaded his acting from beginning to end. Irving the realist – Craig demonstrated – had a personal technique similar to that which Meyerhold, fully aware of the choice he was making, formulated for his school and in his writings.

There is not an obligatory cause–effect relationship between technical procedures and forms of expression. Very different buildings have their foundations in the same ground. The illusion that the ground explored by Stanislavski could give birth only to a 'realistic' actor is based to a large extent on American Stanislavskiism influenced by the demands of cinema.

The psychotechnique, the mental technique which Stanislavski synthesized in the word *perezhivanie*, is not limited to the identification of the performer with the supposed feelings and states of mind of the character. It certainly can be used with the aim of giving the spectator a 'verisimilitude effect', giving her/him the illusion of watching a piece of real life. This draws attention, however, to a general and essential problem: whatever the aesthetic of the *mise en scène* may be, there must be within it a relationship between the score of the physical actions and the 'sub-score', the sub-text, the points of support, and the performer's internal mobilization. It is, in other words, the problem of the body-mind, of the psycho-physical entirety of the action.

This explains why Jerzy Grotowski is a true successor to Stanislavski even though, as a director, he always oriented himself in a direction opposite to 'Stanislavskiism', searching for a rigorous artificiality of the expressive form, negating the psychological justification of the character, and avoiding 'verisimilitude effects' in his performances.

The expression 'body-mind' is not an expeditious formula to indicate the obvious inseparability of one from the other. It indicates an objective which is difficult to reach when one passes from daily behaviour to the extra-daily behaviour which the performer must know how to repeat and keep alive night after night. The performer who begins from the inside must deal with the risks inherent in an accidental sequence of movements which tends to succumb to entropy and, with time, to be carried out mechanically.

The performer who begins from the outside, who uses a design of movements, or what the Japanese call a *kata*, modelled by her/himself or others, is in danger from the outset of submitting mechanically to pure dynamism, instead of living in it. Does this mean that the two ways are equivalent? No. It is more probable that an internal movement can be condensed from a well-executed and incorporated *kata* than the contrary, that a *kata*, with precise and repeatable form, can emerge from an internal movement. Without the precision of the external shape, the action cannot be fixed and therefore repeated independently of the performer's state of mind.

It is understandable, however, that the two ways are equivalent when the performer is working for film or television. In such a case, the action must be photographed, once and for all, in its best moment. What counts most is the intensity and the photogenic quality of the action, not its precision-repeatability. The intensity and emotional versatility of the film actor – who can *live* without a score for a series of brief, separate moments which s/he will not have to assemble – can effectively be reached with equal probability of success whether begun from the inside or the outside.

In one of his first writings on the theatre, Grotowski stated:

> Practice has convinced me that the school of *perezhivanie* is partly correct. In the theatre of which I speak, the result of the actor's work must have a quality of artificiality, but in order for this to be achieved in a dynamic and suggestive way, a certain internal engagement of the actor is necessary. No result is achieved, or something wooden is achieved, if there is not a conscious intention in the actor's acting, not only during the process but also during the moment of representation.

And he added:

> The physical action must be founded on and rest on the actor's personal, intimate associations, on his psychic batteries, his internal accumulators.[15]

Some years later we find the same obsession with technique – artificiality, score and internal engagement – expressed with greater determination:

> The search for artificiality in its turn requires a series of additional exercises, forming a miniature score for each part of the body. At any rate, the decisive principle remains the following: the more we become absorbed in what is hidden inside us, in the excess, in the exposure, in the self-penetration, the more rigid must be the external discipline; that is to say the form, the artificiality, the ideogram, the sign. Here lies the whole principle of expressiveness.[16]

Until he worked with the actors of the Berliner Ensemble, Brecht criticized 'the mystical and cultist' nature of the Stanislavski system.[17] Later, practical experience made him realize that the divergence between his ideas and Stanislavski's concerning the actor was not due to a real contraposition but to a different point of view: Stanislavski looked at the author's text from the actor's point of view; Brecht, on the other hand, looked at the actor on the basis of the author's demands.

In other words, Stanislavski's method was work on the pre-expressive, on which Brecht could also construct the form of expression based on alienation.[18] 'Now it will be my turn to defend Stanislavski from his supporters', Brecht exclaimed, after having seen a Moscow Art Theatre performance (Ostrovski's *Burning Heart*), based on the precision of the actors' scores which made their acting unrealistic and 'alienated'. Since he identified Stanislavski's 'theory' with *perezhivanie*, he added: 'Now I will have to say of him what is said of me – that the practice contradicts the theory.'[19]

At the pre-expressive level, there is no realism/non-realism polarity, there are no natural or unnatural actions, but only useless gesticulation or *necessary* actions. A 'necessary' action is one which engages the whole body, perceptibly changes its tonus, and implies a leap of energy even in immobility.

Neither does the identification/alienation polarity exist at the pre-expressive level. No matter what the effect the performance ought to produce on the spectator may be, the distance between the body and the mind, the sensation that there is a mind which is commanding and a body which is executing, must be reduced until it disappears.

Let us return to Stanislavski and watch him carry out the exercise of 'the man buying a newspaper'. Scenography and props were missing, there was no newsagent and no news-stand and Stanislavski's hands, with their precise movements, held neither money nor newspaper. We might have seen a recognizable pantomime. However, the myriad variations with which Stanislavski went through the same sequence of actions again and again, leaping from one rhythm to another, destroyed the literalness of the action and its realistic epidermis (a traveller who buys a newspaper on his way to catch a train). When each individual variation of the scene was executed on its own, it kept its pantomimic verisimilitude. But when these variations were executed in an uninterrupted flow, they transformed the realistic action into a kind of abstract ballet.

Here is the paradox: the more the action was 'abstract' for the spectator, the more 'realistic' it was on the mental stage of the performer who executed it. In order to establish the clarity of the flow of the actions, he had to represent vividly in his mind details which were always new and surprising: the sudden whistle of the departing train, the too-slow answer of the newsagent, a moment of uncertainty in the choice of newspaper, a coin which slipped from his fingers, the search for something with which to fill the waiting time, or the sudden memory of other times spent waiting and other departures. All this was achieved without disarranging the form of the exercise. The improvisation took place within the form, it did not de-form. Stanislavski was exploring an ever wider gamut of nuances, rhythms, connotations, different meanings.

We have already examined the improvisation occurring within the form, when we discussed *jo-ha-kyu*. When *jo-ha-kyu* is being used, improvisation is not guided by the variation of mental images but by the way of thinking the rhythm. From this, we deduced that beyond a certain limit, the segmentation of the action into separate elements is no longer feasible and becomes a rhythm of the thought. This is another of those particular cases which lead us to the understanding of a general principle. Every action is like a garment with a lining. The lining, which is not usually visible from the outside, is for the performer's use. Some performers prefer to begin with the lining, others with the garment. There is no lining–garment duality. Where the performer begins is not a deciding factor. In the end, lining and garment must be one entity: a body-mind.

This complementary dimension of the action is one of the recurring principles in performers' transcultural behaviour, even when they wish to obtain realistic effects and therefore seem to take their inspiration from the so-called reproduction of reality. It is easy to be realistic but even in realism it is difficult to carry out *real* actions.[20]

It is also difficult to present the theatre as theatricality, as fiction. This, too, always requires *real* actions. Otherwise there is the risk that they will simply appear simulated or overdone.

The effect of truth sought by Stanislavski, the theatricality sought by Meyerhold, and the alienation effect sought by Brecht, indicate opposite objectives on the level of results, but they are not divergent criteria in the process. These different objectives presuppose, within the coherence of the score's actions, an equally coherent organization of a 'sub-score', of a sub-text, of a lining-thought which the performer stitches together for her/himself. This is made up of circumstantial images or technical rules, of stories and questions asked of oneself, or of rhythms, of dynamic models or lived or hypothetical situations.

It is true, therefore, that the pre-expressive does not exist materially in a form of its own and can only be thought *as if* it did exist on its own. But this *as if* is operatively effective, it is concrete.

Indeed, not only that which is material is *concrete*. Numbers, measurements, conceptual categories, and all those immaterial entities which make it possible for us to operate effectively, to intervene in reality and to transform it, are also all concrete. The pre-expressive is only one of the levels of organization of the performer's technique. We discuss it, disembodying it from the organicity of the whole. But this level of organization has, within its limits, a quality of completeness.

The pre-expressive has to do not only with the physical aspect but also with the body-mind complementarity. It reproduces within its most restricted and basic scope a totality equivalent to that which must characterize the broader level of organization of expression. The body-mind totality of the performer on the pre-expressive level is equivalent, on the expressive level, to the totality of the performer-spectator system, with its perceptive and kinaesthetic circuits and with all the meanings which it can produce.

We have seen how, in the course of the history of the theatre, exercises have had the tendency to break off from the continent of rehearsals and performance. When this happens, they become a theatre of performers only which does not take the spectators into account. We can imagine the performers leaving the stage and entering a room of their own, where what they work on is not intended for representation. But also when they act in the public space of the theatre, they still, with a part of themselves, in ways that are theirs alone, conceal themselves from the spectators at the very moment in which they offer them the performance.

Borges says of Ariosto:

> Como a todo poeta la fortuna
> O el destino le dió una suerte rara
> Iba por los caminos de Ferrara
> Y al mismo tiempo andaba por la luna.[21]

> (As it does to all poets, Fortune
> Or Destiny allotted him a rare lot:
> He walked along Ferrara roads
> And at the same time trod the moon.)

Performers find this 'rare lot' in the daily practice of their profession. They can only be ubiquitous, otherwise they offer only an obvious display of themselves, of the words of an author, the intentions of a director or the score of a choreographer or of a tradition.

Secret points of support, sub-scores, hidden paths which lead to ubiquity can be:

– Stanislavski subtext;

- the systems of specific rules which give a distinct face to each of the so-called 'codified' theatres;
- the continuous dialogue with which performers – according to Brecht – must question themselves regarding the structural and historical truth of which their characters are, without knowing it, a mystified subjectivity;
- certain personal techniques of South Pole performers; for example, basing the details of one's actions on a different, contradictory or secret 'double' of a character (St Francis as a 'double' of Tartuffe).

It makes no difference that some of these hidden paths or sub-scores, as well as the many others which could be listed, have to do with the 'physical' aspect and others have to do with the 'mental' aspect. All of them involve the body-mind. It makes no difference that one of these means might be superimposed on the other. What does matter is to observe that all of them, although by different routes, lead to the practice of ubiquity. They all indicate how one can weave the lining of the action which is then made visible.

The performer follows several roads at the same time. It is not important which roads they are, what the *method* may be, which way is the 'way to the beyond'. It is important that at least one of these roads be secret, shielded from the spectator's gaze.

This place of their own, where performers walk in safety is not the moon, it is Ferrara. It is a town whose corners and colours are familiar, a personal and intimate sequence of images, rhythms, and sounds, composed of details which they assemble, repeat, accelerate, slow down; the faces they see and see again; the conversations they have within themselves; the experiences which, told to someone else, would seem banal; the perceptions of the impulses, of the changes of direction, of varying orientations. A private horizon of their own. A land on which one can solidly place one's feet, and then fly.

The vivid face of the moon is what the spectators will see.

The mother's smile

At this point, the question is: how does the performer work towards a future performance by concentrating, at the right moment, only on the pre-expressive level?

By forgetting what they want their actions to say, and what these actions must represent.

They will work, therefore, on the actions of the performance, dealing with each one on its own, almost as if each action was part of a micro-sequence of dance. That is, they will concentrate on the design of movements, on the segmentation, on the scansion of the *sats*, on the temperatures of the energy, on the dynamo-rhythm, protecting the details which render the action *real*.

Is it useful, during the process, to think in categories of form–content? In the creative process, the fertile polarity is that between form and precision, between design of movements and detail.

118

The moment in which it is essential to work on pre-expressivity, is when, during the creative process, our claim to become the authors of the meaning, its owners, is emerging. This demand is manifest in two opposite and equivalent ways: by knowing too much/being afraid of knowing too little; knowing in advance the results one wants to achieve/being completely disorientated, having lost the thread which leads one through the labyrinth, and therefore feeling the need to impose a definitive direction on the work.

The 'right moment' is that in which it is necessary to disorientate an order that is too evident, or to introduce a thread of order into the disorientation which threatens to pulverize the work.

It is the moment in which we must work with the greatest attention on every detail until room has been made for a new collaborator: Chance.

Louis Jouvet suggests the use of certain empirical procedures when collaborating with Chance. He says that the work must go through two phases: a period of dissolution of order, acquired knowledge, and certainties; and then a moment of recomposition. The phase which he calls 'dissociation' consists of a conscious fall into disorder, into the fragmentation of the materials, into the abandonment of the interpretive plans, into refusal of technical principles and stylistic experimentations, until one arrives at a 'mobile irresolution', at an uncertainty which he defines as 'necessary in order to free the intelligence'. It is this state of voluntary turmoil which makes possible the 'multiplication of ideas, attempts, points of view, until a paradox is reached'. It is the moment in which one declares war on everything one knows, not just because of a taste for the different, but 'to create doubt within oneself, to elicit the mystery'. It is a voluntary ruin, a systematic deterioration and destruction which recall the alchemists' way of thinking, but which in Jouvet are precise indications of work.

The subsequent phase is the work of 'association', of the synthesis of the loose elements, when the performer works to construct action sequences, *mise en scène* proposals using the fragments which emerged during the destruction phase. The assembling of these fragments releases the wonder and the sense of novelty and adventure which guide the work. Jouvet concludes: 'This puzzle game, this *reconstruction*, is the discovery of the role.'[22]

One proceeds in this way in order to prevent over-planning, limiting ideas, and a certain premature plan of work from suffocating the process, in which there should always be a dynamic balance between fortuitousness and organization.

Bertolt Brecht described the good director in this way:

He does not want to 'realize an idea'. His task is to stimulate and organize the actors' work [. . .]. He must provoke *crises* and not be inhibited by the fear of confessing that he does not have ready-made solutions. The trust his collaborators have in him must be based on his ability to discover what is *not* a solution. He must relieve doubts, solve problems, propose a quantity of possible points of view, comparisons, memories, experiences [. . .] He must organize the actors' *attitude of wonder*. He must make everyone ask himself: 'Why do I say this?' He must ensure that the wondering hesitations, the initial contradictions, once a given answer has been obtained, do not completely disappear as rehearsals progress. The uniqueness of the words spoken and the actions done must, time after time, remain clear within the definitive form.[23]

Here is Brecht during rehearsals of *The Caucasian Chalk Circle*, one day in September 1954. It is the ninety-fourth day of rehearsal. Hans-Joachim Bunge notes in his diary:

Brecht rehearses the bridge scene over and over again for almost two hours. He always goes back to the beginning. The dialogues are moved around, cut, re-introduced, shortened, and then, finally, put back where they had been at the beginning.

The same work of de-composition and fragmentation is carried out on the actors' gestures, their designs of movements are taken apart and put back together again. Every element put back in order in this way shows new facets. Bunge adds:

Brecht is creating the usual chaos. He is always suggesting new possibilities. Finally, no-one knows what is happening anymore. Not even Brecht knows.

He then stops the rehearsal because neither he nor the others can go on. Situations of this kind often happen. The rehearsals seem disastrous. But Bunge is obliged to recognize: 'From this confusion, however, more often than not, something new emerges.'[24]

Even in daily life, Chance seems sometimes to collaborate with us, disrupting our plans, which are threatening to petrify the flow of life, or indicating a way out of a confusion which is drowning us or a spider's web of contradictions in which we are entangled. Then, if we are lucky, Chance intervenes and suggests an unexpected solution. Some psychoanalysts say, in their imaginative language, that when this happens we have experienced 'the mother's smile'. Basavanna said it with other words: the 'Lord of the meeting rivers'.

All this, however, must be translated into technical procedures. Work on pre-expressivity serves to create a body-in-life, which is not idolized as a value unto itself. It has value because it guides the performer and the spectator to the discovery of non-obvious meanings in the performance.

The question and the answers which appeared at the beginning of this section have taken on the aspect of direct advice. They condense into explicit form the core of the solutions which are implied in the thick skeins of the uses and rules of the different theatrical traditions. It is up to scholars to unravel those skeins.

The fact remains that the constellation of norms, recommendations and artifices elaborated by the scenic traditions, by both North Pole and South Pole performers, have as their ultimate objective the individuation of practical ways of collaborating with the unforeseen by means of the foreseen and *of giving life to the drama*. This *life* must not be confused with vitality. It is that which becomes meaning for the spectator. The study of pre-expressivity is one way of putting into motion the apparently evident meaning in the work of an author, in a story already told, in the songs of a poet, in the interpretation of a director or in a choreographic score fixed by tradition.

In its original language, Basavanna's poem, which says

> Listen, O Lord of the meeting rivers,
> things standing shall fall
> but the moving ever shall stay

is constructed around the antinomy between the verbs *sthavara* and *jangama*.[25] *Sthavara* refers to what is there and can be possessed. It is the root of such words in Indo-European languages as 'stay', 'static', 'statue', 'status' and 'estate'. *Jangama* refers to what is moving, what is becoming. It is the root of the English 'go' and the German 'gehen'. We could translate *sthavara* and *jangama* with 'to build' and 'to act':

> things built shall fall
> but the action ever shall stay.

The pre-expressive, seen in its separateness, is a cognitive fiction which allows for effective interventions. It is not limited to the performer's pure physicality but has to do with the body-mind totality, and makes it possible for the performer to concentrate in a separate area which contains her/his laws, systems of orientation, logics, just as the larger area of the contents of the performance also has its own laws, systems of orientation and logics.

Details, traces, symptoms, clues, which attract the performer, director and spectator towards meanings which are not obvious emerge from the pre-expressive dimension when it is worked upon with precision and according to its own principles.

But the point where the two rivers meet, where the mother smiles at you, eludes all your plans and expectations.

To live according to the precision of a design

The essence of the pre-expressive has to do with the *real* nature of the performer's action, independently of the effects of dance or theatre, of realism or non-realism which can be achieved with it.

The *real* nature of the action derives from the quality of the process. It is what makes the performer exist as a performer and is not that which characterizes her/his performative style. It is not a stylistic choice. It gives a foundation to the choice of a given style. It is worth repeating, even at the risk of being boring: to say that the performer's action must be *real* does not mean in any way that it must be realistic.

The performer's action is *real* if it is disciplined by a score.

When applied to the performer, the word *score* (first used by Stanislavski and taken up by Grotowski), refers to an organic consistency. It is this organic consistency which allows the work on the pre-expressive to be conducted as if it was independent of the work on the meaning (the dramaturgical work), and can be oriented according to its own principles, leading to the discovery of non-obvious significations and establishing the dialectic of the creative process between organization and fortuitousness.

The term *score* refers to:

- the general form of the action and the outline of its course (beginning, climax, conclusion);
- the precision of the fixed details: the exact definition of the individual segments of the action and the joints which connect them (*sats*, changes of direction, different qualities of energy, variations of speed);
- the dynamo-rhythm, the speed and intensity which regulate the *tempo* (in the musical sense) of every individual segment. This is the metre of the action, the alternation of long or short, accented or unaccented segments;
- the orchestration of the relationships between the different parts of the body (hands, arms, legs, feet, eyes, voice, facial expression).

According to a term which probably comes from Decroux, the last point could be defined as 'orchestration of the anecdotes', given that the essential part of the action, its seed, is in the torso.

The orchestration of the anecdotes can consist of concordances, complementarities or contrasts. For example:

- *concordance*: the different parts of the body all collaborate in the composition of a soft, delicate, introverted physical–vocal action; or
- *complementarity*: the general form of the action is soft, delicate, introverted, *and* the voice (or the eyes, the hands . . .) maintains an extroverted relationship with the outside; or
- *contrast*: a delicate walk *but* a voice which intervenes in an overbearing way in the space; calm and confident hands, nervous feet . . .

(One should not forget the deceptive nature of examples: they refer to one case from among a hundred but risk transforming that one case into a model the use of which is particularly advised. The richness of the creative process does not derive from the application of an example but from the application of the exploration of the logic behind the example, making hundreds of other cases possible, all of which ought to be explored.)

In chapter 5, 'Energy, or Rather, the Thought', we saw a particularly subtle case of orchestration in one of Michael Chekhov's exercises: the opposition between internal and external rhythms.

Both the different parts of the body and the score can be organized in relationships of concordance, complementarity or contrast: the parts of the body in their reciprocal and simultaneous connections, and the score with the meaning of the words, the dialogues, the scenic situation. A page from Meyerhold's writings furnishes us with a particularly clear example of the complementary montage between dialogue and physical score.

The text in question was written in 1906. From when he first began to work as a director and teacher, Meyerhold treated the score (which he referred to in his terminology with the expression *risunok dvizhenij*, 'design of movements') as a coherent and virtually autonomous whole, comparable to the music of an opera in relation to the libretto. Wagner had explored one of the traditional uses of the orchestra (the way it can comment on events, reveal the hidden thoughts, feelings, emotional reactions of the characters) and taken it to its extreme limit. Similarly, Meyerhold reinforced the autonomy of the physical score with respect to the written text:

> Just as Wagner employs the orchestra to convey spiritual emotions, I employ plastic movement.

Even in the 'old theatre', Meyerhold recognized, there was an elaborate plastic art. Tommaso Salvini astonished spectators with the refined plastic composition which he used to bring the characters of Othello and Hamlet to life. But that plastic art, Meyerhold said, was rigorously harmonized with the words. He, on the other hand, was interested in a plasticity which did not correspond to the words:

> What do I mean by this [plasticity which does not correspond to the words]?

> Two people are discussing the weather, art, apartments. A third – given, of course that he is reasonably sensitive and observant – can tell exactly by listening to this conversation, which has no bearing on the relationship between the two, whether they are friends, enemies or lovers. He can tell this from the way they gesticulate, stand, move their eyes. This is because they move in a way unrelated to their words, a way which reveals their relationship.

The observer's individuation of relationships between the characters, independent of the content of their dialogue, is made possible by a whole series of details (small hand movements, ways of looking at each other, of adjusting distances, of assuming specific postures) which depend on the quality of the relationships between them and which do not illustrate the words they are saying. The director, says Meyerhold, must make the actors act in a way that makes it possible for the spectator not only to understand the words written by the author but also to penetrate the implied inner dialogue of the situation:

> The essence of human relationships is determined by gestures, poses, glances and silences. Words alone cannot say everything. Hence there must be a *pattern of movement* on the stage to transform the spectator into a vigilant observer. [. . .] Thus the spectator's imagination is exposed to two stimuli: the oral and the visual. The difference between the old theatre and the new is that in the new theatre speech and plasticity are each subordinated to their own separate rhythms and the two do not necessarily coincide.[26]

The actors who Meyerhold called the 'old theatre' elaborated their scores by harmonizing them with the words of the text. This concordance was, however, neither slavish nor tautological. Meyerhold himself, when describing this procedure, let it be understood that there were at least two different possibilities: to harmonize the gestures with the words as spoken by a particular character or with the words as understood on their own. This distinction remains obscure until it is compared with other observations which show us how the (great) actors of the 'old theatre' composed an extremely varied score while yet respecting the illustrative criteria.

A character is always a specific individual who speaks with a specific intention about something specific to a specific listener.

Each of these elements could constitute a different point of view for the illustration. The actors could leap from one point of view to another. They synchronized the words of the text with particular postures elaborated on the basis of the traditions of dance, painting or sculpture and assembled them in sequences which sometimes had a very rapid rhythm. Each individual segment of the score, like a photogram, illustrated a part of the text but did so by leaping from one facet to another: at one moment, it visualized the character, the condition or intention of the speaker, at another moment, the object of the discussion; at one moment, the stated intention, at the next, the hidden intention and even the attitude of the actor towards the character.[27]

Let us imagine, for example, Iago's speeches in the third scene of the third act of *Othello* (lines 390–420). Othello asks Iago for proof of Desdemona's betrayal. Iago says, first of all, that having seen how jealous Othello has become, he regrets having told him of his suspicions. Then he states that if Othello so wishes he can have proof of Desdemona's adultery with Cassio. But, it will never be an absolute proof. Perhaps Othello would like to spy on his wife at the very moment she lets herself be mounted by Cassio? It would be very difficult, he says, to create a situation which would make it possible for the Moor to see the two in bed. Even if they were as 'prime as goats, as hot as monkeys, as salt as wolves in pride, and fools as gross as ignorance made drunk', it would still be difficult to surprise them in flagrante. But, Iago adds, he has a few clues.

Urged on by Othello, he claims to be reluctant to assume the role of the spy. Then he gives in. One night he was sleeping in the same bed as Cassio and had such terrible toothache that he was unable to sleep. Cassio is one of those people who talk out loud when dreaming, and in his dreams, he talked about Desdemona and said, 'Sweet Desdemona, let us be wary, let us hide our love!' Then, Iago relates, Cassio reached out, and in the unconsciousness of sleep, took one of Iago's hands, and dreaming about Desdemona, whispered 'O sweet creature!' He kissed Iago. He flung his leg over Iago's thigh, kissed him again and finally cried 'Cursed fate, that gave thee to the Moor!'

The actor illustrates. But what does he illustrate? He can choose. The text, in fact, offers him several opportunities. He can illustrate the cunning, deceitful, slippery, bitter, vindictive character of Iago, the wounded snake. He can illustrate Iago as he appears to the Moor: an old, loyal companion compelled by his very loyalty to denounce the outrage which his friend Cassio is perpetrating on his master. He can illustrate the various subjects referred to in Iago's speech: the lasciviousness of animals in heat, the brutality of a drunken peasant, himself – Iago – sleepless because of toothache; his reactions to the behaviour of the sleeping Cassio; or Cassio dreaming of Desdemona, his kisses, his caresses ... He can repeat Cassio's words, colouring them with the astonishment and indignation he himself felt when he heard them, or with the cunning reluctance he pretends to feel when he reports to the Moor, or he can throw the words in the Moor's face as if he was Cassio saying them at that moment.

The actor of the 'old theatre' could in fact compose his score by leaping from one illustrative line to another, choosing his photograms in a varied manner, weaving a living tapestry, alternating the images of a loyal lieutenant, of a diabolical cheat, of a lascivious monkey, of a night of love, of the contempt shown by the young lover to the no longer young Moor, of the reaction of disgust or hesitancy to the involuntarily homosexual advances made by the dreaming Cassio. It was this refined plastic art which, even though it followed illustrative criteria, fascinated the spectators, revealing to them unexpected aspects of the text. And it fascinated Meyerhold as well.

Meyerhold is substantially right. There is a profound difference between his vision of a plastic art separate from the logic of the words and that of the actors of the 'old theatre'. The complex embroidery of their illustrative scores, which could leap from one perspective to another, gave emphasis to certain particularly important scenes. In such cases, the line of plastic representation acquired a certain autonomy with respect to the text. But in general, it remained illustrative in a univocal and undiversified way.

Still, it is useful to remember the procedures employed by the performers of the great European tradition. The variety of their scores could be increased by the use of poses or brief sequences of movements which could be enjoyed by the spectator for what they were, for the elegance, the energy, the virtuosity of the form. In short, these actors applied a complex dramaturgy to their performance scores.[28]

We find the same basic procedures in the scores of performers from classical Asian theatres. These scores are also based on the alternation of non-narrative and illustrative segments which are constantly changing the point of view, now illustrating the subject, now the object, now the character, now what the character is speaking about, now the contours of a landscape, now a fine detail (a woman watching . . . a lake; the mist on the lake; an approaching boat; the woman becoming afraid; a soldier on the boat; his helmet shining in the first rays of the sun; the soldier looking up to the sky; a bird . . .). The complicated dramaturgical refinement of the scores of Asian performers is often dizzying because of the orchestration of different points of view assembled with an equally varied orchestration of the relationships between the different parts of the body (the hands and the ways they move, the gait, the face, each of which can illustrate a different 'photogram').

At this point, it is obvious that to speak of 'illustration' is no longer completely justified. The illustrative criteria explains the performer's mental process, not the result which s/he achieves in the eyes of the spectator. The latter does not see an illustration. The more the spectator's competence increases, the more s/he becomes able to penetrate the multiplicity of the details, and the more the performer reveals to the spectator a microcosm of actions and reactions, a complex dramatic interweaving which brings the presence of her/his scenic persona alive.

It is also obvious that this complexity is not made cohesive and consistent because of the narrative thread. It is the organicity which makes the action *real*, because the individual photograms are assembled respecting the pre-expressive principles which render the performer's body a body-in-life.

Dario Fo, when he explains the principles according to which he designs his own scenic presence, speaks of zooms, background shots, wide shots, close-ups, reverse shots. He imagines a film camera in the brain of each spectator. The performer must know how to direct this camera, sending the correct impulses, so that the spectator can change the 'lens' and the angle of the 'shot'.[29] He adds that the spectator is not aware of this complicated montage of different points of view. It is this montage, however, which makes the action precise, alive, and interesting.

The dramaturgy of the score is first of all used to fix the form of the action, that is, to animate it with details, détours, impulses and counterimpulses. This elaboration is important for the performer. Upon it depends the precision and thus the quality of the presence.

The aim here is a microscopic dramaturgy. It is one of the means used by the performer to pass from a design of movements conceived of in general to a design which is defined in its most minimal particularities. It suffices to remember Stanislavski's obsessive demand to his actors: 'None of your actions made must be in general.'

This is why it is difficult to distinguish clearly – using Stanislavski's terminology – between 'the actor's work on himself' and the 'actor's work on the character'. Using the terminology of Theatre Anthropology, we could ask: is the performer who follows the research of Stanislavski's last years working on the pre-expressive or on interpretation?

During his last years as a teacher and director, Stanislavski, rather than beginning from the text, sets up a draft. Work on the character's words, which before had been the starting point for the actor, is now postponed to the final phase of the process. A simple outline of actions is extracted from the text, scene by scene, situation by situation. Stanislavski begins to direct the actor on the basis of this outline.

Each character's action, as it emerges from the draft extracted from the text, could result in conventional pantomime. In order to develop and deepen the action, it is divided and subdivided into its various segments. The simplest stage directions (to enter a room closing the door behind one, to have a conversation seated on a sofa, to present oneself politely to a stranger . . .) generate innumerable segments, each one of them suggesting dozens of possible micro-actions. At each point, the actor must decide which micro-actions to make her/his character execute, how, and why. The actor makes her/his decision and proposes it to her/his colleagues and to Stanislavski by means of scenic actions, not words.

Whereas a writer uses mental processes to transfer the summary draft of a plot into the pages of a novel, a performer uses different tools for her/his craft, but analogous criteria. The analogy lies in the process. When the result has been achieved, that is, when the performance has been put together, only a limited number of those micro-actions will be discernible to the spectator. Most of them will function as barely perceptible bacterial flora whose pulsation gives substance to the action's life and precision.

When the characters are speaking, the actors – who Stanislavski has energetically urged not to learn the words of the text – extemporize, retelling the contents of the author's written dialogues in their own way. All the goldsmithing which the author has done with the language will only be allowed to shine again at the end of the process.

The text is a ready-made *result* waiting to meet, at the right moment, the other *result*, autonomously reached by means of the complex work of weaving the various performers' scores together.

Stanislavski maintained that with this method, one did not lose the principle of *perezhivanie* ('revivification'). Tracing the line of the physical actions, he said, meant also tracing the line of the *perezhivanie*.[30] We have already referred to Grotowski's comments in this regard.

The meeting between *the final phase of the* performers' *process* and the author's *result*, the written words, puts the text in a new light, freeing it from obvious interpretations.

This strategy for the creative process does not apply only to realistic theatre, based on so-called psychological interpretation. Its fundamental principle is also found in theatres which belong to different traditions or which are inspired by completely different perspectives. It is the strategy of the search for meaning. This is why I stated that during the process it is not appropriate to reason on the basis of the form–content polarity and that it is useful instead to keep the form–precision of details polarity in mind.

The performer's soul, intelligence, sincerity and warmth do not exist without the precision forged by the score.

Here is how Copeau comments on Diderot, objecting to the rigid contra-position, often raised to a dualism, between the warm performer and the cold performer, between the performer who feels and does not compose and, on the contrary, the performer who composes because he does not feel:

> I can imagine an actor confronted with a role he likes and understands. [. . .] The first reading that he gives of it is surprising in its correctness. Everything in it is masterfully indicated, not only the overall intention, but already even the nuances. [. . .]
>
>
> Now he gets down to work. He rehearses, in a hushed tone, cautiously, as if he were afraid of upsetting something within himself. [. . .] The actor now has the role committed to memory. This is the moment when he begins to be a bit less in possession of the character. He can see what he is trying to do. He is composing and developing. He is setting in place the sequences, the transitions. He reasons out his movements, classifies his gestures, corrects his intonations. He watches himself and listens to himself. He detaches himself from himself. He judges himself. He seems no longer to be giving anything of himself. [. . .] He is trying to find the means to put himself in the right attitude, a state of feeling: a starting point which might sometimes be a hand movement or a vocal intonation, a particular contraction or a simple intake of breath . . . He tries to tune himself up. He sets out his nets. He is organising in order to capture something which he has known of and anticipated for a long time, but which has remained alien to him, has not yet entered into him, taken up residence inside him . . . [. . .]
>
> For the actor, the whole art is the gift of himself. In order to give himself, he must first possess himself. Not only does technique not exclude sensitivity: it authenticates and liberates it. It is thanks to our craft that we are able to let ourselves go, because it is thanks to our craft that we will be able to find ourselves again.[. . .]
>
> It is at this stage of the work that is born, matures and develops a sincerity, an acquired and achieved spontaneity, which we can say acts like a second nature, inspiring in its turn the physical reactions and giving them control, eloquence, naturalness and freedom.[31]

In one of his notes on the theatre, published in 1910, Meyerhold wrote:

Henry Louis Lekain writes to M. de la Ferté: 'The actor's first gift is the soul, the second is the intellect, the third is the sincerity and the warmth of interpretation, the fourth is *the refined design of the physical movements*.'

Meyerhold drew attention to how much time had passed between the beginning of the eighteenth century, the time of Lekain, and the beginning of the twentieth century, when Gordon Craig and Georg Fuchs again insisted upon the need for refined design of scenic movements. And he asked himself:

Is it possible that two centuries were not enough to make obvious the importance of the design to which the body on stage must conform?[32]

Every theatrical generation seems destined to repeat Meyerhold's question, making the time even longer: 'How can it be that *three* centuries . . . '

To Meyerhold's way of thinking, the design of movements is the *conditio sine qua non* of being a performer. Meyerhold investigates its criteria throughout his career. He makes it increasingly autonomous from work on the text, no longer modelling the score with the instrument of dramaturgical thinking but by means of musical knowledge. His working language is made up of musical terminology and words like 'rhythm', 'dance', and 'bio-mechanics', which take the place of 'interpretation' and *'perezhivanie'*.[33]

In 1925 he writes:

We are sometimes accused of not using psychology. And, indeed, some of us shrink from this word and fear it. But, to the extent that objective psychology effects us, we also obviously deal with psychology. Except that we do not let ourselves be governed by *perezhivanie*, but rather by a constant faith in the precision of our acting technique.[34]

Igor Ilinski, who acted in many of Meyerhold's performances, recalls in his autobiography the severity with which Meyerhold demanded that the actors 'marry a precise design to their gestures and body positions'.[35]

The value of a precise score had such priority for Meyerhold that he foresaw the possibility of its transmission from one actor to another.

In the programme of work for his 1914 Studio he had written:

The absence of a subject in the study chosen as an exercise (a scene without text), underlines the importance of the form as a self-sufficient scenic value (design of the movements and of the actors' gestures) [. . .]

The actor-graphic artist and his predominant thought: to live according to the precision of a design. Or the actor himself designs it, or can reproduce the design of another actor, like a pianist can decipher a score which he has not himself written.[36]

We should pay particular attention to the expression 'to live according to the precision of a design'. It is one of the clues which helps us understand that there is a common ground which unites – above and beyond individual idiosyncracies and profound differences of taste, style and aesthetics – Stanislavski, Meyerhold, Craig and later Grotowski.

The theatrical kinships do not correspond to similarities of aesthetic choice. They derive from having questions and obsessions in common. As far as his aesthetic choices were concerned, Meyerhold appeared, and appears, to many as being anti-Stanislavski. But, exactly like Stanislavski, he was stubborn, iconoclastic, never satisfied, unable to accept principles and teachings which had not been empirically verified, independent in his way of thinking and behaving. At the end of his life, Stanislavski considered passing on to Meyerhold his entire legacy, both his artistic and his empirical research.[37] 'To live according to the precision of a design' was Stanislavski's life-long obsession as actor, director and teacher.

A score of physical and vocal actions in which the succession of details is fixed in an irrevocable way imposes a discipline which seems to contradict the free flow of life, the performer's spontaneity, even her/his individuality. On the contrary.

> The score is like a glass inside which a candle is burning. The glass is solid; it is there, you can depend on it. It contains and guides the flame. But it is not the flame. The flame is my inner process each night. The flame is what illuminates the score, what the spectators see through the score. The flame is alive. Just as the flame in the glass moves, flutters, rises, falls, almost goes out, suddenly glows brightly, responds to each breath of wind – so my inner life varies from night to night, from moment to moment. . . .

This is the unforgettable Ryszard Cieslak, speaking about Jerzy Grotowski's *The Constant Prince*. The form of the score, the details which have been fixed, that must not be varied in any way; this is the 'theatre not made of stones and bricks' in which the performer – or *something in* the performer – lives the precision of a design, his extra-daily life.

> I begin each night without anticipations. This is the hardest thing to learn. I do not prepare myself to feel anything. I do not say, 'Last night, this scene was extraordinary, I will try to do that again.' I want only to be receptive to what will happen. And I am ready to take what happens if I am secure in my score, knowing that, even if I feel a minimum, the glass will not break, the objective structure worked out over the months will help me through. But when a night comes that I can glow, shine, live, reveal – I am ready for it by not anticipating it. The score remains the same, but everything is different because I am different.[38]

Jacques Copeau wrote the following to his actress Valentine Tessier, recognizing the score that remained the same and the flame which made it different on one particular evening:

Yet another aspect of your nature, courage. I remember it from *Le carrosse*. You performed it the night of your father's funeral. And one can certainly not say it was because of lack of sensitivity. *Grand Dieu!* I remember that evening. Since I was sitting and nearly always immobile in my seat, it was easy not to lose sight of you. You fluttered about me like a huge butterfly. All the movements, all the gestures of the character had been inscribed in your body for so long, you had done them so many times and assimilated them so profoundly, that they didn't need you any longer, and could, so to speak, enact themselves.[39]

We have seen how, at the beginning of the century, Gordon Craig fired broadsides against the concept of the 'actor's art'. He lamented the absence of physical scores which were sufficiently refined, rigorous and complete. He concluded that the word 'art' when applied to the actor was unjustifiable. He was the son of Ellen Terry, the student of Henry Irving, a devoted spectator, in Italy, of Tommaso Salvini, Giovanni Grasso, Ettore Petrolini and Eleonora Duse. He said that they were more than actors – and something less than artists.

Acting is not an art. It is therefore incorrect to speak of the actor as an artist. For accident is an enemy of the artist. Art is the exact antithesis of pandemonium, and pandemonium is created by the tumbling together of many accidents [. . .]

In the modern theatre, owing to the use of the bodies of men and woman *as their material*, all which is presented there is of an accidental nature. The actions of the actor's body, the expressions of his face, the sounds of his voice, all are at the mercy of the winds of his emotions: these winds, which must blow for ever round the artist, moving without unbalancing him. But with the actor, emotion possesses him; it seizes upon his limbs, moving them whither it will [. . .] emotion is able to win over the mind to assist in the destruction of that which the mind would produce [. . .] emotion is the cause which first of all creates, and secondly destroys.[40]

In his first books on the theatre, Craig had strongly refuted the preoccupations and needs which had nourished Stanislavski's and Meyerhold's empirical research. Craig presented the ideal image of the Über-Marionette, capable of incarnating Form. Stanislavski, Meyerhold and all those who followed them and will follow the roads opened by them, spoke of rigour in physical actions. Copeau defined the actor as one who knew how to be a natural human being and a marionette at the same time.

With the hindsight of our perspective, these words of Decroux are almost an answer to Craig with respect to the destructive force of the emotions:

The mastery of emotion? When the actor undertakes to express himself in lines of meticulous geometry, risking his balance and thus suffering in his flesh, he is indeed forced to hold back his emotion and behave as an artist: an artist of drawing.[41]

From Meyerhold's working language to that of Decroux, the design of movements assumes different nuances, according to the two men's different artistic biographies, and yet remains substantially the same: a principle which is unavoidable for the performer who refuses the self-indulgence which our society confers upon the theatre. This principle is found throughout the entire twentieth century tradition, from Stanislavski to Grotowski, and in others after him.

Meyerhold retraced this same need going back in time, and quoted Voltaire, for whom the actor – as opposed to the dancer – is not an artist. 'Dance', Voltaire said, 'is art because it is bound by laws.'[42]

To have a score, defined in every detail and disciplined in its form, is one of the performer's primary needs. This is one of those evident truths which we usually call a 'Colombus egg'. In order to see this truth clearly, all one has to do is lift the veil of commonplaces created by theatrical self-indulgence.

The word *kata* is found throughout the tradition of Japanese theatre and dance. It could be defined as a message from the past, transmitted from one generation to another by means of small or large vocal and movement sequences. Some of these sequences of fixed details have a title or are accompanied by a suggestive comment. For example: 'the moon on the water', which is explained as follows: 'the action is not calculated, it springs forth without visible force, it is the unity of separate elements, not overshadowed by the clouds of thought'. The poetic images which describe the *kata* also serve to hide it, to protect its secret from being penetrated by competitors and adversaries.

On its own, the word *kata* has nothing mysterious or esoteric about it. Semantically, in common speech, it corresponds more or less to words like 'form', 'stamp', 'pattern', and 'model' in European languages. For the performer, it can refer to a single movement, a single position, a structured sequence of actions, or to an entire role. A *kata* can transmit the detailed version of a realistic action – making us think of Stanislavski's 'physical action'. And it can transmit a design of symbolic movements – and hence the thought which seeks out analogies turns to Craig, who maintained that actors, in order to avoid the state of servitude in which they find themselves, must create a way of performing made up of symbolic gestures:

> To-day they impersonate and interpret; to-morrow they must represent and interpret; and the third day they must create.[43]

In some cases, the title and comment which accompany a *kata*, this sort of hieroglyph-in-action, has been lost, and the *kata* has become a kind of score without evident content. It is executed and appreciated for its dynamic, rhythmic and aesthetic qualities – and hence our thought turns towards the choreographic work which is closest to it, to Meyerhold, to his work on rhythm, to his use of music during rehearsal in order to impose a tempo on the design of movements.

Experience teaches us that if a performer learns to execute a *kata* which is for her/him a precise but empty score, repeating it over and over again, then s/he will succeed in personalizing it, discovering or renewing its meaning. An empty score does not in fact exist. Ideoplastic precision, the sensation which passes through the body of the performer who has mastered a precise pattern, makes it possible, with time, to extract a meaning from what seemed to be pure form.

Extract *a* meaning or discover *the* meaning?

Whichever it may be, to learn to execute a *kata* is not an intellectual task, but requires corporal effort, in which, however, mental activity is always present. This is why the *kata* – like the design of movements in Meyerhold's school – can be passed on. And it is useful if it is passed on from the person who has composed it to someone who will know how to recompose it.

James Brandon affirms that the process by means of which performers from one generation to another learn the same *kata* is an essential part of the art of *kabuki*. From the point of view of the individual performer, to learn to represent a *kata* is a process which is closely connected to the search for his own personal and artistic individuality. This leads to a fertile dialectic between conservation and innovation, because the performer must create a new *kata* in order to assert his own individuality and so doing contradicts his own profound respect for the traditional *kata*. These two opposing tendencies are in contraposition in every artistic society, but when they are present in physical scores with rigorous form, they can transform the contrast into harmony:

> The two forces tend to check each other, with the result that in the actor's work neither unregulated newness, applauded by some segments of the audience, nor slavish adherence to tradition, rewarded by family elders, becomes dominant. They are balanced in a state of healthy tension. The balance will differ for each actor – some inclining toward new ideas and some toward established forms – and according to circumstances, but it has always been maintained. As long as actors can continue to create within the framework of traditional *kata*, *kabuki* will remain the living theatre art that it is today.[44]

The quote refers to the *kata* understood as the score of an entire role. It does, however, also apply to the *kata* understood as scores or segments of actions (a *nō* performer, for example, will never move from a seated position to a fast walk without two intermediate *kata* which elaborate the micro-action of standing up and the micro-action of beginning to walk).

The term *shu-ha-ri* defines the process of apprenticeship and development

133

by means of the *kata*. *Shu* indicates the first phase of work: to respect the form, to learn it in all the accuracy of its details. *Ha* (one is reminded of the second phase of *jo-ha kyu*) refers to the moment in which the performer becomes free of the technique, not because its dictates have been transgressed, but because they have been respected and the performer can now move with a new 'spontaneity', as if with a 'second nature'. The *kata* has been incorporated. *Ri*, the third phase, refers to the moment in which the performer moves away from the form: he models the form which modelled him.

Following the design of the *kata*, the performer's thought seeks to find out *how* to avoid the fixity of the form which offers a resistance to him, *how* to dilate the form without exploding it. A technically elaborated and fixed behaviour becomes a means of personal discovery. Some commentators define the *kata* as a 'physical *koan*'.

When referring to the performer who has discovered how to dominate the various phases of this process, one speaks of 'ability which has no ability', of 'technique which has no technique', of 'art without art'. Images which have strong echoes and relationships with those used by Craig when he spoke of the actor as the Über-Marionette. He recalled an ancient axiom, one repeated *ad infinitum* and very difficult to understand: 'The highest art is that which conceals the craft and forgets the craftsman.'[45] Intellectually, it is easy to believe that one understands what this means. But in practice, what does one do? How does one help the performer 'give her/himself', 'burn', go beyond her/himself, and, at the same time, hide the artifice?

The answers to these questions, formulated at different times and in different working languages, all converge towards the procedures necessary for the construction of a *real* action. The pre-expressive appears to us, then, as the dynamic matter circumscribed and worked on by those principles which, in a transcultural dimension, help *bring alive* the precision of a design.

Thus, when the design of a movement is organically developed and brought alive, it leads to a leap of meaning. A word or phrase can change colour, an action can reveal an unthought-of aspect of the behaviour of a character or a situation. We call it Chance. But it is the mother smiling at us.

134

8

CANOES, BUTTERFLIES
AND A HORSE

Words, seemingly stable, have one particular weakness: their apparent stability. Behind every definite statement, a misunderstanding lies in wait.

In one's work, certain words shine like lightning on water. When they are written down, their nature is dangerously changed. The act of writing untangles the skein; it becomes more linear and less truthful. Experience, on the other hand, is contiguity of actions, of simultaneous perspectives. When one acts, one is present on different levels of organization at the same time.

Those who have built theatres, but not with stones and bricks, and who have then written about them, have also generated many misunderstandings. They wanted their words to be bridges between practice and theory, between experience and memory, between the performers and the spectators, between themselves and their heirs. But their words were not bridges: they were canoes.

Canoes are slight craft; they fight against the current, cross the river, can land on the other bank, but one can never be sure how their cargo will be received and used. We write with the precision of a good craftsman and then, incredulously, re-read our texts, which are now far removed from the tensions that generated them.

But what, then, is good communication? 'Good management of misunder-standings', Jean-Marie Pradier, one of the readers of this book when it was yet unfinished, judiciously answered me.

Canoes navigate the currents of misunderstanding. One would like them to be the stable pages of a book and instead they are letters. And we do not know if or when they will reach their destination, nor how they will be understood if they are read, nor by whom.

Only the action is alive, but only the word remains

Letter to Jerzy Grotowski, on the occasion of the first performance of *Itsi Bitsi*.

Holstebro, 1 June 1991

Dear Jurek,

Here the wind is blowing, darkness falls at midnight, the summer is coming.

You once said that you are like Aramis, who when he was a musketeer always talked about becoming a monk, and when he then began his religious career always talked about his life as a soldier. Nowadays you often analyse your productions of twenty and thirty years ago. For a long time, you haven't wanted to make any more productions. Those who have seen your work know that you could make marvellous ones.

You, however, are weaving other threads. You have fulfilled – you say – the task which was entrusted to you.

In my theatre, new productions now grow with greater frequency than they once did. You have let such things slide out of your life, like the clothes of the woman who rose at dawn and ran towards the voice of her god. While she ran, her dress came undone, slipped off her shoulders and was left behind at the edge of the road: the vestige of another time.

You have often explained your choice. But you owe us no explanations. You ask new questions. Do you still ask *my* questions?

As a way of presenting the production which Iben and I have made, I write about it to you. I ask myself: 'What does a production mean to me? Why is it necessary for me?'

The answer to these questions came almost on its own: 'It is a thread made of artifice and guile. Pull it, but do not break it.'

Iben is performing her life story, her biography. The word 'biography' suggests something graphic: a design, a drawing, a thread. It is representation, not confession.

What did we believe in so many years ago, when you were weaving your productions and I imagined that I was learning about theatre and, instead, was discovering myself while discovering you? You probably already believed in what you believe in today.

Is there, then, something which is steadfast and absolute? If so, it is found in the depths of a labyrinth. The thread thus becomes sacred because it does not bind us but connects us to someone or to something which keeps us alive.

When people talk to me about you, I recognize you, with your intransigent wisdom.

When we meet, we speak an old language and parallel languages.

I have become Danish, you have become French and Italian. But it is not our houses which are important. It is the stories we live in.

Here, in this performance, you will see an actress who says: 'The story must be told.' She is not *an* actress. She is Iben. I did not know that before she came to Odin Teatret, someone had baptized her 'Itsi Bitsi' and had made that name shine in a rock song.

It is a name full of joy. You will see Itsi Bitsi dance when she tells about the day she heard that Eik had died. I myself was astonished by this dance. I tend to look for contrasts, for knots of oppositions, for the grotesque. And here instead radiates the amusing joy of a masked child, a child older than we who are learning to grow old.

We doubt, but the masked child knows: everything is present, time does not exist. One can criss-cross an entire labyrinth in a passionless hour.

The child's face is a broken, corroded, wounded mask. It has no reason to rejoice. But there is joy. The masked child seems to have freed itself of our stubborn hands, the hands of artisans of the grotesque. It seems to be saying: 'Smile – and laugh no more.'

Is this the theatre's artifice? Or reason's guile?

On the thread of the performance, we hang the figures of everyday tragedies: veins, tortured and seduced; the blossoming of indifference; clean-faced youth escaping from the gloomy fever of serenity at-all-costs which in Denmark they call *hygge*.

These stories are probably foreign to you. The boy who invented that name – 'Itsi Bitsi' – is part of Iben's life. He was a skinny kid with red hair, the first beat poet to write in Danish, a model for his generation. Young people today, those around you, those around me, know nothing about that meadow which was mowed down in the sixties. They refer to those years the way we, in Opole, referred to the civil war in Spain. In 1968, the skinny kid with red hair swallowed his poison, in India, alone.

You and your actors (there were seven of them, four are no longer alive) worked in the brick-walled room in Wroclaw on a production which was to take its title from a book of woodcuts by Dürer. We, in the black room in Holstebro, worked on Alcestis and thought of Jan Palac. Iben was a girl without words. I watched her grow, fly and fall. She fell seven times; she got up eight.

She followed me. She followed us. Then we watched as others followed her. And you as well, in spite of being far away, commented from time to time on her journey.

Now, in the theatre, she defends the right of the dead to stay alive: neither mourned nor forgotten.

It is said that a performance is images and metaphors. I am certain about one thing. That this is not so. A performance is real action. This is why I do not allow the thread to be pulled until it breaks.

The real letter I am sending you is not the one on this paper but the flimsy white cloth on which Iben and her two companions, Jan and Kai, dance fragments of life to prevent them from being buried.

I ask myself once again: 'Why send a performance to you?'

We are united by the past, but also by the harsh experience of the discordance and alliance between the *action* and the *word*. We know that only the action is alive but only the word remains, in the spectacular desert of dirty cities and outsized museums.

Eugenio

Quipu

Do we want solid words? Or do we want to smash the solidity of words?

Theories become macabre when they tie one's thought down to concepts and words which were no more than provisional vehicles – canoes.

Provisional does not mean casual or uncertain. It means that the flow of terminology follows the flow of thought according to changing circumstance.

Our 'ancestors' also speak with sardonic and mocking voices.

In short, I said *cruelty* like I could have said *life* or like I could have said *necessity*, because I want to indicate that for me the theatre is an act, an uninterrupted emanation, and that it contains nothing fixed. For me, it is comparable to a real act, and is therefore alive, therefore magical.[1]

It was the theoretician of the 'theatre of cruelty' himself who purged his definition of the excited and violent extremism which had given him a dubious fame.

One day I said that the words are an embroidery on the canvas of the movements. This was one of those metaphors which one happens to use when speaking to students. But the pedants took that image literally and still today, twenty years later, they scientifically denounce my light-winged aphorism.

This is Meyerhold. *Bio-mechanics* and *grotesque* are also light-winged words. We should learn to let them fly. I can imagine Meyerhold watching them fly up into the air, with that derisory (or arrogant?) smile on his face which he sometimes used in order to avoid questions – so much so that, said Eisenstein, one wanted to spit in his eye.

Meyerhold, meanwhile, is observing other butterflies:

And Craig? He is pilloried because he once dared compare actors to marionettes!

And he warns us:

Avoid expressing yourselves with metaphors when dealing with a pedant! He takes everything literally and then torments you.[2]

But it is impossible not to use metaphors. To do so would be to renounce the transmission of experience.

Joining the pedants, the police now also enter the scene:

> I agree with you – Stanislavski writes to Aleksei Ivanovich Angarov, theatre critic and member of the Cheka, Stalin's secret police – I agree with you: there is nothing mystical about the creative process. One must speak clearly. But there are creative experiences, sensations, which cannot be cancelled out without doing great harm to art. When something inside (the subconscious) takes possession of us, we are not aware of what is happening [...] These are the best moments of our work [...] I must speak of these things to my actors and students, but how do I do so without being accused of mysticism?[3]

This was written in 1937, in the Soviet Union, at the height of Stalinism: it could be dangerous to be accused of mysticism. In other times, it would be innocuous or even advantageous. As customs change, spies, police and pedants are dangerous to varying degrees, but their methods of listening and reading remain similar.

At the preface to the Russian edition of *An Actor Prepares* (*Robota Aktera Nad Soboj*, 1938), Stanislavski repeats the words which had already appeared in the letter to Angarov and continues:

> The terminology which I use in this book was not invented by me, but is taken from practice, from students themselves and from beginning performers. In the midst of their work they defined their creative feelings with words. Their terminology is valuable, since it is familiar and understandable to beginners.

Let us draw attention to: 'the terminology [...] is taken from practice'. We continue to read:

> Don't try to find scholarly roots in it. We have our own theatrical lexicon and our own actors' jargon, which life itself has created. To be sure, we do make use of scholarly words – for example, 'the subconscious' and 'intuition' – but they are used by us not in a philosophical, but rather in the simplest workaday meaning.

Now even Stanislavski permits himself a little irony:

> It's not our fault that the domain of stage art is disdained by scholars, that it has remained unexplored and that we have not been given the words for practical work. We had to do what we could, so to speak, with home-made means.[4]

What happens to our words when we speak of technical experiences? They began as simple or ingenuous words which flew effectively when we used them during our work. Taken literally, they become leaden and fall on top of us.

It is not the metaphors which make everything difficult. The 'legs of the

139

table' is a bold metaphor which becomes almost a literal expression through common use. 'Influenza' is a word which stems from mystical thought, but we all know what it means to be in bed with influenza or to be influenced by someone. No one suspects that this word contains a reference to astrology or mesmerism.

When Stanislavski speaks of the 'subconscious', Meyerhold of the 'embroidery on the canvas of the movements' or Craig of 'Über-Marionette', misunderstandings do not arise from the imprecise or figurative nature of the expressions but from the fact that among those who hear or read their words, only a few *have experience of the craft*. It is difficult to understand the concrete, technical, circumstantial references of these expressions which become voluble metaphors.

Our 'ancestors' speak through *quipu*, messages made of knotted strings which, for the Incas, were simply accounting records. When we peer at them through the glass panes of a museum display, they look like esoteric symbols or magic embroideries.

It is not only our predecessors who speak with *quipu*.

I leaf through a booklet from thirty years ago: *Moźliwosc Teatru* (The Possibility of the Theatre). Twenty-four pages, half of which quote excerpts from the writings of Polish critics about the performances at the Teatr 13 Rzedów, the Theatre of the Thirteen Rows, in Opole. The other half of the booklet contains writings by Ludwik Flaszen, its literary director, and some by its artistic director, Jerzy Grotowski. The booklet is the latter's first attempt at synthesis. It was put together in 1962. Grotowski insistently repeats certain general affirmations which sometimes seem obvious and sometimes pure philosophy: what is particular about the theatre is the live and immediate contact between actor and spectator; it is necessary to find a unifying spatial structure for actors and spectators, without which the contact between them is left to chance; the performance is the spark which flashes from the contact between these two ensembles: the actors and the spectators; the director consciously models the contact between the actor ensemble and the spectator ensemble to designate and attack an archetype and thus reach the 'collective subconscious' of the two ensembles; the two ensembles become aware of the archetype by means of the dialectic of apotheosis and derision.[5]

Smoky and suggestive images and concepts, *wishful thinking*: looking back, Grotowski appears to be a dreamer, an incurable utopian. I was beside him in those years and remember something very different: a director who applied himself to the practice of his craft, a technician who only later searched for the words to describe his own procedures.

When I say that he *searched for*, I mean the simple act of looking around to find what one needs.

Reading the 1961 review of his production of Mickiewicz' *Dziady* ('The Ancestors'), Grotowski is struck by the expression 'dialectic of apotheosis and derision' used by critic Tadeusz Kudliński.

In those years, using irony and applying precision, Grotowski amalgamated divergencies, tensions, and paradoxes to shatter the univocal meaning of the theatrical action. He constructed systems of collision between the different scenic elements in order to elicit a con-fusion in the spectator's mind, to compel her/him to react to two or more irreconcilable chains of associations.

He gives his work method various names: 'dialectic of *divertissement* and poetry' or 'dialectic of confirmation and surpassing'. But he also uses the reactions of his spectators, like, for example, the Swiss author Walter Weideli, who writes about a method based on 'testing the pros and cons'. A Polish critic writes about 'love which manifests itself in blasphemy', and Ludwik Flaszen about the 'dialectic of blasphemy and devotion'.

Grotowski tries all these different formulations. He knows the direction in which he wants to go and he knows the technique to get there. But he does not yet know what name to give to the road he travels on. He finally settles on the phrase by Kudlinski, 'dialectic of apotheosis and derision'. For some years this will be his canonical expression, his trademark.

How overbearing are the words which linger on. When one reads 'dialectic of apotheosis and derision', one has the impression that one is confronting a theory: take a text, a character, an idea. Confirm them, exalt them, make them triumph in the spectator's mind, and then overturn and deride them, possibly simultaneously.

Result: actor–shamans and shocked spectators.

This is the reader's intellectual abortion. The reality, unfortunately, is exactly the opposite.

'Dialectic of apotheosis and derision' says nothing technical. It is a good memo, not a good explanation of 'how to do'. It is the right sign on the street, but tells us nothing of the street's topography. And as a street sign, it has been astutely chosen, in a country with marxist or clerical bosses.

Grotowski has nearly always selected from other sources the formulas which have made his theatrical revolution famous. Just recently, he extracted the definition 'art as a vehicle' from a conference by Peter Brook and adopted it as the official denomination of his current research. He even found the historical definition 'poor theatre' in an article by Ludwik Flaszen on the *mise en scène* of *Akropolis*.[6]

Grotowski does not look for the definitions for his own work, he finds them. From time to time, he throws away the entire arsenal of words and renews his language.

The struggle against the fixity of words is characteristic of masters of the stage. They do not defeat the overbearance and insufficiency of words with mutism but with mutation.

In some cases, circumstance and prudence have suggested a change of terminology. Stanislavski got rid of 'soul', 'spirit', 'psyche', and from a certain point on, spoke of 'physical actions'. Meyerhold called the same field of work 'dance', then 'the grotesque', then 'bio-mechanics'. His language became more and more materialistic but was not, however, indicative of any substantial change in the perspectives of his work.

There is a certain volubility in the use of words which is not due to the artist's incoherence or whimsical temperament. It is the only suitable way of evoking technical experience: by means of shadows and reflections. Something absent must project its shadow onto the word-screen which is presenting technical advice, artistic politics, poetic visions, scientific hypotheses.

The branch of a tree in flower trembles in the breeze at dusk and its outline is projected on a cloth. The cloth is hiding two clandestine lovers. There is no butterfly on the branch. And yet I see the shadow of a butterfly land on the shadow of the branch. A book on Theatre Anthropology must conclude by clarifying its own attitude with respect to words.

Words become *presence* if we know how to recognize and accept the nature of their shadows. It is difficult to protect their fragile wings, to let them fly, glide, and metamorphose from translation to translation. We must not be concerned if, sometimes, still too connected to the experience which sets them in motion, their outlines are magnified and become a grey haze. The closer the butterflies are to the lamp, the more their shadows on the wall blur. They need only fly a short distance from the source of light for their shadows to acquire a recognizable and precise outline.

The people of ritual

Letter to Richard Schechner.

Holstebro, September 16th, 1991

Dear Richard,

What is most valuable in each one of us cannot make direct contact with the other. Inner lives don't communicate with each other. I am not interested in technique. Yet, in order to achieve what does interest me most, I must pay attention to essential problems related to technique. What I am searching for lies on the other bank of the river. This is why I am preoccupied with canoes.

Last night marked the end of the *Festuge* (a Danish word meaning 'week of festivities') in Holstebro, which this year was called 'Culture Without Borders'. In order to emphasize that the absence of borders is linked to freedom as much as to fluidity, we merged the nine days and nine nights of activities into one continuous performance event entitled *Vandstier*, 'Waterways'.

The title 'Culture Without Borders', which might seem optimistic, has a malicious undercurrent. When the delineation of borders is lost, identity is threatened. And insecurity over identity leads to rigour, to an exasperated attempt to give oneself a profile by opposing others. Intolerance, xenophobia and racism come out into the open.

142

On the other hand, borders are sheer illusions, and they are sometimes imposed. Then, they lead to suffocation.

During the *Festuge*, a symposium was held on Danish cultural politics. Politicians, administrators, journalists, an anthropologist and a professor of literature spoke. They discussed culture as a means of conquering and safeguarding identity in a Europe which is in the process of abolishing borders.

One of the speakers said: 'Look what happens when the contours of a state are obliterated. Look at Yugoslavia, where nobody knows any more what it means to be a Yugoslav: old divisions, nationalisms, and ethnic fundamentalism are revived.' Somebody else replied: 'This happens for the very opposite reasons, not because of the loss of a solid profile, but because the profile was artificial. It was a straitjacket, imposed in the name of an abstract ideology to repress a reality which is now exploding. The explosion is violent because the union was violent.'

Something similar has happened in the theatre of this century which is now about to end: the erosion of the definite borders which gave identity to theatre of European origin; the invention of small traditions; the growth of separate cultures.

In order to understand the theatre of the twentieth century, it is necessary to keep in mind that some theatres and groups have functioned, and continue to function, not only as ensembles, but also as tribes. Tribe is the wrong word, though, because it evokes archaic images. It is better to speak of 'theatres which invent small traditions'.

The invention of traditions can lead to sectarianism and ideological intolerance. The theatre has also had its fundamentalist movements (Stanislavskian, Brechtian, Grotowskian . . .). When fundamentalist movements cannot sustain themselves by force, when they are restricted to the use of cultural weapons, they become substantially innocuous and are weakened by their own rigidity; it is enough for fashion to change and they disappear in smoke.

When we think of interculturalism, we have the tendency to think in terms of the cultural divisions we learned in school (Europe, Asia, Africa, popular cultures, the cultures of people studied by anthropologists, Judaism, Islam, Hinduism . . .). We forget, however, that the abstract term 'theatre' in fact refers to non-homogenous phenomena, each with boundaries created by itself and by its context. Limited boundaries sometimes generate a superiority complex; in other cases, they may encourage exchange, create the need to go into depth and to venture forth into the different.

You would have enjoyed being here in Holstebro during these days because you like to move in that no-man's-land between daily life and the organized performance situation, between performance and ritual.

We remained in this no-man's-land for nine days and nine nights, dissolving the theatre into the town and absorbing the reality of the town into the theatre. But mixing with others puts the consistency of one's own borders to the test. It is a way of deepening the differences and of defining oneself. When performers throw themselves into the daily life of a street or a market, they are not blending with the local people; they don't establish a communion with them. They are merely solidifying their own identities, and therefore their own differences. This leads to the possibility of creating a relationship.

The intercultural dimension of the world in which we live is not a conquest; it is a state of danger. When it remains inert, awareness of co-existence with diversity generates indifference. It unleashes rage if the stranger comes too close.

You are familiar with the greyness of Holstebro and with its plastic colours. So you can imagine the surprise of seeing it traversed by two camels, carrying a little fellow in a top hat and his child-double on their backs. But surprise made the passers-by turn their eyes away. For me, this is one of the images of interculturalism when it bursts into the routines of our lives. I am talking about the first morning of the *Festuge*. By the ninth day, things had changed. People were accustomed to no longer being afraid of showing their curiosity and the performers could circulate in the streets and supermarkets, schools, churches and barracks, confident of creating a relationship that went beyond the involuntary spectator's usual limits of acceptance.

The more uniform our panorama seems when seen from afar, the more when seen close up it resembles an intricate tapestry of minute and diverse cultures. Perhaps we should say sub-cultures, if only the word could lose its ring of inferiority.

I wonder whether what I am about to tell you pertains to inter-culturalism and theatre. I believe it does.

Every four hours, in a large carpark on the roof of a supermarket, groups of people united by the same profession, hobby, or condition, presented themselves: the archers' and rowers' clubs, the owners of trained Alsation dogs, of old American cars, music students, motorcycle police, the homemaker's association, the firefighters.

A dozen recruits got down from a military truck and stood to attention – in their underwear. They then demonstrated the elaborate 'dressing' procedures which transform men into soldiers: their daily uniform, their off-duty uniform, parade attire, war gear, with their faces painted black and their helmets covered with leaves, ending up looking like armoured extra-terrestrials, their faces deformed by gas masks. Next to these, a *kathakali* performer, made huge by his costume and crown, was dilating his face with the green and white make-up which turned him into a mythical figure.

144

Fox-hunters and their buglers arrived, as well as horses from the riding school. Centaurs appeared: those young men in black leather on motorcycles who intimidate us when they ride through our cities. They roared out their performances to the accompaniment of a violin, at first drowning its sound, and then accentuating it by suddenly switching off their engines. They exhibited their menace, transforming it into vitality and openness. Boys and girls in white pyjamas stopped speaking Danish and shouted in an unfamiliar language, Korean, while they moved according to the martial ballet of *taekwondo*.

It was interesting to notice how disconcerted and astonished the spectators were. They must surely have known that these activities went on in Holstebro, just as they probably know that there are men with four wives, or people who burn their dead and eat the soup they make from the ashes. The sub-cultures they saw were recognizable. What wasn't clear to them was the reason why all these people had come out of their shells and were invading the time and space of this carpark, day and night, with or without observers, even in the rain.

In the middle of the carpark, a fifteen-metre long wooden ship was being constructed according to the elegant design of an architect; it was not seaworthy (it not being possible to build a real ship in only nine days and nine nights). Everything taking place there seemed to be in honour of the ship, without taking the spectators into consideration. The numerous small sub-cultures of Holstebro, once exposed, demonstrated that it was one's next door neighbour who was truly *exotic*.

Here in Holstebro, it starts to get cold around mid-September. On the first few nights of the *Festuge*, there were not many people on the supermarket roof. But as time went by, the place became the centre of the town, a sort of secular temple where the long, unsailable ship was slowly taking shape, and where, after this week, there would be nothing left other than the memory of what had been. In this asphalted, open air 'temple', a ship's bell rang out every half hour, day and night, and *De store Skibe* by Frans Winther was sung. Every four hours, day and night, horses, performers, cars, dogs, soldiers and other representatives of the invisible Holstebro appeared.

It was a lay liturgy, created by the Hotel Pro Forma Theatre from Copenhagen. We from Odin Teatret participated every midnight, with a performance evoking the ghosts of sailors.

On the last day, we carried the long ship to the park and buried it in true Viking style, while a tiny sailboat drifted up into the sky. The trees in the park were decked with crimson flowers and golden apples. Floating islands caught fire in the middle of the lake, while black-clad Death paddled the Trickster's small boat across its still waters. A mother sat in the boat with her newborn child.

During the entire week, the performers spread out into different parts of the town. At dawn, groups of two or three went to greet the town bakers at their ovens with a short performance. Others would show up, unexpectedly, at birthday parties in people's homes. Some met incoming trains. Others slipped quietly into a meeting of the Town Council, first appearing as jesters and then, like influential monks from the past, admonishing the mayor and the councillors.

There were real performances: by Odin Teatret and by the Italian group, Teatro Tascabile, skilled in performing on stilts an elegant waltz from the time of Anna Karenina. The Teatro Tascabile performers are also experts in *kathakali*, so expert that they are recognized as such even in India. They danced with their Indian guru, accompanied by his musicians. This theatre comes from Bergamo, an ancient mountain city close to Milan and Bellagio, the town where you organized the colloquium on interculturalism at the Rockefeller Foundation's villa last February.

In addition to Teatro Tascabile, there was Akadenwa, a group from Aarhus, the second largest city in Denmark. Its performers are members of a mountain climbing club. They give performances climbing the walls of houses, church steeples, town hall towers, tall chimneys. There are no mountains in Denmark.

A Danish mountaineer is, after all, no less strange than a *kathakali* performer who was born and lives in Bergamo. For both, what is important is to find the appropriate context for their professional self-definition. It is said that Harlequin came from Bergamo. But Harlequin, who has become the universal symbol of the fantasy and anarchy of the theatre, was almost certainly invented in France four or five hundred years ago.

There is no *genius loci*, genie of the place, either in theatre or culture. Everything travels, everything drifts away from its original context, and is transplanted. There are no traditions which are inseparably connected to a particular geographical location, language or profession.

What happened this week is something very new to me and my companions from Odin Teatret. Yet it also evokes flavours familiar to us. We have already experienced something similar: the sensation that a metamorphosis is taking place and that we are not yet able to give a name to it. Seventeen years ago, after ten years of giving performances behind closed doors for a few dozen spectators, we burst out into the streets and squares of southern Italian villages. And from there we then toured much of the planet, bartering theatre. I was about to say: 'we went to central places and to isolated places'. But wherever you fix the point of your compass is the centre.

Now we have made a journey in our own home. True travellers know this experience very well: the unknown world is discovered when one returns.

Tomorrow, Odin Teatret's actors will leave for Copenhagen. Essentially, it's no different from touring Poland or Brazil. It takes us just as close and just as far away. This evening, all of us who worked on the *Festuge* gathered in our theatre for a farewell dinner. In these situations, among men and women of our profession, I feel at home regardless of where we are in the world. You also made this point in your essay 'Magnitudes of Performance': performers from distant cultures meet and experience more affinity with each other than with their compatriots.

There is theatre in interculturalism. And there is interculturalism in the theatre.

Dear Richard, I don't want a country made up of a nation or a town. I don't believe in it. Yet I do need a country. This is why, in simple terms, I do theatre.

I ask myself the question Jean Améry (one of the greatest country-less men of our times) put to himself: 'How much country does a man need?' I have been lucky: my country has expanded. It does not consist of land or geography. It is made up of history, of people.

When talking, one often uses generalizations to speed up the conversation. So I sometimes speak of my interest in Indian theatre and of the contributions Odissi dance has made to ISTA, the International School of Theatre Anthropology. In reality, I do not collaborate with Odissi dance or Indian theatre but with Sanjukta Panigrahi, whom I consider a compatriot. Similarly, thirty years ago, I indentified with those children at the Kathakali Kalamandalam in Cheruthuruthy who, before dawn, would burn incense in front of the picture of the school's founder. I have met some of those children years later, as mature men and established performers. They remember me, and I remember them as they were thirty years ago: somewhat frail, with cheeky yet melancholy smiles, their eyes big, enlarged by exercises. Why shouldn't I think of them as compatriots?

Sanjukta is not 'an Indian': she is Sanjukta. After all the years we have been working together, I find it hard to think of her as an Indian. Just as she only rarely, almost as an afterthought, remembers that I am a European.

What would you call this? Interculturalism? Humanism? The culture of work?

It is not only love of the other. It is the need to know oneself.

One night, in Bellagio, I asked you for your definition of interculturalism. You replied that you were not interested in defining it, that you preferred it to remain a gravitational field, an open perspective, a black hole. You were smiling as you said this. It is to this smile which I am now speaking.

The gods have left. We are vessels without a crew, restless vessels carried by obscure currents. And yet, I hold a belief: only by measuring myself against others can I give a meaning to the route and find my identity.

I am interested in a specific intercultural perspective: to explore the pre-expressive level of the performer's behaviour. Sometimes you share my interest. You say that the biologist in you agrees with me, but that the politician in you does not. Sometimes you participate with me in the discovery of this common land that nourishes the roots of diverse performative practices. Other times, you shake your head, preferring your favorite study, the description of social interactions.

It is at the performer's 'biological' level, in the domain of impulses and counter-impulses, the *sats*, and the physical and vocal score, that my individual research and my individual needs have become political; they interweave with the similarly deep and incommunicable needs of those people who have become my companions. Only by learning how to navigate in these technical waters, whose surface is cold, have they become 'my' actors and I 'their' director. And we have acted together, changing something around us.

When we speak of culture, that is, of relationships, the subject of identity is always at the centre of our discourse.

Our ethnic identity has been established by history. We cannot shape it.

Personal identity is built by each of us on our own, but unwittingly. We call it 'destiny'.

The only profile on which we can consciously act as rational beings is the profile of our professional identity.

When we look around us and compare our craft to the technology of the times, or when we compare our small circle of spectators to mass media audiences, we feel archaic. The theatre seems to us to be a vestige from another time.

If we then compare this vestige to the images of what it used to be, our dismay increases: the ritual is empty.

What is 'an empty ritual'? Is it one that is meaningless, characterized by the absence of values, something which is debased?

Emptiness is absence. But it is also potentiality. It may be the darkness of a crevasse. Or the stillness of a deep lake from which unexpected signs of life emerge.

In the stew of cultures, where old borders creak, distintegrate or become sclerotic, theatre is not a people's ritual.

But it can become the people of ritual.

It cannot remain isolated. But it can be an island.

Every theatre is part of an historical and cultural context from which it cannot escape. Theatre can, however, possess a diversity, an energy

148

of its own by means of which it can translate, in its particular way, the mould of the world it is part of, re-inventing and even inverting it.

We could say that in the theatre the seeds of rebellion, refusal and opposition can be preserved. Perhaps it suffices to remember the old saying: the theatre must be a mirror. But the mirror is not only the performance. The mirror is the whole island: the men and women who cultivate it, their relationships, their boldness. Jan Kott reminded us of this a few years ago when discussing the theatre and one of the recent political upheavals in Europe: the mirror reproduces the image but it also reverses it. What on the outside is on the right, in the mirror is on the left. The world can be turned upside down.

In order to realize these possibilities, one has to be able to avoid identifying oneself totally with the present.

The flying houses which I have built with my companions from Odin Teatret and with the people from ISTA are inhabited by ancestors whose presence is invisible but concrete. Every time there is a problem to be dealt with, a difficult step to take, or a new situation to decipher, my thoughts turn to how Brecht behaved, to what Artaud said, to what actors did at the time of the Renaissance and during the Religious Wars. I think of Opole or Moscow, Stanislavski or . . . It is true, those were different times. But our times too are 'different', if we compare them to the times we yearn for.

The present is complex and contradictory. It is enigmatic. Once we look deeply into it, it is difficult to pull our eyes away. We are fascinated by and lose ourselves in the labyrinth of all there is to be seen, pondered and evaluated. Time and generations have not yet eroded the labyrinth to the point of giving it the outline of a landscape. We get entangled as we try to understand, condemn and change the scenery of our present. There is never a moment to raise one's eyes. This is how we tame ourselves to the spirit of our times.

When I was in Opole, Ludwik Flazen used to tell me a story. He would tell it to me, for example, every time I got too worked up about something. One is unable to take one's eyes off something one hates, just as one cannot take them off something one loves. Benvenuto Cellini tells of how, in the streets of Rome, he used to gaze fondly upon his mortal enemy (whom he later killed), devouring him with his eyes, like a lovesick young man staring at a beautiful girl. But it wasn't Cellini's story that Flaszen told me. It was the story of a head and a wall.

A wall was blocking a man's way. He threw himself headfirst against it, determined to knock it down. He hurt his head but kept on. He tried again and again, blinded by the fire of his own rage and pain, banging his head against the wall, banging, banging. Then there was no more resistance. His head had become the wall.

The past is not behind us. It is above us. It is what is left of the vertical dimension.

History, the past that we know, is the tale of the possible. It makes it possible for us to catch a glimpse of the world and the theatre the way it could be. Our dissatisfaction with the present is nourished by this profound dialogue with what was different in the past. This dissatisfaction is what we call our 'spiritual life'.

The dead are the true, diverse interlocutors, Richard. Not macabre corpses, but invisible presences.

The interculturalism which challenges me most is the vertical one.

Eugenio

Shadow-words

For a long time, I played one of the characters typical of our intercultural planet: the man who travels to the most distant places and in the streets around home, with knapsack on his back, glasses on his nose and notebook in hand.

Lumpy notebooks, which after the sweat of the Orient and the Mediterranean summers, have dried out in the pockets of my jeans. Crumpled notebooks, crammed with useless notes, preserved with care, containing the framework of words around which this paper canoe has taken me.

My research into Theatre Anthropology began as translation exercises. I asked Hideo Kanze, I Made Pasek Tempo, Krishna Nambudiri, Tsao Chunlin, Katsuko Azuma, I Made Bandem, Sanjukta Panigrahi, how they translated, into their working languages, words like 'energy', 'rhythm', 'power', 'form', 'score'. I asked Dario Fo, Decroux (through his students), Grotowski, Franca Rame, Maria Casarés, Bob Wilson, what word they used where we from Odin Teatret use the word *sats*.

And how to translate *jo-ha-kyu* into my work experience?

Terms from the different working languages slowly began to revolve, and like in a magic lantern, became each other's shadows. Finally, as they sped up, they broke apart and became superimposed and delineated a unitary design. For a long time, I asked myself if this was an optical illusion, if I was perhaps projecting the already known onto the unknown. I had to accept the evidence: this unitary design was, objectively, the basis of the performer's presence. Beneath the phantasmagoria of the different images there was a pre-expressive level, common to all.

All butterflies are different.

Each language has its own word for 'butterfly'.

And yet we are able to recognize what there is in common among the words 'butterfly', 'motyl', 'papillon', 'chocho', 'farfalla', 'sommerfugl', 'mariposa'. We know how to move from one word to another, we know how to translate.

Every performing artist is different.

Each one uses different words, different metaphors, different aesthetic or scientific orientations. Dissimilar histories navigate a common river.

Do we know how to translate?

On the one hand, the science of the performer is the arid anatomy of the *bios*, of the skeleton-in-life and the body-in life. On the other hand, it is knowing how to vault among the words and with the words, to change and invent them, because even the mind must dance, from thought to thought, around the pattern of the action.

> Personally, I must admit that we do not shrink from using these 'quack' formulas. Anything that has an unusual or magical ring stimulates the imagination of both actor and producer.[7]

This is what Grotowski said to me thirty years ago, in 1963. Was it self-irony? An invitation to treat the words as shadows, light-winged butterflies which could carry us a long way?

Certain words are stimuli. But we must be careful: stimulus is fuel, it works if one burns it. A stimulus is something profoundly different from a description or a definition. One must above all know how to transform it into fuel.

I witnessed the moment at which the first exercises which later developed into the 'famous training' of the Teatr Laboratorium were introduced into the Teatr 13 Rzedów.[8]

Grotowski was working on Wyspianski's *Akropolis*. He had set the action in a place opposite to that foreseen by the author: not in the castle of Wawel, the sanctuary of the Polish nation, but in the sanctuary of extermination – Auschwitz.

There is always a gap between the director's intentions and the reality which the performers present. During the rehearsals, Grotowski had trouble with one of the actresses' faces, which showed an excess of expressivity. He thought of hiding it behind a mask, but this solution didn't work. He then tried to transform the face itself into a mask, freezing it in one single expression. He justified this by evoking the petrified faces of the 'Muslims', the name given to the internees of Auschwitz who had reached the lowest levels of survival.

It was a good solution! He applied it to all the other actors.

In the production, all the actors' faces were frozen into impassivity, in spite of the horror of the situation. The blankness of their faces was in contrast to the vitality of their bodies, which were composed in a detailed design of movements between dance and acrobatics. The unstable base of their acting was the clumsy wooden prisoners' clogs they wore.

The actors had prepared themselves for these performances with daily exercises not dissimilar from gymnastic exercises. Exercises for the voice, traditional plastic exercises, pantomime and certain yoga positions were also introduced into the work schedule. From out of this mixture, the 'training'

151

began to distil and develop, later freeing itself from the functional and episodic purposes which had given birth to it.

Outside the rehearsal room, Grotowski used words like 'holy actor', 'trance', 'self-penetration', or the image of an actor-shaman. In practice, he persistently used the oxymoron, the co-existence of opposites, the contradictions in terms incarnate in the actors' bodies. He translated the postulates of modern poetry into physical actions.

He was, in fact, creating *spatial poetry*.

The word 'poetry' elicits numerous associations confirmed by the dictionary. Poetry = idealism, beauty, grace, fascination, inspiration, harmony, lyricism, the ineffable, as indicated by expressions like 'the poetry of nature', 'the poetry of the sea'.

But when the poet Antonin Artaud became an actor, he defined scenic art as 'spatial poetry' ('*poésie dans l'espace*'). As someone who knew how to use the techniques of 'wordsmiths', he spoke of concrete procedures. He writes:

> This physical language [. . .] this solid material language [. . .] [of the theatre] is composed of everything filling the stage, everything that can be shown and materially expressed on stage, intended first of all to appeal to the senses, instead of being addressed primarily to the mind, like spoken language.

He asserts:

> This language created for the senses must first take care to satisfy the senses. This would not prevent it later amplifying its full mental effect on all possible levels and along all lines. It would also permit spatial poetry to take the place of language poetry.

Today we would use the term 'performance text'. In fact, Artaud claimed that every single expressive means used on the stage (dance, plasticity, pantomime, diction, scenography, lights, music, costumes . . .) has its own effectivness. But that there is, in addition

> [. . .] a kind of ironic poetry arising from the way it [the expressive means] combines with other expressive means. It is easy to see the result of these combinations, their interaction and mutual subversion.[9]

In the early twenties, Artaud worked as an actor at Charles Dullin's Théâtre de l'Atelier. There, Edgar Allan Poe's poems and theoretical writings on poetry had been chosen as a guide for the actors' improvisations. Other 'masters', in addition to Poe, were the Japanese painters. It was possible to recognize, in the poetry of the former and the images of the latter, a common knowledge of the art of isolating details, of subjecting them to opposing tensions, of taking them out of their usual context.[10]

Artaud (like Dullin, like Meyerhold . . . like Grotowski) often spoke of the actor's magic.

152

Edgar Allan Poe, Baudelaire, Rimbaud and Mallarmé also spoke of 'magic', 'incantation', or 'sorcery'. And they did not mean anything vague. They were referring to the indissolubility of effectiveness and precision. The subtle effectiveness of a phrase or an image – they said – has not so much to do with what that particular phrase or image represents or suggests but with the exactitude with which its various segments have been assembled.

From Poe on, poets had dissected the art of deformation, of surprise, of sudden changes of direction, contrasts, dissonances, oxymorons. They had exposed the principles of non-linear montage, the art of de-composing and re-composing phrases in an extra-daily dimension. 'The words I use' – wrote Paul Claudel in the line of a poem – 'are the words of every day, but . . . they are not at all the same.'

There is no doubt that *spatial poetry*, the performer's extra-daily technique, and pre-expressive behaviour are different ways of suggesting the same reality which, however, projects different shadows.

Is Artaud then the same as Grotowski? Grotowski the same as Meyerhold? And do Meyerhold's 'dance', 'the grotesque' and 'bio-mechanics' – as we have repeated several times – refer to the same procedures?

Yes, 'dance', 'the grotesque' and 'bio-mechanics' are synonyms, just as 'cruelty', 'life', 'necessity', and 'uninterrupted emanation [. . .] that contains nothing fixed', were for Artaud synonyms according to his shadow-words.

For Meyerhold, dance, the grotesque and bio-mechanics were not three different stages in his artistic evolution. They were three stimulating ways of referring, at different times, to his analytical work on *znak otkaza* ('the sign of refusal'), on *rhythm* and on *tempo*, on *raccourci*, on *predigra* ('pre-acting'), on principles of precision and distortion in the design of movements.

I repeat once more: the differences which distinguish the results and styles of the various artists whose testimony has been the cargo of this paper canoe are enormous. To throw light upon the hidden, elementary morphology which different performers have in common does not mean joining them together in a unique and universal idea of theatre.

The risk run by Theatre Anthropology is not the homogenization of its sources. This is what historians call that professional deformation which takes hold of the researcher when s/he espouses a scientific theory or ideology and uses it to interpret every phenomenon, measuring everything with the same schemas, always reaching the same results, illusorily adding confirmation to confirmation.

The principle risk of Theatre Anthropology is its readers, if they try to give excessive weight to the wings and shadows of changing words. And among those readers must also be included the one who wrote this book.

In particular, there is the risk that the words which represent the extremes of a range of possibilities will take on too much weight. Let us imagine a film in black and white. The black is hardly ever seen, nor is the white; the film is a symphony of grays. And yet it is correct to define it as being in black and white because they are the limits of a vast gamut. As a way of indicating through concepts the existence of a gamut of possibilities, it is advisable to emphasize the extremes: *lasya* and *tandava*, warm performer and cold performer, identification and alienation, Animus and Anima, North Pole performers and South Pole performers, *keras* and *manis*, introversion and extroversion. *This insistence on extremes facilitates the explanatory clarity and not the practical effectiveness.* In the work situation, opposing poles are considered to be the limits of a wide territory which one must explore. Otherwise the results will be pure mechanics. One must not work on the extremes, but on the range of nuances which lie between them. The body-in-life is a question of nuances.

I have at times imagined Theatre Anthropology as a description of the alphabet, something elementarily practical which guides the performer. At other times, I have imagined it as a path made of words, but able to lead the scholar beyond the words and shadows towards a core which is analogous to experience.

Can the two images be superimposed one upon the other? Can the alphabet be Ariadne's thread?

Silver Horse – a week of work

I never usually work this way. I choose the transcription of this week because someone happened to put my words down on paper and because the situation was anomalous: my ephemeral students were not actors but dancers and choreographers.[11]

Yet more words, none of which I use with my actors at Odin Teatret or when I speak publicly on technique and on theatre.

Behind the closed doors of a work room, words fly with particular intensity, create knots which appear indissoluble and revelatory. And so they are, in *that* moment.

In a work room, one must create a language. A language springing from the situation, part of no system, no theory. An autochtonous and fugitive language.

To repeat dogmatically the terms of Theatre Anthropology can be deceptive and dangerous. But to repeat the words of the 'Silver Horse' would only be ridiculous.

Then why are they here? And why do they conclude this book?

The very language which to you, serious reader, must seem uselessly 'lyrical', 'emotive', 'suggestive', and which you might even reject, is in fact a language fleeing from prefabricated definitions which increase confusion while obscuring the language behind a screen of false precision.

Here we are not making 'poetry'. The poetry is 'spatial'.

Monday

You have been trained not to speak when you are dancing. Let us listen, then, to an author, Robert Louis Stevenson:

> The motive and end of any art whatever is to make a pattern; a pattern, it may be, of colours, sounds, of changing attitudes, geometrical figures, or imitative lines; but still a pattern. [. . .] The true business of the literary artist is to plait or weave his meaning, involving it around itself; so that each sentence, by successive phrases, shall first come into a kind of knot, and then, after a moment of suspended meaning, solve and clear itself. In every properly constructed sentence there should be observed this knot or hitch; so that (however delicately) we are led to foresee, to expect, and then to welcome the successive phrases. The pleasure may be heightened by an element of surprise [. . .]. The one rule is to be infinitely various; to interest, to disappoint, to surprise, and yet still to gratify. [. . .] Style is synthetic.
>
> And the artist, seeking, so to speak, a peg to plait about, takes up at once two or more elements or two or more views of the subject in hand; combines, implicates and contrasts them [. . .]
>
> The web, then, or the pattern: a web at once sensuous and logical [. . .].[12]

Task: Prepare a scene on the theme: *The dark hands of oblivion.*

Comment: *From* blood
                            to the skin
                            to the colour

Those of you who did the scene while seated, will do it again standing. Those of you who prepared the scene standing, will do it again sitting down. The object of this exercise is to retain the *blood* while changing the *skin* in space. It is necessary to keep the *blood* from coagulating when this change is made. The *blood* is the internal motor, the motivation, the personal image, the invisible. The *skin* is its visible manifestation, the action in the space. Practically speaking, I am asking you to find an equivalent for each of the actions from the original scene and to present them in a different situation. The ability to create equivalents while still conserving the same *blood* is the first sign of your craft.

Task: Now we have a sequence enacted in two different ways, but with the same internal current: with one *blood* (motivation) and two *skins* (the form). Now take the actions from both *skins* and assemble them in a sequence which allows you to reveal the density of the *blood* more clearly.

Comment: *To be in life
                            a step?*

a beat?
an image?

In the human organism, the smallest living unit is the cell. And in dance? In dance, the smallest unit is the action.

It is necessary to define the action in a functional way so that it can help us in our daily work. By action we mean *that which changes me and the perception which the spectator has of me*. What must change is the muscular tonus of my entire body. This change engages the spinal column, where the impulse of the action is born.

When this happens, there is a change in balance and in the pressure of the feet on the floor. If I move my hand and start the movement at the elbow, this movement does not change the tonus of my whole body. It is a gesture. And the elbow joint does all the work. But if I do the same thing trying to push against someone who is resisting me, then the spinal column comes into play, the legs exert a pressure downwards. There is a change of tonus. There is action.

Task: Transform everything that in the previous sequence was only gesture and redundant movement.

Comment:

Above
and below
the sea

I notice two tendencies: you act like marine currents concealed beneath the surface of the sea, or else you move like waves.

Task: Those who belong to the species of the underwater currents will now work by tripling their rhythms. Those who belong to the 'surface waves' must withhold their rhythm, diminishing them three-fold.

Comment: *There is a breathing/transition*
knowing . . .

When one works slowly, one tends to lose the breathing of the rhythm. It becomes uniform, monotonous. The rhythm's breathing is a continuous alternation – inhalation, exhalation – a continuous and assymetrical variation, perceptible in every *action-cell* of the sequence.

BEWARE! There is one kind of fluidity which is continuous alternation, variation, breathing, and which protects the individual, tonic, melodic outline of each action. There is another fluidity which is monotonous and has the consistency of condensed milk. This latter fluidity, instead of keeping the spectator's attention alert, numbs it.

The secret of a 'rhythm-in-life', like the waves of the sea, leaves in the wind, the flames of a fire, is in the pauses. They are not static stops but dynamic preparations, transitions, changes between one action and another. One action ends and is held for a fraction of a second at the same time as it changes into the impulse for the successive action.

When the pause–transition loses its withheld pulsation, which was ready to continue, it coagulates and dies. Dynamic transition becomes a static pause.

The totality of the human being is made up of the complementarity between the invisible and the visible.

The invisible is the psychic, mental process.

The visible is its physical manifestation.

Every time I think of something, although I may not realize it, my thought has repercussions in my muscular tonus.

BEWARE! In general, dancers or actors know very well what their next actions will be. *While carrying out one action, they are already thinking of the next action and are mentally anticipating it. This automatically involves a physical process which affects their dynamism and is perceived by the spectator's kinaesthetic sense.* Now we can understand why a performance often does not succeed in stimulating our attention: because, on the sensory level, we foresee what the performer is about to do.

The performer must carry out the action by negating it.

To carry out an action by negating it means inventing an infinity of variations within it. This obliges you to be one hundred per cent inside the action so that the next one can be born as a surprise for the spectator and for yourself.

Task: Repeat the same sequence by negating it. To achieve surprise, you must surprise yourselves. Make the action happen a second before or a second after one would expect it to do so.

Comment: *The transformation*
                                of prose into poetry . . .

If I take a balloon filled with gas and reduce its size by a third, I increase the internal tension. You can also reduce the dimensions of your actions and at the same time increase the tension of the *blood*. You can 'absorb' your action to the point of immobility, while still retaining the impulse which models it precisely in space. In ethology, this would be called a 'movement of intention': someone sitting down but ready to stand up.

Performers can reduce an action to its essence, to its impulse. They know how to distil each sequence, keeping only the essential actions, elaborating them phase by phase, transforming – to use literary terms – prose into poetry.

Task: Absorb the actions of the previous sequence by a half.

157

Comment: *The presence of the cells*
or the sorcery of the mosaic

When we see a living organism, we perceive it in its totality. But this totality has different levels of organization. Just as in the human body there is the level of organization of the cells, the molecules and the organs, so there are also three distinct levels of organization in a scenic situation.

The first is the *level of the action which is*. Like a living cell.

The second is the *level of the action in relationship*, which does not necessarily signify anything for the spectator.

The third level, *the action in the context*, is that of the totality from which distinct functions and meanings develop.

The work we have done until now belongs to the first level, that of *the action which is*, without any relationship with a context. It is the level of presence, or of pre-expressivity. It is the foundation of the second level (that of the action in relationship) and of the third level (that of the action in the context) which re-awaken the spectator's energy in the form of images, reflections, affective reactions.

Task: Work on the first level, that of *the action which is*. Repeat the original sequence, *The dark hands of oblivion*, applying all the principles which we have defined.

Comment: *A dialogue of colours*
and blood . . .

When one performer's actions come into contact with those of other performers, a relationship is born. The logic here is similar to that of a dialogue: action and reaction. I speak, someone listens to me (dynamically executes the action of listening) and then reacts, that is, responds, and I listen. This alternation, or dialogue, of dynamisms ends up being impregnated with expressive potentiality for the spectator.

Two performers, with their individual action sequences, can follow the dialogue principle by concentrating on keeping the internal tension of the *blood* (the motivation) and the conciseness of the *skin* (the form), while respecting the rhythm of the action/reaction dynamic, but without injecting meaning into the actions/reactions.

Task: Work in pairs on the second level of organization, that of *relationship*. Each dancer, while holding on to her/his original sequence, must establish a relationship with her/his partner. This relationship must not pretend to express or signify anything. It simply respects the logic of the dialogue: I say (do), the other is receptive (listens, reacts, although immobile).

Comment: *Between the visible*
and the invisible . . .

BEWARE! Your *skin* (the form) changes and your action loses its internal tension. You are losing *blood*, losing precision. Inert pauses suffocate the action/reaction dynamic.

The pauses–transitions, when they alter the original dynamism of the individual sequence, create a new dynamism, a new fluidity/variation. The relationship which results from the fortuitous meeting between two individual sequences elicits associations in the first spectator (choreographer or director), who begins to interpret what s/he sees and to project a meaning onto it. The performer works by manipulating two parallel orbits: one invisible, the *blood* (images, rhythms, sounds, concepts, sensations), the other external, which models the actions with precision, absorbing and dilating them to untangle the thread of the chosen theme.

Task: Elaborate the fortuitous relationship which you have obtained and justify it on the basis of a theme which each pair must choose for itself.

Comment: *Between loyalty*
                                                        and betrayal

It is not the theme which makes a scene artistically alive, but its structure, the conscious organization of its different levels.

In your scenes, there are 'suggestive' fragments combined with stereotyped elements. The 'suggestive' fragments are made up of elaborated actions, each with its own profile, with a vibration which stimulates my perception as spectator and induces in me an interpretive process which is personal creation.

The stereotyped elements are the consequence of generalized sensations lacking nuances, scantily detailed and produced using previously learned technical schemas.

BEWARE! *Avoid abstract titles and themes* which are emotionally gratifying but which do not dictate precise actions. For example, one of your titles was *Power*. There is no such thing as 'power' in general. There is a twelve-year-old child, as blond and chubby as a cherub, who has a sparrow in his hand with a string tied around its claw. He makes it fly and holds it back with a precise impulse, laughing gleefully. He dances, seated on a chair, delighting in the bird's warm, soft feathers because he loves it, and his fetid breath (he has not brushed his teeth) asphyxiates the bird.

BEWARE! *Betray the action.* If, in this process of elaboration, you do not protect your actions, if you are not loyal to them, to what makes them breathe, to their *blood*, then you become a toy in the hands of the choreographer or director. You become mercenaries who only execute and not artisans/artists who give life to their actions by negating them.

Tuesday

Task: Create a three-minute sequence. Its title is *Silver Horse*. Do not be deceived by the apparent meaning. Go deep down into the mine of the possible meanings and dig out your own truth, evoked by this title. Perhaps it is about a centaur, or a lover who gives this name to the loved one, about a Cheyenne warrior whose name it is, about an alcoholic and his bottle of White Horse whisky or about the solitude of a poet who is waiting for his Pegasus to inspire him.

Comment: *A knot*
                                                                     of light . . .

When we speak of text, we immediately think of written words. But the excerpt from Stevenson which we read the first day guides us back to the origin of this term: text as texture, as a web, as the result of weaving, of an interlacing of distinctly coloured threads and heterogenous materials. Weaving words on paper leads to 'written text': to a poem, a novel, a play.

Weaving actions in space and time leads to a 'sensuous and logical' text: to theatre and dance. The actions which are woven together are the words (in both their logical and sonorous aspects), the physical actions, the relationships, the changes of light, the fragments of music, the various ways of using the costumes, the proximity or distance of the spectators.

Stevenson the craftsman gives us an exceptional piece of advice for increasing the richness of the 'sensuous and logical' text: to take two or more elements, two or more distinct perspectives of the theme being dealt with, and to move from one to the other, creating changes of vision and leaps of tension. An alternate current which transforms the *linear flow* of the 'telling', the 'performing'. Like a river which makes a loop and turns back on itself, broadens into a lake and then plummets resolutely as a waterfall. Like those paintings by Picasso where he has woven his threads of line and colour, leaping from one perspective to another.

Task: Now we will work on the third level, that of *the actions in the context*. Take the *Silver Horse* sequence and re-elaborate it using two or more points of view, leaping from one to another, refining and enhancing the innumerable variations and nuances, details and micro-rhythms of the 'sensuous and logical' text.

Comment: *A web*
                                                                     of leaps . . .

The precision of the performer's tonic changes and leaps of energy makes the spectator live the experience of an experience and project a multiplicity of interpretations.

During this construction of the text/web, we can use the 'mistakes' or uncertainties which suddenly spring up, as well as the 'certainties' we are consciously looking for. One must develop the ability to integrate 'mistakes', misunderstandings, fortuitous comments and reactions into the 'sensuous and logical' text.

Task: Work with your *Silver Horse*, controlling it and, at the same time, letting it become wilder. Control it by tidying up the actions, chiselling them, distilling them, eliminating those which are not essential. Transform it into a wild animal, making it bound from one perspective to another, from the foreseeable to the surprising, from the obvious to the paradoxical.

Comment: *A language*
                                  of loyalty . . .

I can say in English: 'I was born in a small village.' If I want to translate these words into another language, I must preserve their *blood* (their internal logic), even if the external form changes.

In English: I was born in a small village.

In Italian: *Sono nato in un paesino.*

We have translated one language into another, looking for equivalents. Following the logic of translation, one can say that there is a language of the 'feet', another of the 'hands', another of the 'torso'.

Every action is a precisely modelled knot of energies and can be translated into its equivalent in another language.

Task: Translate the *Silver Horse* actions into the 'language of the feet'. Each action of the sequence must be transposed into the corresponding step according to the rhythm and dynamism of the original action.

Comment: *A language*
                                  in space . . .

You moved in space according to a dynamic sequence in which each step is distinct from every other, just as each word in a sentence is different from every other. You have invented a dance: the *Silver Horse* tango-rock.

Task: Do this sequence in relationship to the music. Pay attention to the particular profile of each step. You must establish a relationship with your partner (in this case, the music) always respecting the *dynamism* and the *design* of the steps you have created.

Comment: *A language*
                                  in danger . . .

You cannot create equivalents or 'translate' a sequence if you have not first assimilated it perfectly.

BEWARE! When we move from one language to another, the action tends to lose precision, its particular tonus is deformed, it becomes an empty movement, a kinaesthetic amoeba. An improvisation fulfils its function only if it can be repeated in all its details, so that it can be elaborated. Even when there are major changes, the action must keep what makes it alive: the *blood*, the motivation, the rhythm, the invisible, internal logic.

161

Task: Translate *Silver Horse* into the 'arm–hand–finger' language. Don't turn into policemen directing traffic. Avoid movements which begin in the joints. Work with precision, looking for the exact equivalent of the muscular tonus of the original action.

Comment: *The continuous*
                                 trembling of life . . .

I look at your hands and fingers and think of marionettes. In theatre and dance, the hands and fingers are often stiff with inorganic tensions and do not show precise impulses. Each action must construct a labyrinth of multiple tensions in every part of your bodies. I do not see this when I watch your hands.

The 'body-in-life' is a polyphony of tensions, tied together by an invisible, internal consistency.

Task: Translate *Silver Horse* into the language of the 'torso'. The spectator must feel the uninterrupted flow of the absorbed actions, the tensions, impulses, 'movements of intention', as we perceive it in the armless torsos of Rodin's sculptures.

Comment: *Without the fluidity*
                                 of drowsy milk . . .

To act, in the theatre, means to intervene in time and space in order to change and to be changed. The impulse of an action, that is, the 'movement of intention' begins in the spinal column. The energy necessary to give rise to precise actions is concentrated in the torso and withheld as an impulse. The actions are born here. One can see that performers are working with actions when even their trunks also execute them in miniature. Arms, hands and fingers are extensions, waiting to intervene. Each cell of this web-in-life, each piece of the sequence-mosaic, has its own specific charge of energy.

Task: Choose one of the *Silver Horse* incarnations and elaborate each one of the leaps of energy which link the actions together. Try to arrive at a fluidity which is different from that which would be born spontaneously. Don't forget the *blood*.

Comment: *Not walls*
                                 of cement, but . . .
                                    the melodies
                                 of your temperature

I don't want to see dance. I don't want to see theatre. I want to find myself face to face with that which 'is-in-life' and which reawakens echoes and silences. I watch you, and in spite of your refined technique, you are like walls of cement. What I miss in your work is a mirror I can enter into, like Alice, where I can encounter the universe of your experiences and mine.

I admire you. I see years of discipline, dedication and research in your virtuosity. But I don't hear your melodies because I can find no nuances, details, micro-rhythms.

When you create a sequence of actions, you must protect it like a newborn child who can be injured by the slightest pressure. You must be aware that there are two kinds of tension: one which aids life and another which suffocates it. At times, your actions are too rapid and breach the transitions. You give the impression of a redundant and unmotivated force. Your actions are *indifferent*.

The artistic process is a process of selection. The spectators may or may not understand the logic of your actions, but they must be sensorially taken by them. This logic must be rooted in your internal space/time. These roots, these ties with what lies underneath your actions 'individualize' that which is technical and reveal the melody of your temperature. It is the most imperceptible tensions in each action which reveal temperament, biography, nostalgia.

Our first obligation as social beings and professionals is to learn to see, to avoid letting ourselves be dazzled by the surface, and to bring the hidden forces into the light.

Wednesday

Task: Sing a song dear to you.

Comment: *Who has lost*
his soul?

The flow of our energy, as a physical and mental process, is materialized in the action of speaking and singing. There are vocal actions just as there are physical actions. Our 'being-in-life' manifests itself through song. There are peoples who believe that the soul is found in the throat: those who cannot sing have lost their souls.

Task: Translate the physical actions of *Silver Horse* into vocal actions. Find the equivalent of the tonus of the physical actions in the tone of the songs. Avoid inert pauses. The pause/silence is a transition in the continual process of the *bios*. Carry out the vocal action with your whole body just as in a physical action. You must sing with your liver and your guts, your genitals and your spinal column. When you sing, rediscover all the tensions, however small, of the *Silver Horse*.

Comment: *Who has lost*
his ancestors?

BEWARE! For those of you who spoke or sang in a language not your own: language is connected to an emotional system. The newborn child moves according to the rhythms of the language spoken by its parents. In this way, our dynamic temperament, our 'vitality', our way of behaving, is connected to the rhythm of the language we speak. When the language of an individual or a people is taken away, an integral part of the affective behaviour contained within speaking and singing is amputated.

Any physical action has its equivalent vocal action. Precision is essential to both of them. There is always the temptation to change, to make variations, that is, to improvise. Anyone can improvise. It is part of the human being's ability to adapt.

It is very difficult, however, to repeat each of the thousand variations of the multiple physical and vocal actions of an improvisation while still conserving its *blood*; to reproduce it exactly, in an immediate way, and make it live as if every action was new and surprised us. This is the performer's craft: to create a structure which holds the spectator's attention and which can be repeated with all the vigour of its *blood* for months and for years, every night.

Task: React with your song to the simple and exact movements of my hand as I raise it, move it sinuously, slowly, forcefully, gently. Follow me with your song as if I was a conductor.

Comment:
> *Singing the space*
> *there are meetings*
> *and I am transformed . . .*

The secret of our work is not in acting but 'reacting'. Vocal actions are reactions. Modern composers use blots, rough sketches, intersecting lines, abstract signs, as the 'notes' of their scores. The interpreter does not read (sing) recognizable notes but reacts with the voice to these graphic stimuli.

A singer once explained to me that her principal exercise consisted of 'singing the space'. The voice grows until it reaches the wall, and then returns. It slides along the floor, clambers up to the ceiling, walks on electric wires like a tightrope walker, rests on the window, jumps out. All this by means of a song or text.

When one sings or speaks a written text, it becomes a fabric of sounds. It is a continuous flow of energy which respects neither full stops nor commas, those conventional pauses used in writing which do not exist when one speaks: when speaking we make only pause–transitions, that is, inhalations. It is important that the convention of the written text does not suffocate the organic process of speaking. It is essential to protect its flow, the fabric of sounds, and bring it to life in vocal actions, *without trying to express anything*.

The *Silver Horse* physical actions can be transformed into vocal actions: dark clouds spreading, white suns burning, dolphins playing, bears dancing, hands scraping the ground and digging deep into the earth, where the darkness is hot, soft, round.

BEWARE! You simulate the physical actions which accompany the vocal actions, gesticulate redundantly, distort the muscles of face and mouth, move incessantly without respecting the exact impulse of the action. The voice must emerge from the stomach/mouth, from the neck/mouth, from the skin/mouth, from the body/mouth, and not only from the face/mouth.

Task: Vocal actions can be absorbed in the same way as physical actions. The energy is withheld until the voice becomes a whisper. Do this with your songs, and then, choose partners and do your individual *Silver Horse* sequences. Establish a relationship, have a dialogue using your vocal actions, while protecting the pauses–transitions. Make the whole space reverberate, even when you are whispering; the corners, the ceiling, a metre beneath the floor, as if spectators were all around you and each one of your actions had to shake and caress them at the same time.

Comment: *Forgetting,*
                 I find memory intact again . . .

When an experience hits us in the stomach, we do not ask questions. We are oblivious to what we see in the scenic space and are overwhelmed by memories from our mental, physical and sensorial space-time. We do not ask ourselves if what we are seeing is theatre or dance. The more we strive to reach this depth, the more the marrow of the action must be defended. The more we reduce the external pattern, the greater is the need to safeguard its essence.

I asked you to absorb your actions during the work in pairs. The objective was to destroy automatisms, to make you concentrate and keep the core of each action, its DNA. When you passed from the individual level to that of relationships, you did not manage to preserve the impulses and internal tensions.

You have practised dance for years and I see only movements. They may be interesting, but they become monotonous because they always rotate in the same energy orbit. I don't see the two distinct perspectives of which Stevenson writes. I don't see tenderness, vigour, doubt, decision. I don't see *you*. I see only learned movements. One action can blossom with a multiplicity of meanings. The biographical context of each spectator determines the perception and interpretation of what happens on stage.

BEWARE! Do not confuse the execution of the actions with the intention to express. Emotion is a reaction. There is an internal or external stimulus and the reaction manifests an emotion. I see a dog. I keep completely still. My immobility makes visible a terror which paralyzes. I see a dog and I begin to run; this reaction expresses the same emotion of terror which makes me flee.

165

For the performer, emotion is always materialized through an action which 'moves' the spectator. The secret of artistic discipline consists of eliminating the superfluous and of distilling the essential, which one must be able to repeat in a chosen context.

The action comes first and is the basis of everything else, with its *blood* and its *skin*, with an invisible motivation and a perceptible form. It is the simplest cell of a complex organism. But if the cells are fragile, the organism, in time, will collapse.

Task: Write your definition of the word 'action'. This definition, image, sound or concept, must be functional for you in your practical work.

Comment:
*To see the light
by switching it off . . .*

To negate by acting. This principle must be applied to the terminology we have learned. We must negate the terminology by forging our own definition of each concept fundamental to our work. We must have a terminology made from our own images, both pragmatic and poetic. Improvisation. Rhythm. Relationship. Tension. Context. *Blood. Skin.* Your task is to refuse, negate by acting. Negate my definitions, invented here with you during these days. Negate them by acting, *creating your own.*

Thursday

Task: Choose an object and find four ways of using it.

Comment:
*Sky
sea or
earth . . .
Rebirth or transition?*

To introduce a prop means working with an active presence which helps us react. You must know how to discover the object's hidden 'lives', its multiple possibilities for use, its most surprising 'incarnations'.

What is its spinal column? How does it move? Can it walk? Dance? Fly? And its rhythm? It is fast? Slow? Heavy? Can it become light? What is its temperament? What associations does it elicit, which can then be immediately negated? How can it be made to live following the logic of contrasting associations? The object has a voice. How can its sonorous possibilities be brought out, how can they be structured melodiously, with accents which underline or contradict the action?

If I work with a scarf, to which universe does it belong? To the sky? To the sea? To the earth? Or does it belong to all these universes together? Then it can become rain, a bird, a snake, can be incarnated in one form or another, with that form's particular spinal column, with its dynamism and its particular rhythm, with that maximum precision which prevents the rain from resembling the snake, and even less a crumpled scarf, manipulated haphazardly.

Task: Use the object in four distinct ways to discover four of its 'lives'. Then a partner will propose two new ways to use it – two new 'lives'.

Comment:
It is raining
a scarf . . .
and I get wet

To establish a relationship with an object (like with a person) means respecting the principle of dialogue. The object acts (speaks) and the performer reacts (listens). In order to act, the object must have its own life. If we control it, if we make it do only what we impose, if we treat it as an inanimate object, a slave which must submit to our will/violence, then the relationship is not fertile. It does not permit the moments of adjustment, of sudden interference, of pauses–transitions which oblige us to be in a state of alertness.

One essential principle which determines the 'life' of the object consists in allowing it to escape our orbit of control so that it can manifest all its temperament and caprices. We must adapt to it.

The scarf is cloud or rain. I must throw it into the air with the precision which will make it acquire an autonomous life, floating softly and falling like innumerable drops which I gather, collecting them in the palms of my cupped hands.

In the relationship with the object, it is necessary to choose different points of departure and different anchorages for each action. Then one must be consistent with these choices. This makes it possible for us to have a dialogue with the object while conserving its wild nature.

One must outline one's energy in specific actions and relationships which confront the wild and rebellious object. We want it to reveal all its lives. Only the impulse of a well-modelled energy can tame the prop. The precision and surprise arise from the 'resistances' we have created, by giving the object a temperament which is independent of our will.

Task: Work with an object, making it pass from one 'life' to another, and direct the spectator's attention/tension through the object's actions/reactions.

Comment:
Navigating
in living matter
the skin *does not suffocate*
the blood . . .

There are certain principles of craftsmanship which every artist uses in relationship to her/his own reader/listener/spectator. Stevenson asserts that

167

the writer must compose her/his sentences like knots which suspend and conceal the meaning which, when it becomes clear, leads the reader towards the unforeseeable and the unexpected. The unforeseeable is not an inert mental condition. It is an attention/tension which follows the themes and paths which the writer traces by means of sentences. The unforeseeable is a sinuous labyrinth of oppositions, a dynamism which 'moves' the reader or spectator: experience.

In his diary, Paul Klee describes the refined strategy, the calculated meanderings of his paintings; the way in which he directs the observer's eye by means of line and colour, fractures and deformations, in order to create, within the pictorial structure, an invisible route which guides the leaps of the observer's gaze.

The objective of the choreographer/director is similar to that of the writer and painter: to guide the spectator's attention. To direct or choreograph means steering the spectator's perception by using the performer's actions.

Stevenson's advice concerning the craft of writing is valid for all artistic disciplines: the two or more perspectives, on the basis of which the theme is developed, and their contrasts, generate 'leaps' of vision. They are like the changes or 'leaps' of function of an object when a performer suddenly transforms it into something different from what the spectator was expecting.

The substantial difference between an actor and a dancer is that the former often works by making use of a narrative logic, with justifications based on a text or concrete situation. But an actor's reactions often remain within the realm of the daily without arriving at the quality of energy of extra-daily technique.

Dancers work with 'themes', 'emotions', with vague and abstract sensations, relying often on codified models, on an explicit extra-daily technique. In the case of the actor, only a personal temperature can break the daily stereotype. In the case of the dancer, the learned codification, which is a technical stereotype, is not enough to give a personal life to their 'theme' or 'pure' dances. A narrative logic can help the dancer personalize each action and give it a profile. But there is the danger that the dancer will then 'do theatre', illustrating the situation and losing the power of the extra-daily technique.

The dancer's struggle is similar to that of the actor; the former struggles against technical stereotypes, the latter against the stereotypes of daily behaviour (which we call 'spontaneity').

A technical pattern which can be repeated is not negative in and of itself. It is like a word in a language which we master well and which we pronounce without having to think about it. Only the intensity, the way we use words, their reciprocal connections, the context, the montage, decide whether or not stereotypes are broken, and transform the words into the Word, act, personal reaction.

Task: Create a story which justifies the object's four lives and your four different ways of using it.

Comment: *Massacre*
                                                    never surprises . . .

During their apprenticeship, dancers learn to withhold their energy, to sustain the end of the action. This makes them 'alive', even in immobility. You use this knowledge, this intelligence of the body, in situations with which you are already familiar. But when you have to invent, to think paradoxically, to astonish yourselves, you forget this ability of yours, as if you had assimilated the technique, but not its principles. It is as if you have learned to add two plus two with oranges; when you are asked to add three plus eight with birds in flight, you get lost.

Your work with the props is chaotic, it lacks discipline, balance, rhythm, the ability to dilate or contract the space. I see redundancies, superfluous or inert movements; the various alternatives which permit the discovery of distinct, unexpected trajectories are absent. There is no precision either at the beginning or the end of each action, the pauses/transitions do not breathe. You massacre the object instead of reacting in relation to it. You can only react if the object surprises you.

Sometimes I insist on the external shape of the action, the *skin*. Other times, I claim that the *blood*, the motivation, determines the action's *bios*. Do not be confused: any living process consists of this polarity. Both theatre and dance require external precision. But this precision has deep roots in the *blood*. And the *blood* must flow in visible ramifications.

The work can begin from a technical detail which then sends roots towards the inside. Or the sequence can begin by means of images, associations, sounds, thoughts, rhythms, and then develop its organic *skin*: the perceptible form of the action. What is important is that this polarity is reached and co-exists in the performance in a symbiosis which is nourished by the reciprocal oppositions.

Task: Tomorrow you will come dressed in your best clothes, rich in light and colour, as if for a rendezvous with your loved one. We will form four groups, North, South, East and West. Each group will prepare a performance called *Velorio en la Navidad* [in Spanish, 'Christmas Eve', but also 'Funeral Vigil at the Birth']. You can bring props with you. You must create a sonorous universe without recorded music, with dialogues and songs in an uninterrupted flow.

Comment: *And the child*
                                                    never grows up . . .

Experience has taught me to reject the differentiation between dance and theatre. My work with Odin Teatret, which could be defined as a 'theatre which dances', and with ISTA, the International School of Theatre Anthropology, has confirmed for me that the only real difference is between daily technique and extra-daily technique. There is a distance between the way we use our presence in life and the way we use it in a performance situation.

All traditional Asian forms are 'theatre which dances'. Their codification is based on an explicitly extra-daily technique. Western dance has also accentuated the first level of organization of the performance: that of *the action which is*, which strikes and fascinates the spectator's senses.

But the theatres which dance, in Asia, have gone beyond this fascinating level. They have given life to a dramaturgy, to a way of weaving time, space, stage design, lights, costumes, objects, colours, movement, music, songs, monologues, dialogues, choruses, to introduce the spectator into a macrocosm which is not only energy modelled into actions but stories reflecting on human existence.

Some dancers claim that dance is merely movement, a kinaesthetic, expressive form of its own. The fundamental difference betwen Asian theatre which dances and Western dance is that the latter has yet to invent a dramaturgical knowledge which develops the molecules, the organs, the systems, in short, the totality which is characteristic of a living organism. The sensuous and logical text of dance is often limited to virtuosity, to the inventions of the *skin*, to a flow of energy whose variations of muscle tones are in danger of becoming conditioned reflexes which imprison the dancer.

The pureness of dance – in its modern or folkloric versions – has an immaculate beauty. It is like a little girl who decides to remain a child all her life and never grow up.

Friday

Task: The four groups, North, South, East and West, prepare the performance *Velorio en la Navidad*.

Comment: *In this*
                              distant proximity

The other day, someone remarked to me how strange it was to work without knowing where the work was going. This is the proof that we are in a process which is experience and unexpected knowledge, which stimulates us to ask questions and to question ourselves. It is difficult to work without knowing what the conclusion might be. It gives one the impression of wandering without an objective. We know very well how important the final knot, the arrival point of the process is. But when it appears, it is like a sudden exit from the labyrinth which the process of work has constructed. When we think we are getting close to the exit, we find we are moving further away. When we despair that we are far away from it, it is very close.

The end is a knot which draws together all the threads that have been woven and interwoven during the work, sealing the 'sensuous and logical' text. The true end is the one which finds its beginning, a rare experience where oppositions embrace and polarities seem to co-exist in the same situation, in one body, in one action.

We cannot plan any of this seated at a table. It does not happen in a conscious way. One cannot prepare it in advance. It is a gift, a moment of grace, which fills us with gratitude because we do not know why we have earned it.

There is no discovery if the route is already fixed. One can learn to hoist and furl the sails, to fight against the currents, to use the crosswinds. This is the craftsmanship of the work, the first and second levels of organization, those we have spoken of during these days. But the third level, that of the totality, of the co-existent polarities, of the actions in a context, the moment in which our temperaments and our life-stories guide us to construct and cross a labyrinth, to weave the threads together, to tighten the final knot, is the result of an existential injustice: some reach it, others do not.

We can reach a new shore by sailing without a clearly defined route. We know only the techniques of sailing. We don't know if we will reach the dreamed-of continent. Our awareness of our limitations worries us: this time, perhaps, we will not get there. In this discouraging haze, the Ariadne's thread is our daily work, our ability to concentrate on the apparent but concrete simplicity of every action. With the essential precision of the action, which could be our last.

Where the pause
is discernment

For some of you this experience has provoked a kind of paralysis, and disorientation. Obviously, none of us wants to suffer, to expose ourselves to insecurity, to live in a state of crisis. But a new orientation is possible only as the consequence of a disorientation. Crises in our lives can be pause/transitions in which our experience prepares itself to leap into a new orbit which revitalizes our energies.

To be disoriented means that the solutions and answers which we already possess are no longer satisfying. It is the birth of something new, a gestation, with the nausea, the vomiting, and the sensation that the physical and the psychic bodies are being deformed. In this period of confusion, all of our previous experience tries to find a new way to manifest itself, abandoning the safe shell of habits which now fetter us.

When it is necessary to seduce
to the point of reflection . . .

When I saw your four *Velorio en la Navidad*, I felt as if I had been carried back in time, to the end of the sixties. At that time, in Europe, a multitude of groups, dissatisfied with traditional theatre, sprang up. They were trying to

171

find a new way of using the relationship which is theatre. Certain experiences took place, and, after having passed through crisis, they led to the discovery of new horizons: Grotowski's theatre and the Living Theatre. 'Grotowski-ism' and 'Living Theatre-ism' became cardinal points for an entire parallel theatre.

I remembered all of this when I saw your work. It is as if you are on the verge of moving into a new no-man's land, as if you had abandoned the territory of known dance but had not yet reached the country you longed for.

You often speak of Dance-Theatre. For you, the solution cannot be collaboration with directors or actors, who use concepts, texts, and linear, narrative logics which risk suffocating dance's quality of presence. Your extra-daily technique must remain your point of departure. You must invent a dramaturgy of your own in order to weave the actions in sequences while conserving their backbones and melting the metal of technique.

A performer 'in-life' becomes sensual. S/he seduces the spectators, leads them to the meeting between experience and reflection. This sensuality attracts, captures, 'enamours' the spectators, makes them react emotionally, transforms their reactions into reflection. The Asian or Western 'theatre which dances' captivates us with its sensuality. Here, I see your bodies move with vigour, but I am not 'enamoured', I am not seduced into reflection. You are silver horses. You have covered your ability to 'be-in-life' with refined plates of technique. You have taken care of the muscles, but you have suffocated the life.

I don't know how you will be able to save yourselves from your silver skin. In the theatre, actors use their characters to conceal or reveal their own vulnerability. For dancers, energy often obscures the transparency and the vulnerability. It is the anonymity of technique.

When I watch you I ask myself if your reactions correspond to the freedom you live with someone you love, someone who inspires you with confidence, with security. It is the moment in which the polarity we are manifests itself, and our energies, soft and strong, not 'masculine' or 'feminine' but 'vigorous' and 'tender', are incarnated in actions, becoming individual destiny and history.

There are simultaneous solitudes
that will make us fall in love ...

I can only say: use your disorientation to discover your face, the face which is hidden behind the mask of dance. Do not forget: your work and your presence must 'enamour' someone else.

We have arrived at the end, and we all begin the return to our own solitudes.

NOTES

1 THE GENESIS OF THEATRE ANTHROPOLOGY pp.1–8

1 Eugenio Barba, *Alla Ricerca del Teatro Perduto: Grotowski, una proposta dell'avanguardia polacca*, Padova, Marsilio, 1965. [This book has not been translated into English. R.F.] This was the first book on Grotowski and was published in Italy and Hungary. The French translation circulated as a manuscript in theatre circles and excerpts from it were printed in French, German and Scandinavian magazines. Excerpts in English were published by Richard Schechner in *Tulane Drama Review* as early as 1964.

2 Between 1980 and 1994, the following sessions of ISTA were held, varying from a week to two months: 1980, Bonn, Germany; 1981, Volterra and Pontedera, Italy; 1985, Blois and Malakoff, France; 1986, Holstebro, Denmark; 1987, Salento, Italy; 1990 Bologna, Italy; 1992, Brecon and Cardiff, Great Britain; 1994, Londrina, Brazil. In 1990, ISTA began a new activity, the University of Eurasian Theatre, which held its first seminar in Padova in March of 1992. The results of ISTA's research have been collected in *The Secret Art of the Performer*, by Eugenio Barba and Nicola Savarese, London and New York, Centre for Performance Research-Routledge, 1991.

3 RECURRING PRINCIPLES pp.13–35

1 Louis Jovet, *Le Comédien désincarné*, Paris, Flammarion, 1954, p.138. *S'imposer des règles simples et qu'on ne trahira jamais*. [This book has been translated into English. R.F.]

2 I have not been able to trace this statement of Decroux', which I believed was to be found in the pages of 'Words on mime'. It has always managed to escape me in spite of numerous re-readings. It is also possible that it comes from the numerous conversations I have had with Decroux' students: Ingemar Lindh (Swedish), Yves Lebreton (French), Luis Otavio Burnier (Brazilian).

3 Etienne Decroux, 'Words on mime', trans. by Mark Piper, *Mime Journal*, Claremont, California, Pomona College, 1985, p. 129.

4 From a conversation between Pierre Verry and dancer Lulli Svedin. Lulli Svedin, *Den Klassika Ballettens Byggstenar*, Stockholm, Rabén and Sjögren, 1978, p. 84.

5 Ranka Bijeljac-Babić, 'Utilizzazione di un metodo scientifico nello studio dell'espressione sportiva e teatrale', in *La Scuola degli attori. Rapporti della prima sessione dell'ISTA*, edited by Franco Ruffini, Firenze, La Casa Usher, 1981. An essay based on experiments conducted with a statokinesimeter. [This essay has not been translated into English. R.F.]

6 Junko Sakaba Berberich, 'Some Observations on Movement in *nō*', in *Asian Theatre Journal*, I, Autumn 1984, n. 2, pp.210–11. The author bases her article on the teachings of Nomura Shiro, *nō* performer from the Kanze family.
7 Konstantin Stanislavski, *Building a Character*, trans. by Elizabeth Reynolds Hapgood, London, Max Reinhardt, 1950, pp.49–53.
8 Vsevolod Meyerhold, *Écrits sur le théâtre, Tome II 1917–1929*, translation, preface and notes by Béatrice Picon-Vallin, Lausanne, La Cité-L'Age d'Homme, 1975, p.72. [This book has not been translated into English. R.F.]
9 Béatrice Picon-Vallin, *Meyerhold*, Paris, CNRS, 'Les voies de la création théâtrale', 17, 1990, p.106. [This book has not been translated into English. R.F.]
10 ibid., p.116.
11 Charles Dullin, *Souvenirs et notes de travail d'un acteur*, Paris, Odette Lieutier, 1946, pp.114–15. [This book has not been translated into English. R.F.]
12 Jerzy Grotowski, *Towards a Poor Theatre*, Holstebro, Odin Teatrets Forlag, 1968, p.143.
13 Decroux, 'Words on mime', p.48.
14 ibid., p.52
15 Jouvet, *Le Comédien Désincarné*, p.241.
16 Junichiro Tanizaki, *In Praise of Shadows*, Tokyo, Charles E. Tuttle, 1977, p.24.
17 Decroux, 'Words on mime', p.56.
18 ibid., pp.38–40, 68–9, 125–30.
19 Charles J. Dunn and Bunzo Torigoe (eds), *The Actor's Analects*, University of Tokyo Press, 1969, p. 94.
20 Quoted in Frank Hoff, 'Killing the self: how the narrator acts', in *Asian Theatre Journal*, II, Spring 1985, n.l, p.5.
21 Decroux 'Words on mime', p. 30.
22 Bertolt Brecht, *Buch der Wendungen, Gesainmelte Werke, Band V*, Frankfurt, Suhrkamp, 1967, p.493.
23 Tage Larsen, 'Dalla parte degli attori', in Eugenio Barba (ed.) *Il Brecht dell'Odin*, Milano, Ubulibri, 1981, p.109. [This book has not been translated into English. R.F.]
24 George Gamow, *Tredive aar der Rystede Fysikken*, Copenhagen, Gyldendal, 1968, p.59. [This book has not been translated into English. R.F.]

5 ENERGY, OR RATHER, THE THOUGHT pp.50–80

1 Etienne Decroux, 'Words on mime', trans. by Mark Piper, *Mime Journal*, Claremont, California, Pomona College, 1985, p.12.
   In the original French text, Decroux' argument is more subtle because of the almost identical pronunciation of *pouce* (thumb) and *pousse* (press, push): *notre pensée pousse nos gestes ainsi qu'un pouce de statuaire pousse des formes; et notre corps, sculpté de l'intérieur, s'étend.*
2 Louis Jouvet, *Le Comédien désincarné*, Paris, Flammarion, 1954, p.182. [This book has not been translated into English. R.F.]
3 ibid., p.182.
4 ibid., pp. 174 and 184.
5 Sergei Michaelovitch Eisenstein, *Memorie*, Italian translation, Rome, Editori Riuniti, pp.76–7. This is a collection of texts taken from the first volume (*Memoirs*) of Eisenstein's *Collected Works* in six volumes, published in the USSR between 1964 and 1971. [These texts have not been translated into English. R.F.]
6 This is an observation made by Meyerhold, as reported by Alexander Gladkov, quoted in Vsevolod Meyerhold, *Le Théâtre théâtral*, French translation and

presentation by Nina Gourfinkel, Paris, Gallimard, 1963, p.283. In the chapter, 'Meyerhold Speaks', Gourfinkel presents pages taken from a series of articles published by Gladkov in 1961 in the magazine *Novi Mir* and in the collections *Tarussa Pages* and *Theatrical Moscow*. [No translation of this material exists in English. R.F.]

7 Decroux, 1985 op.cit. p.79.

8 Quoted from the English translation (anon.) of 'Bertolt Brecht: A short description of a new technique of the art of acting which produces an effect of estrangement', in *World Theatre*, Brussels, IV, 1, 1955, p.24.

9 Jack D. Flam (ed.), *Matisse on Art*, Oxford, Phaidon Press, 1973, p.138.

10 Quoted in Béatrice Picon-Vallin, *Le Théâtre juif soviétique pendant les années vingt*, Lausanne, La Cité-L'Age d'Homme, 1973, p.94. [This book has not been translated into English. R.F.]

11 J. Thomas Rimer and Yamazaki Masakazu (trans.) *On the Art of Nō Drama: the major treatises of Zeami*, Princeton, Princeton University Press, 1984, p.75. It is the second part of the treatise *Kakyō* (A mirror held to the flower).

12 Vsevolod Meyerhold, *Ecrits sur le théâtre, Tome II 1917–1929*, translation, preface and notes by Béatrice Picon-Vallin, Lausanne, La Cité-L'Age d'Homme, 1975, p. 13. [This book has not been translated into English. R.F.]

13 Béatrice Picon-Vallin, *Meyerhold*, Paris, CNRS, 'Les voies de la création théâtrale', 17, 1990, p.113. [This book has not been translated into English. R.F.]

14 Jerzy Grotowski, 'Pragmatic laws' in Eugenio Barba and Nicola Savarese, *The Secret Art of the Performer*, London and New York, Centre for Performance Research-Routledge, 1991, p.236.

15 Decroux, 'Words on mime', p.51.

16 Meyerhold, *Ecrits sur le théâtre*, pp.128 and 141.

17 This is another sentence attributed to Meyerhold by Alexander Gladkov and translated in the book by Gourfinkel, cit. in note 6, p.255.

18 Kunio Komparu, *The Noh Theatre, Principles and Perspectives*, New York and Tokyo, Weatherhill/Tankosha, 1983, p.216.

19 In his book *Vakhtangov and His Studio*, published in Moscow in 1926, Boris Zachava recalls that in 1921, while working on his production of *The Miracle of Saint Anthony*, Vakhtangov

> declared that no-one had the right to move on the stage when someone was speaking: as soon as one actor began to speak, all the others had to freeze, in absolute immobility, making neither gesture nor muscular movement, in order not to attract the spectator's attention onto himself, because the attention at that given moment had to be concentrated on the character whose turn it was to speak.

> This immobility was not supposed to appear to the spectator as something artificial. Each actor had only to *justify* the stopping of the movement for himself, to find that *reason* which necessarily (organically) would provoke the stop. The immobility had to be internally justified.

> The *external* immobility was not supposed to be interior immobility: *the exterior static state had to be internal dynamics*. Vakhtangov demanded that each actor act in such a way that he took his cue from his partner at exactly the moment when the latter's action was not yet concluded. The movement remained half done, absolutely *expressive*, dynamic in its immobility. The composition of the bodies in this case (especially in crowd scenes) became expressive through immobility; on this background, the one character who had the right to do so moved and spoke.

The excerpt is quoted by Fabio Mollica in the essay, 'Tappe della vocazione teatrale di E.B. Vachtangov', in *Teatro e Storia*, 9, October 1990, p.244. Mollica also recalls some solutions chosen by Vakhtankov for the mise en scène of *The Dybbuk* at the Habimah Theatre of Moscow in 1922 (the text was in Hebrew): 'Zavadski, who was helping Vakhtangov at the Habimah to develop the actors' make-ups remembers that one of the techniques used by Vakhtangov was that of asking the actor, at the moment in which he stopped moving in order to say his line, to do so in precarious balance, "like a photograph of a person in motion". In this way, Zavadski claimed, Vakhtangov achieved a "continuous movement", even with the actors who weren't moving. A sort of flow of tensions and relaxations was created which affected the spectator's attention and made up for his lack of understanding of the text (p.250)'. [This essay has not been translated into English. R.F.]

20   Here as elsewhere, recognition of the same 'biological' nucleus behind different formulations and uses can lead to the suspicion of a homogenization of the sources. This will be discussed in chapter 8, 'Canoes, butterflies and a horse'.
21   Vasily O. Toporkov, *Stanislavski in Rehearsal (1949)*, New York, Theatre Arts Books, 1979, p.62.
22   The list of the twenty-five phases for the application of the Method of Physical Actions is a manuscript memorandum for directors written by Stanislavski at an unknown date (probably around 1936). It is reported on by Mel Gordon in *The Stanislavski Technique*, New York, Applause Theatre Books, 1988, pp.209–12.
23   Heinrich von Kleist, *Über das Marionettentheater, Samtliche Werke*, München, Winkler-Verlag, 1967, p.949–50. [This book has not been translated into English. R.F.]
24   Rimer and Masakaza *On the Art of* Nō *Drama: the major treatises of Zeami*, pp.120–1.
25   ibid., *Fushikaden* (Dictates on the style and the flower) p.58.
26   ibid., *Shikado* (The true way of the flower), p.64.
27   *Nikyoku Santai Ezu* (Two arts and three illustrated types) is translated into French in Zeami, *La Tradition secrète du* Nō, translation and commentary by René Sieffert, Paris, Gallimard, 1960, p.151–61. [This book has not been translated into English. R.F.]
28   *Fushikaden*, in Rimer and Masakaza *On the Art of* Nō *Drama: the major treatises of Zeami*, pp.11–12.
29   Toporkov, *Stanislavski in Rehearsal*, p.63.
30   For many Odin Teatret performances, especially in the first ten years of our activity, from 1964 to 1974, the work was based on the scenic elaboration of 'materials' deriving from the actors' improvisations. Looking back, one realizes that the essential moment was not the improvisation itself, but the immediately successive phase, when the improvisation was memorized and fixed by the actor in a precise score. At that stage of our experience, improvisation was the most effective way of constructing a design of movements rooted in the actor's personal and professional history. When the performer has gained more experience and command of her/himself, when – as is said in many traditions – s/he has become a 'master', s/he can then, on her/his own, elaborate materials which will be structured in the performance. This phase of elaboration thus consists of a personal work of composition which resembles an auto-choreography.
31   Picon-Vallin, *Meyerhold*, p.275.
32   Michael Chekhov, *To the Actor: on the technique of acting*, New York, Harper and Row, 1953, p.xi.
33   ibid., p.7.
34   ibid., p.7.

35 For Katsuko Azuma, as we have seen, it is a ball of steel, covered with cotton, in the triangle formed by the hips and the coccyx. For *kabuki* and *nō* performers, it is *koshi*, the area of the hips. Stanislavski wrote: 'Our spinal column, which bends in all directions, is like a spiral spring and needs to be firmly set on its base. It must be, as it were, well screwed in place at the lowest vertebra. If a person feels that this so-called screw is strong, the upper part of his torso has a support, a centre of gravity, stability and "straightness".' (Konstantin Stanislavski, *Building a Character*, trans. by Elizabeth Reynolds Hapgood, London, Max Reinhardt, 1950, p.43). Here is how Grotowski confronts the problem: 'I believe one must develop a special anatomy of the actor; for instance, find the body's various centres of concentration for different ways of acting, seeking the areas of the body which the actor sometimes feels to be his sources of energy. The lumbar region, the abdomen and the area around the solar plexus often function as such a source.' Jerzy Grotowski, *Towards a Poor Theatre*, Holstebro, Odin Teatrets Forlag, 1968, p.38.
36 Chekhov, *To the Actor*, pp.8–9.
37 ibid., p.10–11.
38 ibid., p.11.
39 ibid., pp.11–12.
40 ibid., p.13.
41 Konstantin S. Stanislavski, *My Life in Art*, Harmondsworth, Penguin Books, 1967, pp.439–40.
42 Chekhov, *To the Actor*, p.83–4.
43 ibid., p.84.
44 ibid., pp.130–1.
45 Meyerhold, *Ecrits sur le théâtre*, p.91.

6 THE DILATED BODY pp.81–100

1 Arthur Koestler, *The Sleepwalkers*, New York, Macmillan, 1959.

7 A THEATRE NOT MADE OF STONES AND BRICKS pp.101–134

1 *Le Rouge et Or*, a stimulating work by Georges Banu, Paris, Flammarion, 1980, is based on this way of considering theatre buildings.
2 Cf., p.44.
3 Gordon Craig, who was living in Genoa at the time, presented his opinions in two articles published by *The Times* of London on 14 and 15 February 1935, entitled respectively, 'Doctors of the Theatre, gathering in Rome' and 'Maecenas and the poet, the real physic'.
4 *Drama* = dramatic literature, *theatre* = theatre buildings and performance.
    When he defines Shaw's words as a brilliant advertisement (a lie from the world of business), Craig is referring to the campaign in defence of the rights of dramatic writers and their corporate enterprises against the power of the theatrical companies. All over Europe, during those years, playwrights, who wanted to make a living from their profession, felt that they were at the mercy of the actors, who could ignore them and present texts from the past, or mediocre scripts revitalized by interpretation and *mise en scène*. In order to defend themselves and to make the most of their own work, the writers expounded the idea of the theatre as a means of diffusion for contemporary dramaturgy and of the priority value of the text in the performance.

5 This speech was given during the fifth session of the congress, presided over by Taírov (the morning of 11 October 1934). Translated from *Teatro Drammatico: atti del convegno di lettere, 8–14 ottobre, 1934*, Fondazione Alessandro Volta, Roma, Reale Accademia d'Italia, 1935, p.211.

6 Mario Corsi, Le Prime Rappresentazioni Dannunzione, Milan, Treves, 1928, p.8. [This book has not been translated into English. R.F.]

7 Cf. Richard C. Beacham, 'Appia, Jaques-Dalcroze and Hellerau. Part One: "Music made Visible"', in *New Theatre Quarterly*, 1985, I, May, n.2, and id. 'Appia, Jaques-Dalcroze and Hellerau. Part Two: "Poetry in Motion"', in *New Theatre Quarterly*, 1985, I, August, n.3.

8 Cf. Georg Fuchs, *Die Sezession in der Dramatischen Kunst und das Volksfestspiel*, Munich, Georg Müller Verlag, 1911, p.55.

9 In a text from 1907 published in *On the Art of the Theatre* (1911), Gordon Craig had asserted: 'So we have to banish from our mind all thought of the use of a human form as the instrument which we are to use to translate what we call *Movement*.' (London, Mercury Books, 1962, p.50).

10 Etienne Decroux, 'Words on mime', trans. by Mark Piper, *Mime Journal*, Claremont, California; Pomona College, 1985, pp.29–30. In the chapter from which these quotes have been taken, Decroux discusses the objections made by Gaston Baty (his first director), who maintained that Decroux' mime was a limb amputated from the body of the theatre. The importance which Decroux assigns to mime as an autonomous artistic genre explains the insistence with which he separates it from the 'genre' of dance (cf. in particular pp. 65–9). Cf. also above, p.23.

11 Cf. Jean Benedetti, *Stanislavski: a biography*, London, Methuen Drama, 1990. Concerning the Studios and *studijnost*: Fabio Mollica, *Il Teatro Possible: Stanislavskij e il Primo studio del Teatro d'arte di Mosca*, Florence, La Casa Usher, 1989.

12 The 'schools' founded by the reformers of twentieth century theatre changed from being places of training into centres of autonomous theatrical vision. Regarding this cultural dynamic, cf. Fabrizio Cruciani, *Teatro nel Novecento: Registi pedagoghi e comunità teatrali nel XX secolo*, Florence, Sansoni, 1985.

13 Patrice Pavis presented a report on training, based on a series of interviews with performers, at the seminar 'Techniques of Representation and Historiography' which was held at the University of Bologna (13–14 July 1990), as part of the sixth international session of ISTA, the International School of Theatre Anthropology, Bologna, 28 June to 18 July 1990.

14 Edward Gordon Craig, *Henry Irving*, New York, Longmans, Green and Co., 1930.

15 Jerzy Grotowski, *Możliwość teatru*, Opole, Materialy warsztatowe Teatru 13 Rzedów, February, 1962. A booklet of twenty-four unnumbered pages. The quote is on page twenty-two. This text was Grotowski's first attempt to present his ideas and his activity at Teatr 13 Rzedów, Opole, which he had been directing since 1959. Two-thirds of the booklet is made up of statements by Ludwik Flaszen (Grotowski's *dramaturg* and close collaborator) and of excerpts from reviews. It is interesting to note how Grotowski constructed his own terminology using the most effective formulations made by other people. Cf. also pp.139–40.

16 Jerzy Grotowski, *Towards a Poor Theatre*, Holstebro, Odin Teatrets Forlag, 1968, p.39.

17 Bertolt Brecht, 'Über das Stanislavski-System (Kultischer Charakter des Systems), (1939)', *Gesammelte Werke, Band VII*, Frankfurt, Suhrkamp Verlag, 1967, pp.381–3.

18 Ibid., 'Stanislavski-Studien, (1951–1954)', pp.862–6.

19 Claudio Meldolesi and Laura Olivi, *Brecht Regista, Memorie dal Berliner Ensemble*, Bologna, Il Mulino, 1989, p.119. [This book has not been translated into English. R.F.]

20 For an analysis of Stanislavski's 'work of the actor on himself' as work on the pre-expressive, cf. Franco Ruffini, 'A propos du niveau pré-expressif du drame', in *Bouffonneries*, 22–3 (1989), pp. 68–93. (See also: Franco Ruffini, 'L'attore e il dramma: saggio teorico di antropologia teatrale', in *Teatro e Storia*, 5 October 1988; Franco Ruffini, 'Romanzo pedagogico: uno studio sui libri di Stanislavskij', in *Teatro e Storia*, 10 April, 1991.)

21 Part of Borges' poem 'Ariosto and the Arabs' in Anthony Kerrigan, (ed.) *Jorge Luis Borges, A Personal Anthology*, New York, Grove Press, 1967, p.98.

22 Louis Jouvet, *Le Comédien désincarné*, Paris, Flammarion, 1945, pp.211–18. [This book has not been translated into English. R.F.]

23 Brecht, op. cit., pp.211–12.

24 Meldolesi and Olivi, *Brecht regista, Memorie dal Berliner Ensemble*, pp.303–4.

25 Cf. the introduction by A. K. Ramanujan to the collection *Speaking of Shiva*, London, Penguin Books, 1973, pp.20–1. Ramanujan's translation into English of Basavanna's poem is on page 88.

26 Edward Braun (trans. and ed.) *Meyerhold on Theatre*, New York, Hill and Wang, 1969, p.56. Braun translates Meyerhold's *risunok dvizhenij* as 'pattern of movement'. The literal English translation of the Russian phrase is 'design of movements', the same expression used by the French actor Henri Louis Lekain (*dessin de mouvements*) which had originally inspired Meyerhold. See also p.128.

27 For historical reconstruction of the procedures used by the actors of the great nineteenth century tradition, cf. Ferdinando Taviani, 'La danse occulte: enseignements d'acteurs disparus', in *Bouffoneries*, 22/23, 1989, p.105; Ferdinando Taviani, 'Energetic language', in Eugenio Barba and Nicola Savarese (eds) *The Secret Art of the Performer*, London and New York, Routledge, 1991, p.144; Claudio Meldolesi and Ferdinando Taviani, *Teatro e Spettacolo nel Primo Ottocento*, Roma-Bari, Laterza, 1991.

28 If by 'dramaturgy', one means the technique and art of weaving actions together, one can speak of a performer's dramaturgy to refer to the way in which s/he weaves her/his compositions into the general framework of the text and the *mise en scène*. See Eugenio Barba, 'Dramaturgy' in *The Secret Art of the Performer*, p.68.

29 Dario Fo, *Manuale minimo dell'attore*, Turin, Einaudi, 1987, p.146. But I am referring above all to Dario Fo's verbal comments during his work sessions with Odin Teatret (since 1968) and later at ISTA.

30 Regarding Stanislavski's method of physical actions, see his notes on *The Government Inspector* (1936–1937) written for the unfinished book devoted to the actor's work on the character: *Creating a Role*, New York, Theatre Arts Books, 1961 translated by Elizabeth Reynolds Hapgood, p.211. But above all, see Vasily Osipovich Toporkov, *Stanislavski in Rehearsal (1949)*, New York, Theatre Arts Books, 1979.

31 Jacques Copeau, 'An actor's thoughts on Diderot's "Paradox"', 1929, in John Rudlin and Norman H. Poul (trans. and eds), *Copeau: Texts on Theatre*, London, Routledge, 1990, pp. 74–8.

32 Meyerhold, *Ecrits sur le théâtre*, volume I, p.179. These notes were published in 1909. The italics are Meyerhold's.

33 Perhaps no-one has understood the importance of music in Meyerhold's vision and technique better than Béatrice Picon-Vallin in *Meyerhold*, Paris, CNRS, 'Les voies de la création théâtrale', 17, 1990 and in *La Musique dans le jeu de l'acteur meyerholdien*, Rennes, Université de Haute Bretagne, Etudes et Documents III, 1981, p.35. [These books have not been translated into English. R.F.]

For the equivalent, in Meyerhold's working language, of 'dance', 'grotesque', 'bio-mechanics', cf. Eugenio Barba, 'Meyerhold: The Grotesque, that is, Bio-mechanics', in *The Secret Art of the Performer*, p.154.

34 Meyerhold, *Ecrits sur le Théâtre*, volume II, p.156.
35 Excerpt from the chapter on bio-mechanics included in Vsevolod Meyerhold, *Le Théâtre théâtral*, trans. and presentation by Nina Gourfinkel, Paris, Gallimard, 1963, p.171.
36 Meyerhold, *Ecrits sur le Théâtre*, vol. I, p.245.
37 Cf. the last chapter of Jean Benedetti, *Stanislavski: a biography*, London, Methuen, 1990. Shortly after Stanislavski's death, Meyerhold was arrested and killed.
38 Quoted in Richard Schechner, *Environmental Theatre*, New York, Hawthorn, 1973, p.295. And also in 'Performers and Spectators Transported and Trans-formed', in *Between Theater and Anthropology*, Philadelphia, University of Pennsylvania Press, 1985, pp.124–5.
39 Letter published posthumously in *Notes sur le métier de comédien*, Paris, Michel Brient, 1955, p.69. [This letter has not been translated into English. R.F.]
40 Edward Gordon Craig, *On the Art of the Theatre*, London, Mercury Books, 1962, pp.55–8.
41 Etienne Decroux, 'Words on mime', trans. by Mark Piper, *Mime Journal*, Claremont, California, Pomona College, 1985, p.7.
42 Edward Braun, trans. and ed. *Meyerhold on Theatre*, New York, Hill and Wang, 1969, p.130.
43 Craig, *On the Art of the Theatre*, p.61.
44 James Brandon, 'Form in Kabuki Acting', in James R. Brandon, William P. Malm and Donald H. Shively (eds), *Studies in Kabuki: its acting, music and historical context*, Honolulu, The University Press of Hawaii, 1978, p.124. Regarding the same topic, see the detailed description of the interpretations of the *kata* of 'Kumagai's Battle Camp' performed by Danjuro IX (1839–1903) and Nakamura Shikan (1830–1899) in Samuel L. Leiter, 'Kumagai's Battle Camp: form and tradition in Kabuki acting', in *Asian Theatre Journal*, VIII, Spring, 1991, n.1.
45 Craig, *On the Art of the Theatre*, p.83.

8 CANOES, BUTTERFLIES AND A HORSE pp.135–172

1 Antonin Artaud, 'Le Théâtre et son double' (1938), in *Oeuvres Complètes*, IV, Paris, Gallimard, 1964, p.137. This is Artaud's response, in a letter written in November, 1931, to objections made to his 'Manifeste du Théâtre de la Cruauté'. [This letter is not found in the English translation of 'Le Théâtre et son double'. R.F.]
2 Vsevolod Meyerhold, *Le Théâtre théâtral*, edited by Nina Gourfinkel, Paris, Gallimard, 1963, p.277. This is one of the statements reported by Alexander Gladkov in the section, 'Meyerhold parle' ('Meyerhold speaks'). [This book has not been translated into English. R.F.]
3 Translated from Fausto Malcovati in the introduction to Konstantin S. Stanislavskij, *Il Lavoro dell'attore sul personaggio,* Bari, Laterza, 1988, p.XV. [This letter is not found in the English translation of *Il Lavoro dell'attore sul Personaggio* (*Creating a Role*)].
4 Cf. Stanislavski's Preface to 'An Actor Prepares', translated and published by Burnet M. Hobgood in *Theatre Journal*, 43, 1991, pp. 229–32.
5 Jerzy Grotowski, *Możliwość Teatru*, Materialy warsztatowe Teatru 13 Rzędów, Opole, February, 1962.
6 Ludwik Flaszen, 'Akropolis: komentaria do przedstawienia', in the programme

for *Akropolis*, October, 1962. Flaszen's text was included in Jerzy Grotowski, *Towards a Poor Theatre*, edited by Eugenio Barba, Holstebro, Odin Teatrets Forlag, 1968, p.61–77.

7 Jerzy Grotowski, *Towards a Poor Theatre*, p.38. The quotation is part of the interview 'The Theatre's New Testament' in which I put together the salient points of a series of conversations I had with Grotowski during the period I spent at his theatre in Opole from 1961–1964. The text, revised by Grotowski, was published for the first time in *Alla Ricerca del Teatro Perduto*, Padova, Marsilio, 1965 (the quotation is on p.97), and later, with some cuts, in *Towards a Poor Theatre*.

8 Grotowski's theatre took the name Teatr Laboratorium 13 Rzedów in the autumn of 1962. The first performance presented under the new name was *Akropolis*. In 1967, after the theatre had been based in Wroclaw for more than a year, it changed its name once again, to Teatr Laboratorium. Instytut Badan Metody Aktorski (Institute of Research into the Method of the Actor).

9 Antonin Artaud, 'The Theatre and its Double', in Antonin Artaud, *Collected Works*, IV, trans. by Victor Corti, London, Calder and Boyars, 1974, pp.25–7. These quotes are from the chapter 'Production and Metaphysics', which is based on a conference given by Artaud at the Sorbonne on December 10th, 1931 and published in *La Nouvelle Revue Française* on 1 February 1932, with the title 'Peinture' ('Painting').

10 Antonin Artaud, 'Charles Dullin's L'Atelier' in *Collected Works*, II, trans. by Victor Corti, London, Calder and Boyars, 1971, pp.128–9. See also the 1921 letter to Max Jacob, ibid., III, p.47.

11 This text is from a seminar for dancers and choreographers organized by the Dirección de Teatro y Danza de la Universidad Autónoma de Mexico (UNAM), from 3 to 7 November 1985. The text was transcribed by Patricia Cardona and revised by the author.

12 Robert Louis Stevenson, *The Art of Writing: technical elements of style*, London, Chatto and Windus, 1908, pp.8–14.

INDEX